PIXÉRÉCOURT

FOUR MELODRAMAS

A theatrical print, published by W.C. Webb of London in 1843, showing the famous American dog Hamlet with Barkham Cony (1802-1858) as Landry in Pixérécourt's *The Forest of Bondy*. Hamlet, like other dogs of melodrama, was trained to jump at the villain's throat and tear open a concealed bag of red ochre to create a horrifying and bloody effect.

Courtesy Harvard Theatre Collection, The Houghton Library

FOUR MELODRAMAS

by

RENÉ-CHARLES GUILBERT DE PIXÉRÉCOURT

TRANSLATED AND EDITED BY
DANIEL GEROULD & MARVIN CARLSON

Martin E. Segal Theatre Center Publications
New York

LIBRARY OF CONGRESS CATALOGING-IN PUBLICATION DATA
Pixérécourt, R.-C. Guilbert de (René-Charles Guilbert), 1773-1844
[Plays. English. Selections]
Four melodramas/ by René-Charles Guilbert Pixérécourt ;
translated and edited by Daniel Gerould & Marvin Carlson
p. cm.
Includes bibliographical references.
Contents: The ruins of Babylon, or, Jafar and Zaida -- The dog of Montargis, or, The forest of Bondy -- Christopher Columbus, or, The discovery of the New World -- Alice, or, The Scottish gravediggers.
ISBN 0-9666152-4-7 (pbk.)
1. Pixérécourt, R.-C. Guilbert de (René-Charles Guilbert), 1773-1844--Translations into English. I. Title: 4 melodramas. II. Gerould, Daniel Charles, 1928- III. Carlson, Marvin A., 1935- IV. Title.
PQ2382.P4 A237   2002
842'.7--dc21   2002020900

Copy-editing and typography by Kurt Taroff
Cover design and graphics by Kimon Keramidas

TABLE OF CONTENTS

Introduction

PIXÉRÉCOURT: FOUR MELODRAMAS

René-Charles Guilbert de Pixérécourt (1773-1844) was the inventor of a new dramatic genre that soon established itself as the avatar of popular entertainment for the masses and the most successful playwright of the first decades of the nineteenth century with some 30,000 performances to his credit. But the public is fickle and tastes change so rapidly that by the end of his life Pixérécourt was already falling into oblivion, shunned by younger generations of theatregoers as a dusty old fossil.

Unacknowledged by Victor Hugo or any of the other romantics (except for Charles Nodier), who appropriated his stage craft and spectacular effects but scorned his earnest moralizing, "the father of melodrama" never entered the pantheon of French writers and artists. You will find scant mention of Pixérécourt's name in the histories of French literature published throughout the nineteenth and early twentieth century. No one took seriously the author of 120 plays, 59 of them melodramas, or felt called upon to discuss his influence on the evolution of the theatrical theory and practice. At best Pixérécourt was patronized as a curious subliterary phenomenon on the margins of artistic respectability.

No more. All of that has changed in the past twenty years. With the postmodern erasure of boundaries between high and low art and the wholehearted embrace of popular culture, Pixérécourt has emerged as an innovative author deserving a place in all the handbooks, dictionaries, and encyclopedias of both French and world drama and theatre.

Our collection is a reflection of this new perception of the creator of melodrama. Pixérécourt is a theatre artist worthy of attention on three grounds. He created a poetics of melodrama; he produced a formidable body of work in the new genre that he pioneered; and he actively engaged in the production, acting, and staging of this work serving as the first full-fledged European metteur-en-scène. He has also been called "a forerunner of the cinema."

For a melodramatist Pixérécourt led an exemplary life, composed of perilous adventures, hair-breadth escapes, sudden changes of fortune, surprising reversals, incredible triumphs, and terrible disasters. A commanding presence on the Boulevard du Crime, the playwright declared himself to possess "a soul in flames, a tender heart, a fiery imagination, and a proud and independent temperament." As a refined connoisseur of the arts, a bibliophile and collector, an editor and annotator of books, it seems most unlikely that Pixérécourt ever said the words often attributed to him: "I write for those who cannot read." In fact, he tells us something quite different about his audience as readers in his essay on the new genre, "Melodrama," published in 1832.

The texts we have chosen illustrate Pixérécourt as theorist of melodrama as well as practitioner. Since his earliest works, *Victor* and *Coelina*, which are adaptations of sentimental novels, already exist in English, we have chosen his historical melodramas — *The Dog of Montargis*, *The Ruins of Babylon*, and *Christopher Columbus* — as more representative of his spectacular stage craft. They also reveal the ethos of what Pixérécourt called "classic melodrama" with its Orientalism and colorful depiction of a non-European "other." The documents that Pixérécourt appended to his historical melodramas (which he sometimes had distributed to the spectators in the theatre) reveal his promotional skills as a showman using his erudition to assure audiences that all the sensational events they will see are authentic. We also include a late collaborative work, *Alice, or the Scottish Gravediggers,* based on a recent sensational crime story of serial murders, revealing Pixérécourt adapting to the taste of the time for "black romanticism." *Alice* bridges the centuries to the modern horror genre in film.

Daniel Gerould
Marvin Carlson

Charles Nodier's "Introduction" to
Pixérécourt's *Théâtre Choisi* (1843)

Translated by Daniel Gerould

Five years ago I wrote the following: "During the Directorate there played in Paris for several years, under the bizarre name of *dialogued pantomimes,* a collection of formless scenes, abortive and monstrous; stormy as a riot, mysterious as a conspiracy, noisy and murderous as a battle; the spectator always saw ghosts, vaults, dungeons, and the marvelous; in short, everything characteristic of an art in its early infancy.

"But melodrama, such as we have seen it, since 1800, come into being, develop, and grow as inspired by the inventive author of *The Wife of Two Husbands, The Ruins of Babylon, The Dog of Montargis, The Daughter of the Exile*, etc., etc., has become a new genre; it is both the true picture of the world which society has created for us and the only popular tragedy befitting the period in which we live.

"Melodrama has never been given its proper place; its birth dates from *Coelina.*

"Until now M. de Pixérécourt's talent has never been appreciated at its just value, and yet the ingenious fluency of this playwright has endowed the stage with a great number of interesting works, remarkable for the clarity of the expositions, the skill of the unfolding, the marvelous integration of the effects, for the concatenation of effects so dynamic and so well managed, the novelty of means so bold and yet so probable, even the propriety of the general style which its solemn and apophthegmatic form makes more suitable, when it is necessary, to leave profound impressions on the soul, but which provides everywhere else enough that is correct, natural and graceful, to do honor to dramas of a more elevated rank. I am less grateful to him, however, for these brilliant dramatic qualities, for which the arbiters of literary glory should have given him credit before me, than for the profound feeling of decency and morality that is shown in all his works. I say this because I have seen them, in the absence of religious worship, take the place of the silent pulpit, and bring, in an attractive form that never failed of its effect, serious and valuable lessons to the soul of the spectators; it is because the performance of these works which are truly classic, in the basic meaning of the word, in the meaning that relates to the moral influence of art, inspired only ideas of justice and humanity, gave rise only to virtuous emulations, aroused only tender and generous feelings, and because the spectators rarely left these performances without being improved; it is because in this difficult period, when the people could begin anew its religious and social education only at the theatre, there was a providential aspect in the application of melodrama to the development of the fundamental principles of any sort of civilization. This powerful action of popular drama, which was unprecedented since the ancients, had begun to reveal itself during the Consulate; it was prolonged during the entire duration of the Empire, and at no other time has the class which directly felt its influence been better behaved morally, never has crime been more rare. Evil-doers would not have dared to show themselves in a place of amusement where everything spoke to them of harrowing remorse and inevitable punishment. Insurmountable anxiety would have betrayed them. I do not know what rank posterity will assign to M. de Pixérécourt among the writers of his century; but for many years the French Academy has owed him the Prix Monthyon. I have no objections to thick books of statistics full of numbers, pretentious metaphysics, and ostentatious philanthropy, whose vogue has succeeded that of melodrama. I believe quite sincerely in the immense advantages that the human race has derived from reading them, if it has read them, either for its material betterment or for its moral welfare; but there is a belief that I would have much more trouble giving up; this is the belief that if a mission of useful and truly social influence has in our time been given to a man of letters, the man who has received that mission is M. de Pixérécourt."[1]

The friendship which has for thirty years united me with M. de Pixérécourt, and which is founded between us on a lively communality of principles, affections, and tastes, has in no way influenced this judgment. I stand by it, and I do better, I have fulfilled the logical duty that this judgment imposed on me by

---

[1] "Du Mouvement intellectuel et littérarire sous le Directoire et le Consulat," *Revue de Paris*, vol. 19, no. 1 (5 July 1835).

accepting the role of editor of these works. Many circumstances removed them from the theatre for a certain time: the disaster that consumed in an hour the theatre that M. de Pixérécourt had created; the fickleness of a public avid for new sensations and profoundly antipathetic to all that it loved when what it loved has grown old; the frightening alteration of national morals and of the mentality of a certain class of people who abhor everything that reminds them of virtue, even in stage performances; the invasion by an eccentric school, carried out with infernal zeal to highlight the poetic beauties of crime, and which is, we must admit, like all literary movements, the true expression of a deplorable age. Therefore I do not delude myself into thinking that the publication of M. de Pixérécourt's *Theatre* is one of those enterprises that guarantee the editor and the bookseller the brilliant successes accorded to what is fashionable. From my point of view, I see this edition as a collection of works whose dramatic destiny is left hanging in the present state of affairs until further notice, but which should hold an honored place in well chosen libraries on two grounds.

I am referring to their vogue and to their influence, neither of which can be contested. It is not solely to one hundred consecutive trials, like Thomas Corneille's *Timocrate*, that the plays of M. de Pixérécourt have been submitted; it is to thousands of performances, frequented by all classes of society, and of which the people have never grown tired, as long as their disposition has not been perverted by the corrupting influence of sophists. As to their effect on public morality, must one repeat that the long stretch of time covered by M. de Pixérécourt's *Theatre* is the most free of every sort of crime of any period, the memory of which has been conserved by the records of our courts? Shall I say yet another time that never has crime been more rare, especially in the lower classes? The reason is that at that time the lower classes sought in the theatre emotions which were always without danger, which were often salutary; the reason is that melodrama was a picture skillfully heightened, where crime appeared in all its repulsive ugliness, where virtue was adorned with all the graces that make it beloved, where the role of providential intelligence in human affairs was highlighted by the most striking and probable circumstances; the reason is that the spectator always came away from the performance better, and in this case this is not an empty boast.

There is no one whose spirits are not uplifted by the touching conversations of those ill-clothed spectators whom an overpowering interest riveted for three hours to all the afflictions of persecuted innocence, and who greeted with a unanimous cry of joy the punishment of the evil-doer. Everyone has had the opportunity to read in the newspaper the profound saying of a witness in a criminal case who recounted how someone tried to get him to commit a crime and how his sole response had been to exclaim: "Wretch, so you've never been to the Gaîté! So you've never seen a play of Pixérécourt performed!" I say that such a *Theatre* is a monument.

In times such as we live in, the theatre has become the school of all the evil passions that it was originally established to correct. Send to the theatre that has been concocted for us a man who has no principles, or who has only weakly held principles (which comes to almost the same thing); he will sharpen a dagger to give himself a dramatic look, and in a month you will see him on the way to the penal colony proudly assuming Robert Macaire's mantle.

The point here is not to make an apology for melodrama as a work of art. In this regard, young and brilliant minds whose abilities no one questions have left me nothing to say, because tragedy and drama of the new school are nothing more than melodramas dressed in the artificial pomp of lyricism; happy the authors of these literary productions, which are in any case truly remarkable, if they have been as faithful to the primitive goal of melodrama as to its form! Whether melodrama is a genre apart and sanctioned, in the narrow sense that classical literature gives that word; or whether it is only an extension of the novel, cut up into dialogue and made to conform to stage practices, is not the point here. What is certain is that in the circumstances in which it arose, melodrama was a necessity. The entire people had just enacted in the streets and on the public squares the greatest drama of all history. Everyone had been an actor in this bloody play, everyone either a soldier or a revolutionary or an outlaw. These solemn spectators who smelled of gunpowder and blood required emotions comparable to those they had been deprived of by the return to order. They needed conspiracies, dungeons, scaffolds, battlefields, gunpowder and blood; the undeserved misfortunes of greatness and glory, the insidious machinations of villains, the perilous devotion of good men. They needed to be reminded, in a theme always new in its context, always the same in its results, of the great lesson, on which all the philosophies are based, in which all the religions are summed up: that even here on earth, virtue is never without recompense, crime is never without punishment. And make no mistake about it! Melodrama was not something to take lightly! It was the morality of the revolution!

By considering it in this fashion, see how it gains in importance; how it approximates Greek tragedy, of which it is a distant and pale copy; how it lends a skillful and powerful helping hand to providence by demonstrating its workings through facts! In the absence of a religion that was truly moral and adequately attuned to the social needs, no one denies that it was the ancient poet who established and maintained the religion of duties among the peoples who lived prior to Christianity. Well, then! At the birth of melodrama, Christianity did not exist any more than if it had never existed. The confessional was shut, the pulpit was empty, the political rostrum resounded only with dangerous paradoxes, the theory of material interests had replaced the idea of any other purpose in the minds of the people. Where would human beings go to imbibe instructions able to guide them amidst the ever-irrepressible anxieties of life, if it were not to melodrama? Go ask the question of what remains of this old generation, and I have no fear of being contradicted: the tireless verve which underlay the performance of these salutary works has nipped in the bud as many evil actions as the eloquence of the Bourdaloues and the Bridaines. Hundreds of times it made the knife fall from the murderer's hands.

A kind of genius was needed to conceive this mission, equal amounts of courage and talent were needed to execute it. It demanded something more, that is to say, an abnegation a thousand times rarer than talent, because M. de Pixérécourt was not unaware that moral utility counted for little in the arts, and that success legitimately attained in the major theatres would not excuse him for having descended to the minor ones. His intellectual calling perhaps lay elsewhere; he answered to the call of duty, and glory be his reward for it, because he has done much good. Fortunately for him, such a feeling has nothing to envy the pleasures of vanity.

The style of melodrama, it is said, is a dangerous innovation in language. It is far-fetched, affected, *periphrastic*, mannered in its locutions, exaggerated in its images. It has nothing of the naïve simplicity of nature which gives so much charm to the language of the grand masters, and that is why it is not difficult to turn it into ridiculous bombast. Although we scarcely have had the right, for some years now, to show ourselves very delicate in matters of style, I am willing to accept this charge in all its rigor. I shall not even insist on the services that M. de Pixérécourt has rendered the language whose resources he possesses so well, by respecting everywhere its correctness and its rules in a genre of which all the licenses cannot be sanctioned by fashion nor justified by criticism. I shall not recall that, in excellent scenes in *Tékéli* and twenty other plays, he has given evidence of an admirable talent for elocution and dialogue. I admit once again that up to a certain point he can be made answerable for the faults and excesses of his school, and this concession is generous enough to put to rest questions about my impartiality; but it is right, at least, to seek with sincere attention the reasons that could have led such a good mind to disregard more or less often, in his melodramas, and much less often than one imagines, the rules of decorum and taste that he has so scrupulously observed in his writings in another genre. This is what I am going to undertake.

The education of the people who went through the revolution was like no other human education. It was accomplished in the sections, in the clubs, on the rostrums of the Convention, where the French language had just undergone an ordeal which threatened to be mortal. The language had been in peril, as had been the entire society. Everyone spoke false, it was the distinctive trait of the period. The expressions of that time matched the empty and incoherent exaggeration of ideas. The logical order of thought had given way to a hollow but sonorous phraseology, whose reverberations had become a habit and a necessity for the public's ear. There was a universal mold, for the use of the rostrum, the bar, the office, the press, where the oratorical period came infallibly to take its shape; there was a banal type whose imprint it was condemned to take before entering into circulation, and to fall like a coin in the popular commerce. The good writers did not let themselves be surprised by the invasion of this artificial verbiage, whose duration could only be ephemeral, but the good writers compose for posterity and are concerned only with it.

It was different for those compositions that live on *topicality,* as we would say today, and whose effect is lost, if it is not immediate and sudden. We cannot even imagine putting a translator between the theatre and the auditorium, and the drama must be spoken in the language that everyone understands, or risk not being understood by anyone. That is why Aristophanes and Plautus, who could be understood so easily by their audiences, are now so obscure. Classical drama in France has not undergone the same changes, but in France classical drama is written for the salons, and the language of the salons changes little, or when it changes, the poet is the one who modifies it. The language of the people is subject to other laws. Its amendment depends only on time.

The people of the revolution appropriated without making any great effort the bombastic rhetoric of the sophists; they regarded it as one of the conquests of their new liberty, and the corruption of their language is actually the most concrete vestige that has been left behind afterwards by those storms of a half-century ago from which the people still have not emerged. It would be a serious mistake to believe that the people are truly susceptible of being moved by the simple and natural beauties of style. They are certainly not and perhaps never have been. At the period of which I am speaking, the people would have regarded those heartfelt expressions which we value so highly as an oblique affront to their intelligence; they would have called for what they regarded as eloquence and poetry, the ornate and redundant phrase, the expression inflated by epithets and figures of speech. Those of a delicate and cultivated nature tremble with emotion at these naïve and touching lines of poetry:

"I have not given him a single kiss today."
[Racine, *Andromaque*, I, iv]

The people are not struck by it, because they know that no mother would express herself in any other way. Replace that with the following:

"I have not pressed him yet in my maternal arms."

Do even better. Replace it with something more mannered, more convoluted, more hyperbolic; and you will hear thunderous applause resound. Such is the taste of the multitude; and this taste that had to be satisfied was a dangerous reef at every moment threatening to the author's talent. We should be grateful to M. de Pixérécourt for having avoided it so often.

I have already spoken of the lofty mission that M. de Pixérécourt has so nobly taken upon himself. It was a veritable apostolate, and the first material condition of any apostolate is the knowledge of the languages proper to the countries for which the benefits of instruction are destined.

After all, the style of melodrama is not as reprehensible as is claimed nowadays by those who have never had any kind of style whatsoever. The melodramatic style has its excuses, and perhaps its advantages. Sometimes it encases the truth in needless ornamentation, but it does not falsify the truth; it half-hides the truth, but it contains it; its sententious and a bit solemn form has something impressive about it which gives it a powerful hold on the minds of the vulgar; its pretentious and mystical turns of phrase seem to command respect; its figures of speech and images strike the imagination and grip the memory.

Among thousands of difficulties solved, there is one for which M. de Pixérécourt has never received any acknowledgment, and which would have been insurmountable for a genius less passionate and less determined than his. In the useful and honorable plan which he designed for himself, he had to invent everything around him. M. de Pixérécourt was not supported by the harmonic knowledge of Luigi Cherubini, Jean François Lesueur, and Henri Montan Berton, by the instantly popular melodies of Nicolas Dalayrac and François Adrien Boïeldieu. He did not have as interpreters the tender sensibility of Simon, the lively and petulant finesse of Mezerai, the engaging ardor of Damas, the profound and spiritual taste of Baptiste, the pathetic and sublime energy of Talma. In addition to writing his play, he had to design the settings, create and execute the staging (*mise en scène*), find the actors to play it, and even a public to be moved by it. For M. de Pixérécourt, the rehearsal was for the education of the actors; while the performance was for the education of the audience. All that got done nonetheless, but it was M. de Pixérécourt who did it; and, if no one has yet said it, there is no one, at least, who could contest it.

The majority of readers must have noticed, among so many dazzling qualities, that admirable integration of scenic effects that no one has carried as far since Sedaine, and the application of which would certainly have given Sedaine much trouble in the same circumstances. The special history of these effects could have a lively interest in the personal memoirs of the author, which he will undoubtedly write, and which I believe are destined to throw a sharp light on the theory and practice of the art, but this history does not belong to external criticism. I shall limit myself to saying that a certain number of his subjects are taken from history and from chronicles, a certain number from the most popular novels of the first years of the nineteenth century, a certain number likewise from the most distinguished works of the foreign theatre, arranged for ours with both skill and judgment. The rest are the author's own creations, and as no mind is more fertile than his in ingenious and striking inventions, these are certainly the most perfect.[2]

M. de Pixérécourt is perhaps the dramatic poet of our days who has produced the most. His collected works would be extremely voluminous if it were complete. You will see by the restricted dimensions that he has given it how circumspect he has been in the choice of works that he believed able to bring back, without too much pride, to public attention. These are those works whose numerous tests, in Paris and in the provinces, have already consecrated the success, and that even modesty has not the right to believe devoid of merit. What he asks of public opinion now is not the annulment of a few more or less negative judgments; it is rather the avowal of an appreciation so often repeated, which has been the most precious fruit of his labors and of which a fatal accident has destroyed all the other results.

I am deeply convinced that public opinion will not invalidate his judgments.

---

[2] The author [François J.M. Raynouard] of *The Templars* [1805] very much appreciated M. de Pixérécourt's dramas. He urged him twenty years ago to become a candidate for the *Académie Française*. "Write," he said, "a tragedy for the *théâtre français*, so as to legitimize your bastards and you will be accepted right away; I promise you my vote in advance."

The Ruins of Babylon

or

Jafar and Zaida

Translated by Daniel Gerould

Translator's Foreword

In his historical melodramas Pixérécourt always strove for authenticity through fidelity to external details. At the time of the premiere of *The Ruins of Babylon* in 1810, critics pointed out that the playwright had incorrectly located the ancient city. In the second edition of 1815, the author, responding to this charge, changed the distance separating the ruins of Babylon from Baghdad to "twelve to fifteen miles" where before he had indicated only "three to four miles." This new corrected edition is also a more complete text in which Pixérécourt has restored a few cuts, including several ideological passages in which the Frenchman Raymond praises the ability of "thought" to defeat the attempts of "power" to silence it and denounces "the inhuman capriciousness" of the "cruel despot" who has overturned "the eternal laws of reason and nature." These passages, extolling enlightenment values, had perhaps been suppressed by the censor in Napoleon's day.

In 1778 Jean-François de La Harpe had written a five-act neoclassical tragedy in verse on the same subject, entitled *The Barmecides*, which played for a respectable eleven times at the Comédie-Française. Pixérécourt's version, which, contrary to the historical record, provides a happy ending for the Caliph's vizier Jafar, enjoyed a run of 318 performances at the Théâtre de la Gaîté, plus 594 in the provinces. In the 1815 edition the author changed the subtitle from "The Massacre of the Barmecides" to the more appropriate "Jafar and Zaida." He also added indications showing where the imposing tableaux occur at the end of the acts.

In *The Ruins of Babylon*, Pixérécourt integrates into his text mime, song, music, and dance (all precisely specified in extensive stage directions) to create a lavish total spectacle. The composer, choreographer, and designer received top billing along with the playwright. Hassan and Nair, the two children's roles, were played by actresses, as was the custom at the time.

In 1811, the ten-year-old Victor Hugo and his two brothers saw *The Ruins of Babylon* performed in Bayonne (on the family's way to Spain). Victor was so enchanted that he returned to the theatre again and again (possibly ten times) until he knew the play by heart. Hugo would draw upon the theatrical magic of its stage effects in his own works. In fact, *The Ruins of Babylon* inspired the future poet to write a melodrama that same year, resulting in the fragment, *Le Château au diable.*

With its triple appeal of Oriental exoticism, sensational action, and spectacular staging, *The Ruins of Babylon* looks forward to twentieth-century sumptuous spectacles with gorgeous ballets and incidental music such as *Kismet.*

Letter from M. Emile Deschamps to M. de Pixérécourt

Paris, 4 May 1841

My dear Pixérécourt,

I hear that you are finally going to give the public an edition of your *Selected Theatre* in four large volumes of 600 pages each, and I assume that you will be judicious and rigorous in your choice of plays. We shall have only around thirty works out of the one hundred and twenty that you owe us! . . . Never mind, we shall accept with alacrity the twenty-five percent of your literary balance sheet. I rejoice on several grounds: you know what a friend I am of the author; and I wholeheartedly seize the occasion of this good news to shake your hand across the eighty leagues that separate us.

The newspapers have announced at the same time that your *Theatre* will be preceded by an introduction by M. Charles Nodier: he is our great leader; we shall go far if we follow him. The chances of a striking success are doubled. I am as impatient to read his preface as to reread your works. He will find, I am sure, a thousand beautiful and fine things, all of them new, to say about melodrama, as you have created it; it is a genre of literature whose popular influence has been great, and which has not yet had its serious criticism. I have often thought about it, since it is a way of thinking about you; but I shall take care not to formulate my ideas: if they were not those of Charles Nodier, they would be very wrong; and, were they the same, they would be wrong, very seriously so too, for being expressed differently. In any case, my dear friend, the title alone of one of your works, which undoubtedly will not have been forgotten in your selection, awakens in me such a fresh memory, such lively emotions from earliest youth, that I shall not try to hold back their onrush. I wish to speak about your *Ruins of Babylon*, and of a reading that you gave of it, before the performance, in the last years of the Empire.

It was at Sceaux, in a charming house, all in white, in the midst of the greenery of its park; a noble sanctuary of friendship, an elegant temple of the arts. The master of the house loved to relax there, far from the cares of public life, in an intimate circle, where he was too well known not to be cherished and venerated; there the lady of the manor came to hold her court of friends upon leaving that of the Empress; she reigned thanks to the charm of her talents and graces, on the strength of her wisdom and goodness: a marvelous secret whereby to maintain her crown.

That day, Madame the countess Duchatel did not make music, and this was a kindness on her part. Who would have imagined it? . . . She did not want to have us hear her voice, after which, you'll agree, it was difficult to listen to anything else; but she led us to the second salon, and asked you for *The Ruins of Babylon*, smiling at the manuscript which had opened of its own accord. The guests took their places on large ottomans; the master and the mistress of the house had at their feet, on silk cushions, their young children who, since . . . Certainly, they deserved the future of their children! — The tripod was brought in, the Sibylline leaves of the book were unfolded upon it, you shook your mighty head of hair, and you gave the prelude to the drama. However, a beautiful autumn sun, gliding among the women, gilded before my eyes young foreheads as beautiful as the sun itself; the cannon of some victory rumbled far away; my father was there close to me; I was sixteen, and the almanac of the Muses was going to publish my first poetry! Anything read would have seemed splendid to me; the reading that you gave us didn't require all that much to please. From scene to scene, from act to act, the interest spread and grew in the audience, as it does in your work: do you remember the adorable flattery and the glorious horoscopes that were sent your way from the most eloquent and the most beautiful mouths? I doubt that the three hundred performances of *The Ruins of Babylon* in Paris and the reports of its success in the provinces and in all the foreign theatres could equal for you that first victory, that matinee for the elite. I said to myself in my corner, in my obscurity: how fortunate that Pixérécourt is!

Alas! My friend, misfortune has come in its turn. If it has not had its reign, it will have it: it is the law of nature. You have been struck in your career, in your affections, in your person; you suffer in both body and soul; but Providence is infinite: thus hope . . . and remember.

And may there be among your memories one for your devoted comrade and faithful friend.

Emile Deschamps

Note on *The Ruins of Babylon*

The title is magnificent, but it is not deceptive: the play all by itself has the where-with-all to sustain the pomp of the title. It is in the nature of melodrama to strike the imagination by famous names that awaken grand memories. Built by Nemrod, beautified by Semiramis, capital of the vast empire of the Assyrians, Babylon enjoys in history that celebrity which the obscurity of the times makes so to speak venerable and sacred, by making it mysterious. We recall only with enthusiasm the hanging gardens of Semiramis; if we had seen them, they would appear to us markedly inferior to the beautiful gardens of modern times. Babylon, with all its marvels, was quite far from equaling Paris; its most brilliant epoch was the time when Alexander held there the States General of Asia. I like to think that the day will come when Paris will have more of a place in history than Babylon; the most far-off centuries will adore her as the queen of cities, for having been the temple of glory and the arts, the center of the States General of the universe, and the seat of another Alexander.

The new melodrama is more historical than most tragedies taken from history. It is true that the caliph Harun-al-Raschid and the grand vizier Jafar are heroes of the *Thousand and One Nights*; but they are nonetheless real characters; they have nonetheless an existence in history, even though they play such a great role in the tales: it is even a kind of advantage for the author who puts them on stage; his actors are already known to both children and adults; there is no child who does not tremble at the name of the commander of the faithful and of his first vizier.

Envious detractors have quibbled with the author over a point of geography: they point out that Babylon, situated on the Euphrates, was at quite a distance from Baghdad, situated on the Tigris, and that consequently it was not exact to place the ruins of Babylon in the vicinity of Baghdad. Several writers, obliged to a greater exactitude than an author of melodrama, have nonetheless fallen into this error, and their opinion, although false, would be enough to excuse M. de Pixérécourt; but what justifies him much better, is that Seleucia, called in the Orient the second Babylon, was situated opposite Baghdad, on the west bank of the Tigris. Baghdad was on the east bank; it was so named after the garden of a monk named Dad. The unhappy people who escaped from the ruins of Seleucia took refuge in Baghdad: the error has its origin in this name of Babylon given to the city of Seleucia. These are then the ruins of Seleucia, the second Babylon, and not the ruins of the ancient Babylon of Semiramis, which were located in the vicinity of Baghdad; but every one will agree that M. de Pixérécourt was authorized to prefer to the name of Seleucia, which is dry and hardly sonorous, that of Babylon, more harmonious and better known. He did well to consult euphony rather than geography. I shall add, to complete this little geographical dissertation, that this name of Babylon went from Seleucia to Baghdad, and that the latter city is the third Babylon: this is the name that Racine gives it in *Bajazet*; if no one has reproached this great poet for having called Baghdad Babylon, who could accuse Mr. de Pixérécourt of a crime for having designated Seleucia under the same name of Babylon, which it had actually borne? Now that everything has been cleared up, there is nothing to prevent this superb title of *The Ruins of Babylon* from having its full and entire effect on the spectators, in spite of the envy of all the geographers hostile to melodramas.

Harun-al-Raschid was a contemporary, but not a rival of Charlemagne. The illustrious emperor of the Occident was always a monarch who was as wise as he was courageous; the caliph of the Orient was too often a mad despot: with a few deeds of justice and generosity, he compounded too great a number of bizarre, extravagant, and cruel actions, sad destiny of Oriental princes who can do whatever they wish: it rarely happens that what they wish is reasonable. This caliph dearly loved both his sister Abassa and his vizier Jafar; but he could only see them separately, because no man outside the immediate family could appear before the princess. To unite these two objects of his tenderness, he conceived the idea of marrying them; but the blood of the Barmecides could not be mixed with the blood of the Abassides without sullying its purity; the child who would be born of this mixture could dispute the throne with the offspring of the race of the great Abas. To overcome this obstacle, the mad caliph exacted the promise from the unfortunate Jafar to live with his wife as with a sister. Jafar swore, and agreed to lose his life if he violated his oath: he believed that he would be able to keep it, because he had not yet seen Abassa's charms. Note that the author has substituted in his play the sweet and agreeable name of Zaida for that of Abassa, which could have provided fools with a bad pun capable of disrupting the performance.

Once Jafar had seen Zaida, politics having made the promise, love violated it. Jafar had a child by his wife; what is the height of joy for ordinary married couples was for Jafar and Zaida the sign of the greatest misfortunes. The princess, on the pretext of a pious pilgrimage, went to be delivered of her child at Mecca. All precautions could not prevent Jafar's enemies from penetrating the mystery: proof had to be given the Caliph; they so effectively made their moves that the monarch surprised Jafar and his wife caressing their child in the secret asylum that they had chosen to hide their love. Any one other than the proud Harun would have been touched by the sight; never was a fault more pardonable, if a despot knew how to pardon. The enraged caliph ordered the execution of Jafar, his son, and the entire family of the Barmecides. He had his own sister driven out of the palace, clothed in the livery of extreme poverty. The dangers of these illustrious outcasts constitutes the interest of this melodrama, rich in pathetic situations, in marvelous incidents, without however being outside the pale of poetic theatrical verisimilitude.

The plot is simple, clear, conducted with much more art and good sense than is usually put in a melodrama, and even than is expected of this genre. I am a bit alarmed at such perfection in a melodrama. I do not have the time to enter into greater detail today; I shall return to this work another time: suffice it for me to say that *The Ruins of Babylon* cost the manager of the Gaîté a great deal, and yet is destined to make him rich.

In the old libertine customs of the ancient Babylonians, there was not too much out of which to make a melodrama, and M. de Pixérécourt has done well to seek a nobler and more serious subject at the court of the caliphs of Baghdad. His heroes are only hapless and guilty for having obeyed the holy laws of matrimony, without regard for a promise made under duress. The author has given the outlaws as a guardian angel a Frenchman named Raymond, all of whose sallies amuse the caliph: this young man, full of wit, gaiety, and courage, is devoted to Jafar's interests, follows him everywhere and extricates him from the greatest dangers. This part is played by Tautin, with a vivacity, a finesse and a sprightliness worthy of the

French nation.

To this young and interesting Raymond, protector of innocence, the author opposes an old chief eunuch, named Isuf; he is an evil-doer, a villain, a cheat; he serves the hate of the Sultana Almaide against the vizier who has rebuffed her advances.

The third act presents a troupe of Bedouin Arabs who are camped amidst the ruins of Babylon; Isuf comes and offers them money to assassinate Jafar and his son; but Raymond gives them more to protect these innocent victims. The unhappy Zaida, overcome by fatigue, dying of hunger, comes to seek refuge in these ruins: a young man hears her cries, and comes out of a nearby fortress; he tries to console this hapless woman, he brings her whatever he can to appease her hunger and thirst. This young man, named Hassan, is the true son of the caliph; his father had him brought up in that fortress, far from the seductions of the court. The young Hassan implores the caliph to pity an unfortunate woman; he presents her to him. The caliph recognizes his sister, and his rage rekindles; he overwhelms her with reproaches and threats. Hassan throws himself at his feet, endeavors to bend him: for long inexorable, the caliph finally opens his heart to compassion; but at this moment he is surrounded by Arabs and about to fall under their blows, when Jafar, friend of the Arab chief, whose life he has previously spared, dashes in to save the caliph, and by this act of generosity, disarms the vengeance of this monarch. There is the gist of the work; but it is not possible to enter into the details in an analysis; they must be seen on the stage. M. Marty plays the role of Jafar with much ardor and sensibility. Mademoiselle Hugens is very touching in the role of the young Hassan; she has a sweet and pathetic tone, her voice is clear; she enunciates well, which is a greater virtue than we realize. The role of Zaida has been assigned to Mademoiselle Bourgeois, who executes it with energy.

The play has two ballets, both composed by M. Hullin, and consequently very delectable; they contribute a great deal to the favor and success accorded this work: the first ballet especially is extremely pleasing and original. The decorations, the costumes, and everything about it has a freshness and brilliance that leaves nothing to be desired, and that makes the spectators forget what country they are in. What would the late Jean Baptiste Nicolet, the founder of this theatre, say, if he could return to the world to see the actual state of his playhouse; he would not recognize it in the sort of palace which has replaced his old shack; he would be dazzled by so much magnificence; he would predict ruin for the manager if he continued his mad expenditures: the good man would not surmise that these very expenditures were what would enrich him.

Julien-Louis Geoffroy

THE RUINS OF BABYLON

or

JAFAR AND ZAIDA

An Historical Melodrama in Three Acts

by

René-Charles Guilbert de Pixérécourt

Music by Gérardin-Lacour

Ballets by Hullin

Decor by Alaux

Presented for the first time in Paris at
the Théâtre de la Gaîté on 30 October 1810

CAST OF CHARACTERS

HARUN al-RASHID, the Caliph of Baghdad

HASSAN, son of Harun

ZAIDA, sister of the Caliph and wife of Jafar

JAFAR, the Barmecide, first Vizier

NAIR, son of Jafar and of Zaida, five years old

RAYMOND, Frenchman, secret friend of Jafar

ISUF, chief Eunuch

ABULCASEM, Bedouin Sheik

MORABEK, Bedouin

AGIB, old Arab

One of the Caliph's GUARDS

ODALISQUES

SOLDIERS

BEDOUINS

SLAVES

EUNUCHS

The action takes place in 796, in Baghdad and in the ruins of Babylon, which are only twelve to fifteen miles from the city.

Act One

The stage represents the interior of the gardens of the seraglio. To the left, ZAIDA's quarters, the casement window of which opens on the garden. To the right, a totally plain kiosk. In the background a highly ornate iron-barred gate. By opening the shutters with which it is equipped, one sees the Tigris, which bathes the walls of the seraglio, and the covered bridge suspended over this river. The other bank reveals a radiant countryside dotted with handsome dwellings.

At the rise of the curtain, the mute SLAVES are busy preparing the feast in honor of JAFAR; they are arranging vases filled with flowers, garlands, etc. RAYMOND directs everything. His advice and his activity lend great vivacity to this tableau.

RAYMOND: I have given you an example of work; now I owe you an example of pleasure and joy. Here is the song that I promised you. But, because it gently mocks the severe laws of the seraglio, I shall sing it very softly and you will dance incognito.

He sings, accompanying himself on the lute.

First Stanza

> At your Mahomet I repress my laughter;
> The Prophet grant me pardon right away!
> Instead of bliss he promised you hereafter,
> I'd choose a kiss that's given me today.

During the refrain, the MUTES dance in a grotesque manner to the accompaniment provided by RAYMOND, who advises them to make as little noise as possible.

Enter JAFAR, disguised as a black slave. He appears at the back of the stage and signals to RAYMOND.

RAYMOND *(aside, noticing him):* Who is that slave beckoning to? He probably did something stupid, and is coming to ask for my support against the chief eunuch. *(The* SLAVES *gather round* RAYMOND *and beg him to continue his song.)* That's right, I haven't kept my promise; I owe you another stanza.

The SLAVES *applaud.*

Second Stanza

> To true believers, in his holy scripture,
> He promises ambrosia — once they die.
> Ah! let's not wait for such uncertain rapture,
> But to the other life let's swiftly fly.

Refrain and dance as for the first stanza. JAFAR, *who has strolled through the gardens so as not to arouse suspicions, comes back at the end of the dance and again signals to* RAYMOND, *but with more insistence; he implores him to dismiss those who surround him.*

RAYMOND *(aside):* That mute again! He is clearly beckoning to me. I am touched by his entreaties. Very well . . . I must oblige him. *(To the* SLAVES.) That's enough for today. Go along to the other part of the gardens, I won't be long in joining you. (JAFAR *thanks* RAYMOND *and keeps to the side during the exit of the* MUTES *who go off to the right dancing.)*

RAYMOND *(to* JAFAR): Approach. What do you want?

JAFAR *(leading him quickly near the kiosk so as not to be seen):* To embrace you and see once more my beloved Zaida. *(He removes the mask covering his face.)*

RAYMOND: Jafar!

JAFAR *(putting his hand over his mouth):* Silence!

RAYMOND: My master!

JAFAR: Say rather your friend. My dear Raymond! *(They embrace.)*

RAYMOND *(after having looked to see if they can be seen):*   Your rashness makes me shudder! If the Caliph . . .

JAFAR: Whatever his mistrust, could he suspect to find his first vizier beneath the clothes of a vile mute? No, it is unlikely. Besides, he thinks that I am busy in my camp. While everything is being arranged for the brilliant and triumphal entry that his lavishness is preparing for me, I secretly stole out of my tent. Thanks to this disguise I passed through the town and entered the seraglio without meeting the slightest obstacle.

RAYMOND: I tremble! If you were discovered here . . .

JAFAR: I know all that I would have to fear from the implacable Harun. Who better than I knows this proud despot, so astonishing in the incredible mixture of the best and the worst qualities? I know that this prince, justly famous in the Orient for his bravery, his generosity, the benefits that he showers on his subjects, has often shown himself to be capricious, ungrateful, even cruel; that he sacrifices, with neither scruple nor regret, the most sacred rights of gratitude and humanity to his unjust suspicions and the bizarre nature of his tastes. I am thus unable to ignore that neither my services for ten years, nor the victories that I have just brought, nor even his friendship could exempt me from the frightful vengeance that he exacts from any one who dares contradict his orders; but I have risked all to see my wife again. After an absence of ten moons, I was compelled to fear that her transports, that mine as well could betray us in the presence of the cunning Argus who watches our every move. She awaits from me the details about our son, about our beloved Nair, whose existence until now we have been able to cloak in an impenetrable mystery. In a word, it is necessary, whatever the price, that I see her and that I speak with her without witnesses. In this important circumstance I have counted on the protection of the Prophet and on the zeal of a sincere friend whose ingenuity has been able to keep me safe from all perils and has obtained for me the only moments of true happiness that I have ever known.

RAYMOND: Oh, Barmecide! My worthy benefactor!   Your expectations will not be disappointed. More than ever I have the means of being useful to you. The sort of folly that I affect and that Zaida deliberately pretends to enjoy pleases the Caliph immensely and gives me the right to tell the truth with impunity. No one dares complain about a man who has the good fortune to make His Highness laugh and to whom His Highness has granted the exclusive right to break the sad monotony of this sojourn by his droll sallies, or by the festivities that he invents. Faithful to our plan, I continue to indicate my coolness, even aversion toward you, and I think I have noticed that it is one of the principal causes of Harun's kindness to me. Although he loves you very much, as a natural consequence of the strangeness of his character, he feels impelled to have the ascendant over you and to instill in me ingratitude toward my former master. Oh how little he knows Raymond's heart: rank, honors, riches could never extinguish the just gratitude that I have vowed to you. Generous Jafar! Remembrance of your benevolence is engraved there . . . in indelible letters. Dispose of Raymond as your most faithful slave; he is devoted to you in life and in death.

JAFAR: So much zeal touches me and does not surprise me. For eight years you have given me proof that your attachment to me knows no bounds. Learn then . . .

ISUF (off-stage): Raymond!

RAYMOND: Someone's calling me . . . (He looks.) It's Isuf.

JAFAR: That eunuch devoted to the favorite? Is he still in favor?

RAYMOND: More than ever.

JAFAR: It's quite simple; he is false and evil.

ISUF *(the same as before):* Raymond!

RAYMOND: What is it, my Lord? *(To* JAFAR.) I'm going to find him. Wait for me. He's coming! . . . Put on your mask again and pretend to be busy arranging these flowers.

Enter ISUF.

RAYMOND *(very gaily):* Here I am, my Lord Isuf; here I am.

ISUF: I was looking for you. I have to speak with you. *(In a harsh tone of voice, to* JAFAR, *who is watering the shrubs.)* Slave, get out of here.

JAFAR *(in an undertone to* RAYMOND): What bad timing! *(He moves off into the gardens to the right.)*

ISUF *(aside):* This Frenchman can be useful to me! I'll try bribing him, reserving his destruction for later on.

RAYMOND *(aside):* Let's be on our guard against this old hypocrite.

ISUF: Most favored Raymond, give thanks for the good fortune that is coming your way.

RAYMOND: Can it bring me anything more delightful than this unexpected meeting?

ISUF: Have done with compliments; only straight talk with me.

RAYMOND *(aside)*: What does he mean by that?

ISUF: I know your schemes. I divined the reason that made you abandon Jafar and seek the extraordinary favor of being admitted to the gardens of the seraglio.

RAYMOND *(anxiously):* You divined it?

ISUF: Yes.

RAYMOND *(as before):* And that reason was . . .

ISUF: Ambition.

RAYMOND *(aside):* He knows nothing.

ISUF: No one has ever fooled me.

RAYMOND *(aside):* Then I'll be the first. *(Aloud.)* Since, thanks to your astonishing perspicacity, you know my secret, I am going to bare my soul to you totally. Undoubtedly, I have great obligations to Jafar: during the visit this minister paid to the court of Charlemagne, I had occasion to experience the goodness of his heart. My family was oppressed, ill-starred; he gave them all the benefits, both honor and fortune. I grew attached to him, and I left France to follow him to Baghdad. He considered me as a second self and divulged his most secret thoughts to me. But through his confessions, I observed the character of the Caliph; I sensed that this prince was beginning to tire of Barmecide, either because he is fickle or perhaps for the sole reason that he had received the most extraordinary services from him.

ISUF: Too loyal to wish to hasten the fall of your benefactor, you could not however repress the hope of raising yourself on his ruins.

RAYMOND: It is true.

ISUF: I had divined all that. I have long observed you, and I was able to discover beneath that mad gaiety of yours a profundity and a subtlety well suited to further my important plans. We both approach a decisive time for our fortune. I accept the augury; but we need a perfect accord, a strict alliance that nothing can sunder, and above all an inviolable secret.

RAYMOND: You could not have better chosen your man.

ISUF: I know it. Then make your choice: either 20,000 sequins and second place in the State after the Caliph, because I shall have the first place . . .

RAYMOND: That's fair.

ISUF: Or death . . .

RAYMOND: My choice is clear.

ISUF: Enter into the vast plan that we have conceived. I say we, because I am only the agent of a jealous and wronged woman, Almaide.

RAYMOND: The wife of the Caliph?

ISUF: For six years Jafar and the beautiful Zaida have been joined in matrimony; but you are unaware of the circumstances that led to this strange marriage, and of the bizarre condition that was attached to it; a condition that is going to become the source of the greatest events.

RAYMOND: Every word redoubles my curiosity.

ISUF: Almaide, before belonging to the Caliph, was smitten with Jafar; but Barmecide was insensible to her charms and to all her enticements. What did that proud beauty do to avenge herself for such indifference? Having noticed Jafar's secret inclination for the Caliph's sister, she advised her husband to unite them. Then, taking advantage of the rights owed her by her husband, whose most cherished wish she had gratified in giving him a son . . .

RAYMOND: That young Hassan who is being reared in a fortress constructed in the midst of the ruins of Babylon?

ISUF: Just so. Under the pretense that the blood of the Alis must not be sullied by a foreign admixture, but actually to assure the throne for her own son, she agreed to that marriage on the cruel condition that Barmecide would never be for Zaida more than a brother and a friend; that, in short, he would never claim his conjugal rights as a husband. Dazzled by such an honor and perhaps deluding himself that the Caliph would one day retract that rigorous order, Jafar submitted to everything. On pain of death, he agreed to total compliance with his master's will.

RAYMOND: A promise of that sort is beyond human strength.

ISUF: And so he broke it.

RAYMOND *(aside):* He knows all.

ISUF: At least, we are thoroughly convinced that he did.

RAYMOND *(aside):* Ah! . . . *(Aloud.)* Unfortunately that's not enough to destroy him, proof is needed.

ISUF: We'll have it. Yes, I'm sure their secret relations have borne fruit.

RAYMOND: What is the likelihood?

ISUF: Nearly fifteen moons after that marriage, Zaida requested her brother's permission to make a pilgrimage to Mecca, on the pretext of fulfilling the vow she had made during a serious illness which had afflicted the Caliph. It was a specious reason. The Princess left; but we kept her surrounded by clever spies who watched all her moves and gave us detailed reports. We knew that she had had frequent secret conferences with the Imam of the temple, and that she had disappeared from the sight of her attendants for an entire day, *(suspiciously with a malicious smile)* so as to stay, it was said, for prayers.

RAYMOND: That last circumstance, I admit it, could make you have suspicions; but if nothing since then has confirmed them . . .

ISUF: After the last battle that Jafar led against the Arabs, he feigned being kept in his tent by a wound, and left his camp for five days. As though by a miracle, he surmounted the enormous distance that separated him from Mecca, where he furtively made his way to seek . . .

RAYMOND: To seek?

ISUF: His son!

RAYMOND: His son!

ISUF: I cannot yet prove it; but some time after this excursion, there was noticed in his retinue a young child whose features very much resembled those of Zaida. In the army he passes for an orphan rescued on the battlefield; a thousand witnesses attest to the fact; but this ruse won't take me in. Jafar is on the very brink of ruin.

RAYMOND *(aside)*: He makes me shudder. *(Aloud.)* Yes, no doubt about it.

ISUF: Now is the time to dissemble. You must be reconciled with Barmecide and appear to repent your ingratitude. He will believe your change of heart to be sincere, and you will soon fathom the mystery that it is so important for us to understand.

RAYMOND: Oh! How thankful I am that you turned to me. You cannot imagine what gratitude . . .

ISUF: I would suspect your candor if your good fortune were not at stake as the result of this treaty. Besides, you know, given Almaide's character and mine, what the reward would be for any betrayal or even the slightest indiscretion. Farewell. I am going to report to the favorite on the success of my mission.

RAYMOND *(seeing* JAFAR, *who is crossing at the back of the stage):* Oh! I'll succeed or I'll lose my life in the attempt.

ISUF: Fine! Fine! I like such ardor. Farewell.

RAYMOND: My compliments to his Highness's first vizier.

ISUF *(taking the compliment for himself)*: Not yet; but that won't be long in coming. Ah! Ah! This Frenchman is quite agreeable! He's totally engaging. *(In a protective tone.)* Rest assured that in my prosperity, I shall not forget you.

RAYMOND *(pointedly)*: I'm counting on it, and I'll make sure you remember me. Good-bye.

ISUF: Farewell. *(He leaves rubbing his hands together.)*

RAYMOND: Ah! Traitor! I'll foil those odious plots. *(He calls JAFAR, who reappears.)* Unhappy Jafar, you are surrounded by spies! Almaide has vowed your ruin; fear everything from her hate. Let us use wariness and guile to thwart the perfidy of her henchmen. Would that I could safeguard you from the traps that are set for you, even at the cost of my blood!

JAFAR: Rare and faithful friend! . . . I entreat you, amidst these anxieties, let me see Zaida for an instant, a sole instant.

RAYMOND: It would be wiser for you to go away.

JAFAR: I cannot. My love, nourished by absence and so many obstacles, is more impetuous than ever. I would pay with my life to have an hour's conversation with my beloved Zaida.

RAYMOND: Once engaged in this sweet interview, will you have sufficient self-mastery to break it off? I fear Isuf's return and Harun's arrival.

JAFAR: What do I care? Your resistance inflames my desires still more.

RAYMOND: Remember, my Lord, that each of you separately has entrusted me to watch over you both, and I must consider for each of you what is most precious in the world.

JAFAR: That is true. Well, then! I consent, I shan't speak with her, but I wish to see her and give her a selam[1] which I am going to compose while you play her the usual signal.

RAYMOND: That is your wish? . . . Then so be it.

He goes and takes his lute, and tunes up beneath the window of ZAIDA's *apartment. Meanwhile* JAFAR *roams throughout the garden to gather flowers and fruit from which he forms a selam.*

ZAIDA *(appearing on the balcony)*: Dear Raymond, what have you come to tell me?

RAYMOND: A message from your husband. *(To* JAFAR.) Come closer.

ZAIDA: When will I be allowed to see him?

JAFAR: Soon.

ZAIDA: That voice!

JAFAR: It is *his* voice!

ZAIDA: Jafar in that disguise!

RAYMOND: What recklessness! Silence!

JAFAR *(showing* ZAIDA *the selam):* This faithful interpreter of my thoughts will tell you what is taking place in my soul, all that I have suffered during our cruel separation, and the means that I have found to reunite us. *(By climbing on a balustrade that is located beneath the window, he succeeds in giving the selam to* ZAIDA, *who leans down to get it.)*

---

[1] In Turkey and the Orient *selam* is the word for a small bundle composed of flowers, fruits, woods, silks and other objects all of which have an allegorical significance. This ingenious means of communication is much used by lovers, inasmuch as it presents no danger, since by disordering the arrangement of the divers objects, or by dividing them up, they no longer convey any meaning. [*Author's note.*]

ZAIDA *(in an undertone):* Our son . . .

JAFAR: This selam will tell you . . .

RAYMOND *(who is looking to the back of the stage):* I see Harun. Separate. Into this kiosk, my Lord, until the danger is past.

JAFAR *(to ZAIDA):* We shall soon meet again. *(He goes into the kiosk, the key to which RAYMOND takes.)*

ISUF *(off-stage, in ZAIDA's apartment):* Princess . . .

ZAIDA *(starting in terror):* Isuf! Heavens!

ISUF *(as before):* The Caliph, your brother, asks that you join him in the pavilion of flowers.

ZAIDA *(She turns to answer ISUF; but over the edge of the balcony she waves the selam which she holds in her left hand so that it will be seen by RAYMOND):* Tell his Highness that his humble slave considers it her duty to obey his orders.

ISUF *(as before):* His Highness has chosen me to escort you myself.

He comes out on the balcony and lowers the blinds. ZAIDA, before going back into the apartment, throws the selam to RAYMOND, who crouches down under the balcony so as not to be seen by ISUF.

RAYMOND *(alone, having picked up the selam):* That old rogue undoubtedly knows the enigmatic language of these flowers, and the Princess was afraid of his discovering her secret. Let us hide them in this vase. *(He puts the selam in a vase beneath the balcony.)* Perhaps during the festivities I'll find a favorable moment to . . . *(He makes a movement to enter the kiosk.)* The Caliph approaches, let us again put on the antic disposition that pleases him and redouble the gaiety to better disguise our distress. *(He sings, accompanying himself to the same tune as in the opening scene.)*

Third Stanza

Ah! Of this dwelling were I at the helm,
To lifelong joy found I the broad highway,
I'd banish stern Mahomet from my realm,
To set up Epicurus there to stay.

Enter HARUN *in the middle of the stanza. His* GUARDS *make a movement to force* RAYMOND *to be silent, but the* CALIPH *commands them to let him finish. He seems to be much amused by the spirit of independence and the gaiety shown by* RAYMOND, *who dances in a droll manner to the refrain, as in the opening scene.*

HARUN: Go to it, Raymond; you seem in cheerful spirits.

RAYMOND: As I always am when I have the good fortune to see his Highness.

HARUN: Do you know I must like you a great deal to let you openly, in my court, express sentiments so contrary to our customs?

RAYMOND: If I had no other proof of the favor with which you honor me, that certainly would not convince me.

HARUN: What do you mean?

RAYMOND (*pretending to be upset that he has said too much*): My Lord . . .

HARUN: Explain yourself.

RAYMOND: Your Highness will perhaps grow angry?

HARUN: What do you care?

RAYMOND: Good gracious! I care a great deal. I'm terrified of the gifts those gentlemen give. (*He indicates the* MUTES *who surround the* CALIPH, *and pantomimes the reaction of a man to whom the hangman's noose is brought.)*

HARUN: Do you like my gifts better?

RAYMOND: There's no comparison.

HARUN: Speak freely. I want to know what you think my reasons are for tolerating your impudence.

RAYMOND: You absolutely want to hear it?

HARUN: Absolutely.

RAYMOND: Well then, there are two.

HARUN: The first?

RAYMOND: The first is that however powerful . . . however despotic the Commander of the Faithful is, thought is still stronger than he is. And that since thought is independent of the human will, it is impossible to subject it to anyone or even for the powerful to place limits on it, and so it is wiser to leave thought a free course.

HARUN: And the second?

RAYMOND: The second is that the great, the sublime Caliph Harun-al-Rashid, who likes everything extraordinary, is not annoyed sometimes to hear the truth, were it only for the rarity of the occurrence.

HARUN *(removing from his finger a costly ring that he gives to RAYMOND):* It is yours.

RAYMOND: Good God! What would become of courtiers if all sovereigns imitated your example?

HARUN: They would become sincere.

RAYMOND: Everyone would gain by it.

HARUN: Here is my sister.

Enter ISUF *and* ZAIDA, SLAVES *and* GUARDS *remain at the back of the stage.* ZAIDA, *veiled, prostrates herself at the feet of the* CALIPH *who raises her up.*

ZAIDA: I beseech his Highness to accept the tokens of my respect.

HARUN: Zaida, your husband has gloriously concluded the expedition with which I entrusted him. Victor over the Arabs, he returns to lay at your feet the spoils of our enemies. His victorious army, encamped since yesterday within sight of Baghdad, is due to enter the city two hours before the setting of the sun.

RAYMOND *(aside):* What are we to do?

ZAIDA *(softly to* RAYMOND): What a dilemma!

HARUN: From here we shall see him cross the Tigris and march beneath the walls of the seraglio. I wished, this once, to have you witness the dazzling honors that my gratitude lavishes on a hero whom we both hold dear and who has seemed to me worthy of being linked to my race.

RAYMOND *(aside):* The hero must first leave his prison, and that is not easy.

ZAIDA: My Lord, if any consideration could add something more to the high esteem that I feel for Barmecide, most assuredly I should not know anything more powerful than the glory with which his latest exploits have just crowned your name and your arms. But I have long been accustomed to find only reasons for admiration in the conduct of the man whom you have given me for husband.

HARUN: No doubt, Raymond, the festivity that I asked you to

arrange will be worthy of its subject. The enmity that you show for Jafar will have given way to the desire to please me by celebrating the victories and the triumph of the first of my subjects?

RAYMOND: I can assure my master *(Quite pointedly.)* that never will my zeal have shone forth more brightly. His Highness will receive this very day quite conclusive proof.

HARUN: I shall not be surprised.

ISUF *(aside):* I understand, that's for me. *(He gives a wink of satisfaction to* RAYMOND.) Let us proceed to our goal. *(Aloud.)* It is true that in this instance the first Vizier has doubly justified his Highness's choice, not only by his worth and his success, but also by the audacious ingenuity with which he conveyed the secret message his Majesty entrusted to him for the Imam of the temple at Mecca.

ZAIDA *(aside, upset):* What is he saying!

ISUF *(staring at* ZAIDA): No one in the army other than he would perhaps have had the noble temerity to cross a distance of two hundred miles alone through the desert infested with Arabs.

HARUN: What is this message you're talking about? I don't know anything about it.

RAYMOND *(aside):* The traitor!

ISUF *(feigning the most ardent repentance):* Commander of the Faithful, pardon my indiscretion; I see too late that this journey was a secret for everyone except you and your minister.

HARUN: I repeat, he did it without my order.

ISUF: In that case too, I would have been no less guilty in divulging another's secret.

HARUN: Jafar can have, should have none from me. Is the reason for this clandestine trip known?

ISUF *(feigning a false reticence):* No, my Lord. But I beg your Highness to forget what I have just said and what is perhaps only the result of an unfounded rumor. *(Aside.)* Zaida has not given herself away, could I have been misled?

RAYMOND *(passing between the* CALIPH *and* ISUF): Instead of listening to the dreams of this old dotard . . .

ISUF *(peevishly):* What do you mean? . . . (RAYMOND *takes him by the hand.)*

HARUN *(to* ISUF): You're not going to take offense? . . . You know he's permitted to say whatever he wants.

RAYMOND: Ho, ho! Yes! Dotard . . . *(In an undertone.)* It's to hide our complicity.

ISUF *(aside):* He's right. *(In an undertone to* RAYMOND.) Excellent! Excellent!

RAYMOND: His Highness should rather tour the gardens to examine the preparations for my festivity. *(Aside.)* If I could get him away from here. *(Aloud.)* That dear Jafar! . . . He'll be so happy.

HARUN *(indicating that* RAYMOND *has lost his wits):* Oh! So now you like him?

RAYMOND *(forgetting himself):* I'll say I do! . . . *(Upon reflection.)* Do *I* like him? A little . . . it's starting to come back. But I'd like him to be far from here.

ZAIDA *(aside):* Would to God it were so.

ISUF *(aside):* I want to put her on the spot. *(Aloud to* RAYMOND.) He won't be as pleased as you think.

RAYMOND: Certainly if he first sees that scowling face, so admirably made to serve as a bugbear to the women of His Highness's seraglio, he would have little reason to be very satisfied.

HARUN *(laughing):* Their quarrels amuse me.

ISUF: It's not about me, it's about the Vizier Jafar. What has just happened to him must somewhat dampen his joy.

ZAIDA *(forgetting herself):* What is it?

HARUN: What has happened to him?

RAYMOND: Another vision. Come, my Lord.

ISUF *(observing ZAIDA):* Vision? . . . Yes! . . . A young child that he brought with him and on whom he lavished all the attentions of the most loving father has disappeared several days ago without any one knowing what has become of him.

ZAIDA *(giving herself away):* Heavens!

RAYMOND *(in an undertone to ZAIDA):* Compose yourself.

ISUF *(who has noticed ZAIDA's reaction. In an undertone):* Ah! No more doubt about it!

At this moment, JAFAR *turns the shutters of the blind behind which he is hidden.* RAYMOND, *located to the right, gets* ZAIDA *to notice this movement of the shutters, where she reads these words that the Vizier has marked on them:* HE IS SAFE.

HARUN *(to* ISUF): What child was that?

ISUF *(in an undertone to the* CALIPH): Observe the Princess's agitation.

HARUN *looks at his sister; but she has quickly regained her composure, and he does not notice the slightest alteration in her facial expression.*

HARUN: What are you talking about?

ISUF *(maliciously; in an undertone):* You'll see. *(Aloud.)* Yes, Princess, the latest word is that he died.

ZAIDA *(laughing):* Ah! ah! ah! What a strange character! I should like to know what interest such an event, real or imagined, can inspire in my brother or me?

ISUF *(disconcerted):* In you? . . . But a very natural interest, I think.

ZAIDA: Truly, my Lord, we are occasionally entertained by Raymond's lunacy; but the madness of this poor Isuf seems to me to be much more amusing.

ISUF *(aside):* Oh! the cunning little creature!

RAYMOND *(passing near* ISUF*):* So now you're mad. Welcome to the fold, comrade. *(Turning back toward* HARUN*.)* Listen, my Lord, it would not be astonishing if he had lost his reason. When one woman alone can sometimes turn the wisest man's head, how can you expect this unhappy creature, whom you have entrusted with the supervision of two hundred, to maintain his sanity? It's impossible.

ISUF *(aside):* I am furious!

HARUN *(to* ZAIDA*):* I rather like his observation.

ZAIDA: It is worthy of a Frenchman.

RAYMOND *(aside):* How can I get him to leave? *(Aloud.)* If your Highness deigns to command my mad colleague to go fetch his pretty flock, I am ready to conduct them as well as the princess to the orange grove where preparations are being made . . .

HARUN: No. I want to watch the festivities from here. We'll be comfortably situated in this kiosk.

RAYMOND *(aside):* Heavens!

ZAIDA *(aside):* He makes me tremble!

ISUF: Your Highness is right; from here you can see the river. I am going to arrange everything . . . *(He heads toward the kiosk.)*

RAYMOND *(stopping* ISUF*)*: With your permission, Lord Isuf: that is not for you to do. To each his task.

HARUN: That's right.

ZAIDA: And you are too officious in executing the task assigned to you . . .

RAYMOND: I still am not doing everything I should like to; but that will perhaps come. With perseverance, courage, and a bit of ingenuity, one gets through everything. Isn't that so, my Lord Isuf? *(He leads* ISUF *back to his place, making signs to him of complicity.)*

ISUF *(in an undertone to* RAYMOND*)*: Yes, yes.

RAYMOND *(aside, as if struck by a sudden idea):* He is saved. *(Aloud to the* CALIPH.*)* I have an idea, my Lord, don't you think it would be suitable to have the Vizier met by the people of your household entrusted with receiving him at the entrance of the seraglio and with greeting him?

HARUN: You are the one in charge of everything connected with the ceremony.

RAYMOND: I know what I owe to the Commander of the Faithful, and even if your ideas were not entirely in keeping with my plan, I would willingly agree . . .

HARUN *(smiling)*: I am obliged to you for this deference; but you are free to act as you see fit.

RAYMOND *(to the* MUTES *who are at the back of the stage and dressed like* JAFAR.) Come nearer, you there.

HARUN: What! You're planning to send mutes to greet Jafar and congratulate him?

ISUF: That's absurd . . . He's mad!

ZAIDA *(aside)*: The idea is altogether droll. *(To* HARUN.) Let him do it.

RAYMOND: Yes. I'm the one who'll serve as spokesman.

HARUN: Fine. Such attentions coming from you may surprise him.

RAYMOND: This is just the beginning. *(To the* MUTES.) Form two rows. *(He has them form in battle array so as to conceal the kiosk.)* In the French style. Stand by; draw up in a line, close ranks . . . Once more . . . There . . . Attention! Forward! (JAFAR *opens the door of the kiosk, takes his place at the end of the row.)* Are you ready? Good! To the left side . . . march. *(He takes his place at the head of the platoon as it passes in front of the* CALIPH *and* ZAIDA.) A quarter turn. Take the door . . . Double time . . . That's it.

By the movements that RAYMOND *has the* MUTES *execute,* JAFAR *ends up at the head of the line, and we see him go off first at high speed. The* MUTES *exit at double time.*

ZAIDA *(expressing her gratitude):* That's very good.

RAYMOND: At least I did the best I could. *(He exits dancing.)*

ZAIDA: That Frenchman is charming.

HARUN: I am infinitely obliged to Barmecide for having ceded him to us; he has provided us with many enjoyable moments.

ISUF *(aside):* He's not playing his role badly. *(Aloud, affecting ill humor.)* It's easy to please when you are allowed everything with impunity.

ZAIDA *(under her breath to* HARUN*)*: Isuf doesn't like him.

HARUN: It's quite simple; they have such different parts to play! The one diverts us, whereas the very sight of the other must inspire terror and constraint.

ISUF *(aside):* Have patience! Soon all the praise will be for me alone! *(He notices the selam that* RAYMOND *put in the vase.)* What's this I see? A selam. *(He takes it and examines it secretly.)* What an important discovery!

HARUN: Yes, Zaida, go find your companions and adorn yourself with my most precious gifts. The triumph of my favorite, of my sister's husband, cannot be celebrated in too lavish a manner. I want this solemnity to be embellished by all the magnificence and wealth that the luxury of the Orient can display; I want, in a word, Harun's court to present a mien worthy of the hero it awaits. You will come rejoin me in this place.

ZAIDA: I obey, my Lord. *(Aside.)* Oh, my beloved Jafar, so I shall see you without having to fear for your life!

HARUN: Isuf, accompany the Princess.

ISUF *(in an undertone):* I implore your Highness to grant me a moment's conversation.

ZAIDA *returns to the seraglio, followed by the* EUNUCHS *who had remained in the background.*

ISUF: The more you dispense blessings to your subjects when they show themselves worthy of them by their services, the more you have the right to expect from them blind submission and unswerving fidelity.

HARUN: At least I should hope so. But most often my favors have produced only ingratitude.

ISUF: Alas! It's only too true; I have just received sad proof to that effect.

HARUN: You carry mistrust and suspicion to such lengths.

ISUF: Would to heaven I had only suspicions!

HARUN: Could I have been betrayed?

ISUF: Because you have what is dearest in the world.

HARUN: Almaide?

ISUF: She is incapable of such a thing.

HARUN: Who then? Could it be my sister? . . . Barmecide?

ISUF: The two of them.

HARUN *(whose anger has been increasing by degrees):* The two of them?

ISUF: Yes. Jafar has broken his oath.

HARUN: Calamity befall him! . . . His death will be the price of his perjury.

ISUF *(aside, joyously):* Ah!

HARUN: But may calamity befall you, over-zealous servant, if you cannot back up this accusation. Remember, I need irrefutable proof . . . within the hour, or I shall have your head. *(Aside.)* Oh! May he never be able to offer me such evidence.

ISUF *(giving him the selam):* I shall not long delay. Here it is.

HARUN: What! . . . These flowers?

ISUF: It is a selam. Look.

HARUN *(with much emotion):* Indeed, this medley of flowers and fruit, the silk that ties them together . . . Where did you find it?

ISUF: In this vase.

HARUN: Beneath Zaida's window! . . . Who put it there?

ISUF *(maliciously):* No doubt Jafar.

HARUN: How can you suppose that this minister, busy in his camp . . .

ISUF: Indeed, that seems difficult . . . Then, it can only be Raymond, that Frenchman in whom you have placed so much trust, and who, in all probability, deceives you, in order to serve his former master.

HARUN: Cruel Isuf! When will you cease to put me in the frightful dilemma of never seeing anyone around me except enemies or traitors? . . . Oh! cursed be the fatal zeal that animates you, since it only serves to trouble the peace of my soul.

ISUF: I agree, my Lord; this news must seem dreadful to you. But it was my duty . . .

HARUN: Your duty could also dictate pointing out to me those to whom I owe rewards; but you are officious only when the need is to punish.

ISUF: Henceforth I shall not forget that I should put limits to my vigilance and my fidelity.

HARUN: Away with that fatal evidence. *(He casts aside the selam; ISUF picks it up.)* Rash Isuf!

ISUF: I beseech your Highness to recall that you have insisted, on pain of death, that I support with proof the warning that I gave you. Then you are not unaware that the mysterious meaning of the objects assembled here depends solely on their arrangement. It is therefore in my interest that the selam remain intact.

HARUN: Who will prove to me that it gives evidence against Barmecide?

ISUF: Its contents. Read it yourself.

HARUN: He absolutely insists on forcing me to punish. *(He takes the selam.)*

ISUF *(aside, joyfully):* I have won.

HARUN *(examines each of the objects that make up the selam and explicates it aloud):* "Sun of my life, incomparable treasure of light and beauty, if the cruel constraint imposed upon us does not allow me at our first interview to give vent to the fires by which my soul is inflamed, and which would betray our secret communications, know that absence has only increased the ardent love that has been awakened in me by our amorous raptures." That is enough! The traitors! . . . In defiance of a solemn promise! . . . It is all clear now; that trip to Mecca; Zaida's journey, muffled in the cloak of religion . . . That child brought back by Barmecide, did you say? *(With concentrated fury.)* Isuf, my vengeance will be terrible.

ISUF: Moderate your anger, my Lord. Oh! How greatly I regret . . .

HARUN: But you realize, there must not remain the shadow of a doubt.

ISUF: Unfortunately it will be easy to dispel them all by spying on the doings of Jafar and Zaida.

HARUN: I charge you with this act of surveillance.

ISUF: Entrust this painful task to another.

HARUN: It is properly your concern since you have provoked the decree. Tomorrow, before the setting of the sun, either the guilty pair, or you, will have ceased to live, I swear it by Mohamet.

ISUF *(aside):* I have no time to lose. *(Aloud.)* Your Highness will be obeyed.

HARUN: Zaida is coming back. I can scarcely contain my anger.

ISUF: Dissemble, my Lord.

HARUN: You are right. They must believe that they are perfectly safe.

ISUF *(aside):* My fortune is assured. I'll employ Raymond until after I succeed; then I'll send him to rejoin Barmecide.

HARUN: Great Prophet! Save Harun from the terrible blow that threatens him; do not allow him to be smitten in the very things most dear to his heart.

ISUF: Slaves! . . . Raise the blinds.

RAYMOND *(running in):* What the deuce, Lord Isuf, look to your own business. I'm the only one who . . .

ISUF *(in an undertone to* RAYMOND): I told the Caliph everything. If you express the wish, Jafar is lost.

RAYMOND *(in an undertone to* ISUF): If I express the wish! . . . Heaven knows . . .

ISUF *(as before):* One of us two must perish.

RAYMOND *(with a very pointed double meaning):* Your business is done.

ZAIDA *(lavishly adorned, comes forward at the head of the* ODALISQUES *covered with their veils):* My Lord, do you hear the sound of the cymbals and the clarions? The air resounds with harmonious songs and cries of glee. From all sides the people come running, they hasten to meet the conqueror of the Arabs, my beloved Jafar! . . . Commander of the Faithful, pardon Zaida's transports, which could not have a more legitimate or beautiful cause.

HARUN (*with constraint*): But, far from blaming your transports, I approve of them and urge you to give them free course. (*Aside.*) Why was it necessary to poison the joy of such a beautiful day? (*To* ISUF.) I do not see Almaide.

ISUF: She charged me with expressing to your Highness how much she regrets not being able to take part in the festivities. (*Aside.*) To participate in the triumph of her cruelest enemy!

RAYMOND: The procession is drawing near. (*In an undertone to* ZAIDA.) All eyes are fixed on you . . . Restrain your joy. (*Aloud.*) I beseech the Commandeer of the Faithful to take the place that is reserved for him.

HARUN: Where is it?

RAYMOND (*turning toward the* SLAVES): Open the blinds so that his Highness can enjoy the view.

They open the blinds that adorn the railing at the back. At a sign from RAYMOND, *the* SLAVES *remove the parts of the kiosk which are between the columns so as to expose it totally and to reveal a platform surmounted by an elegant dome and surrounded by a costly balustrade, trimmed with flowers and scent boxes where delicious perfumes are burning.*

ZAIDA: It is charming!

HARUN: Where do you find these new surprises?

RAYMOND: In the desire to please you, and above all in your approbation.

HARUN *mounts the platform; lower down, to his right,* ZAIDA *is placed; they are surrounded by* ODALISQUES. ISUF *and* RAYMOND *are to the left of the auditorium. To the sound of blaring martial music, the army is seen crossing the covered bridge in an oblique direction. It disappears for a moment, then marches in files behind the gate of the seraglio.* JAFAR, *surrounded by numerous trophies of his victory, is borne on a magnificent palanquin. The people precede and follow him, dancing and throwing him flowers. The army is placed on steps located outside the gate so as to present three rows one above the other.* RAYMOND, *followed by the* ODALISQUES, *goes to meet* JAFAR, *who enters on foot, preceded only by the* EUNUCHS *and* MUTES. HARUN *and* ZAIDA *get up and take several steps toward him.* JAFAR *comes forward and goes down on one knee before his master.*

HARUN: The homage that you render me is due to my birth; here is an honor more flattering and justly merited that I render to heroism.

He places on JAFAR's *head a crown of gold, fashioned into laurel leaves. The people and the army applaud with ineffable transports.*

ZAIDA *(with much emotion):* Barmecide, the magnanimous Harun has just crowned you for your valor and military abilities; but admiration and *(In a timid voice.)* love also wish to present a just tribute to the hero whose exploits bring peace to this empire. Receive this crown of olives, formed by Zaida's hands.

JAFAR *(receiving the crown and eagerly seizing* ZAIDA's *hand, which he kisses ecstatically. This gesture visibly displeases the* CALIPH): Oh! Sweet is this triumph! How could glory be despised when such a flattering reward is its prize.

HARUN, *with marked impatience, separates* JAFAR *and* ZAIDA, *whom he has placed beside his throne.*

RAYMOND *(aside):* What a frightful constraint for a loving couple after such a long separation!

HARUN: Raymond, now it is your turn.

At a signal from RAYMOND, *the* SLAVES *put on the most brilliant festivities, combining everything that good taste and sensuousness can offer that is most seductive and enchanting.   ISUF, crouched between the couple, and watched over by* HARUN, *prevents them from saying a single word to one another.*

Jafar, after your arduous labors, you must have need of some moments of tranquillity. Return to your palace; I allow you to stay there for three days, and until then I exempt you from all service, even from the duties that you perform for me.

JAFAR: Oh, my master! Your concern is touching . . .

HARUN *(to* ISUF*):* I shall enjoy the pleasures of the hunt tomorrow; see that all is ready by break of day.

JAFAR *(aside):* How well he is advancing my plans!

HARUN *(in an undertone to* ISUF*):* They think that they are free, and I shall surprise them easily.

ISUF *(in an undertone to* HARUN*):* The trap is ingenious.

JAFAR *(in an undertone to* ZAIDA, *whom he has approached furtively):* Tomorrow, you will see your son at the pavilion in the forest. *(He moves away.)*

ZAIDA *(aside):* Unhoped for happiness!

HARUN: Let us take our leave. (JAFAR *tries to say good-bye to the* PRINCESS.) Return to the seraglio, Zaida. (ZAIDA *goes off in the direction of the seraglio with all the women.* JAFAR *can only bow to her from afar.)* Barmecide, we shall meet again soon . . . *(With much emotion.)* I hope and I desire to find you always worthy of the favor of your master.

JAFAR *prostrates himself and goes to rejoin the army which has begun its march and again leads him in triumph. Brilliant and animated tableau.*

End of the First Act

Act Two

The stage represents a charming circular or octagonal pavilion in a pleasant woods. Trees can be seen on either side of the pavilion, as well as through the doors and the windows. The windows are furnished with blinds made of painted lattices. This structure must be elegant and above all very light. It takes up the entire breadth of the stage.

A marble flagstone is pushed up in the middle of the stage. Through this opening we see climb out NAIR, *a young child who runs about the pavilion, examining with curiosity all that it contains. He stops in front of several clusters of roses, jasmines, and other bushes, and picks flowers from them, which he casts aside one after the other in order to choose new ones that seem to him prettier or better smelling. From time to time he goes to the edge of the trap-door and indicates by his pantomime that his guardian is asleep and that he has taken advantage of his dozing to escape.*

AGIB, an old Arab, appears at the entrance to the underground vault and follows NAIR's *movements, whose absence had made him anxious. He delights in the joy shown by the child on finding himself free. The youngster, after having explored the pavilion, soon expresses the wish to go out and visit the surroundings. But AGIB catches him on the threshold of the door, scolds him for having run off and tries to bring him back. NAIR laughs at his remonstrances and apprehensions, and announces that he absolutely wants to go for a walk. Finally, the* ARAB, *unable to persuade him to obey, picks the child up and carries him off to the underground vault, despite the lively resistance he puts up.*

JAFAR (*entering*): Nair!

NAIR (*struggling as soon as he sees* JAFAR): Let me go! Let me go! Jafar's here.

AGIB *turns around and recognizes* BARMECIDE. *The child breaks away and runs to his father, throwing his arms around him. The* ARAB *complains about his disobedience and describes his little escapade to* JAFAR, *while* NAIR *makes fun of him and taunts him slyly.*

JAFAR *(to* NAIR): Agib is angry. So you were naughty?

NAIR: He's the one who's naughty. He won't let me go for a walk.

JAFAR: He's right; I forbade him to let you.

NAIR: Why did you forbid him? So you're naughty too.

JAFAR: No, it's because I love you.

NAIR: If you love me, why won't you let me do what I want to? I'm bored down there; I want to go for a walk.

JAFAR: That's not possible, my son. By going into the woods, you could meet soldiers who would kill you.

NAIR *(with naive vivacity):* I don't want you to go there either; stay here with us.

JAFAR, *enchanted by this reply, embraces his son tenderly.* AGIB, *who has been watching in the background, runs up and indicates that he has heard the sound of someone approaching.* JAFAR *gives him back the child and orders him to go back down while he goes to reconnoiter. The* ARAB *descends into the underground vault with* NAIR *and lowers the flagstone.*

RAYMOND *(entering)*: Where is your son?

JAFAR: In his hiding place.

RAYMOND: Is it impervious?

JAFAR: To all eyes.

RAYMOND: May your words prove true!

JAFAR: What causes this uneasiness? Have you come to inform me of some misfortune?

RAYMOND: No. But I fear all the stratagems of your enemies. I do not know what secret foreboding tells me that Harun's departure is only a feint to better discover your next moves. Redouble your precautions, my Lord, or you are lost. Do not forget that a woman's hatred never sleeps.

JAFAR: Who can alarm you to this extent?

RAYMOND: Isuf, you know, was to have accompanied the Caliph on the hunt.

JAFAR: What of it?

RAYMOND: He stayed in Baghdad. On my way here, I saw him as he stole out of the old seraglio, by the little door. He was heading in this direction. I pretended not to see him; but as soon as he recognized me, he hid in a corn field. I continued on my way up to the edge of the woods. There I stopped to observe, in my turn, the enemy who quickened his pace so as to catch up with me. Fearing that he might surprise you, I cut out along less frequented paths, and I congratulate myself on having arrived in time to warn you of the new perils that are threatening you.

JAFAR (leading RAYMOND to the entrance of the pavilion): Stay and observe. (He goes back and raps twice on the flagstone with his dagger.) Open, it is Jafar.

AGIB appears; JAFAR speaks to him in an undertone and advises him henceforth not to open the passageway unless he hears both singing and playing on the lute, then he closes the underground vault again.

RAYMOND: What! So this is where your son? . . .

JAFAR: Forgive me, dear Raymond; this secret, known only to Zaida, was to be a mystery for the whole world, even for you; but the danger that menaces this beloved child has made it a compelling law for me not to hide anything from you any longer. For the sake of his mother, I ask you to protect him and defend him. I entrust you with the fruit of the tenderest and most unhappy marriage. It is not for myself that I implore you; you know that I no longer belong to myself; my life is divided between my son and my wife; so preserve one half of myself for the happiness of the other.

RAYMOND: Oh, my master! If only I had the power or the force to annihilate your enemies, you would soon have no more wishes to make. But are you sure at least that this hiding place . . .

JAFAR: I know your anxiety and I shall dispel it. You are not unaware that there still remain in this country a few descendants of the Chaldaeans. These worshipers of fire have scrupulously preserved the religion of Zoroaster; but not daring to engage publicly in this form of worship, because of the persecutions to which the Mahometans have subjected them, they inhabit the vast underground vaults that are covered by the ruins of Babylon. Surprised three years ago by a violent storm, I came to seek shelter in this forest. Suddenly, amidst the ruins of a temple, I see an old man on his knees; his head and his hands raised toward the heavens, his ecstasy, at the sight of the lightning and thunder bolts that flashed through the clouds and seemed to set the forest ablaze, tell me that he believes himself in the presence of his God. I advance; but he flees when he catches sight of me. More nimble than he, I succeed in overtaking him at the entrance to his dwelling; he throws himself at my feet, begging me to spare his life. I reassure him and soon dispel the fear that my clothes had inspired. In exploring his hiding place, which seems to me vast and commodious, I notice this secret exit, and I conceive both the desire and the possibility of hiding my son there out of everyone's sight, to be shown only to his mother. Alerted to my plan, Zaida appears to notice this site; she often directs her strolls toward this place, and seems to take great delight in the view that one discovers here and the air that one breathes here. Next I suggest to the Caliph the idea of a pleasant surprise for his sister, I advise him to have constructed, on this location, a pretty pavilion where the Princess will be able to repose and devote herself to the arts that she cultivates. My plan pleases him; he charges me with its execution, and thanks to this happy inspiration, by the order of our tyrant, the fierce enemy of my son, I see erected the inviolable sanctuary where the tender Zaida will be able to devote herself without fear to the sweet outpourings of maternal love.

RAYMOND: How resourceful is a father's heart!

JAFAR: The old man, who is devoted to me by a twofold interest, has during my absence fixed a section of the paving stone so that from the inside it can be raised without the slightest effort. Zaida will come here; but given the fears that you have aroused in me . . .

ISUF *(appearing unseen in the rear):* Let's listen. *(He hides behind a blind, near the entrance.)*

JAFAR: I have just forbidden my son . . .

ISUF *(aside):* His son!

JAFAR: And his guardian to obey any signal.

RAYMOND: A prudent course of action.

JAFAR: They will appear only when they hear the sounds of a lute, joined to the tones of the human voice. So, either the Princess or you will give the signal.

RAYMOND: In this way they are protected against any surprises.

ISUF *(aside):* Let us go find the Caliph.

He withdraws, visibly pleased by what he has just heard and indicating the use he plans to make of it for destroying JAFAR.

JAFAR: So I am going to see my dear Zaida without constraint, without witnesses.

RAYMOND: To better thwart Isuf's treacherous surveillance, I think it would be wise of you to return to your palace and adopt the disguise which was so useful to you last night. You will wait near the seraglio for Zaida to come out, and, joining in her retinue, it will be easy for you to get the Princess to notice you.

JAFAR: I approve of this counsel.

RAYMOND: Hurry; but take a circuitous route to avoid meeting that evil eunuch. Your presence in these parts, when the Caliph has exempted you from attending on him only to allow you to rest, would give rise to suspicions which you should ward off with extreme care.

JAFAR: As for you, whose moves are less observed, you will keep at some distance from the pavilion in order to assist us with your counsel or your cunning.

RAYMOND: I shall watch over you, but do not lose a moment.

JAFAR: Faithful friend! What will be your reward?

RAYMOND: The sight of your happiness, and the certainty of having contributed to it.

JAFAR *exits left.*

Accursed be the cruel despot whose inhuman capriciousness, overturning the eternal laws of reason and nature, robs this unhappy man of all the charm attached to the sacred names of husband and father, and makes him prey, within the bounds of the most legitimate marriage, to all the fears and as it were to all the remorse which follow and accompany crime and seduction. I have everything to fear from Harun's unbending pride, if he learns that someone has dared to defy his orders. Who can foresee how far his vengeance will go? . . . Let us be on our guard; let us redouble our cunning and alertness; let's not forget that evil-doers are not put off by reverses: in their longing to do harm, they constantly find the courage and hardiness necessary to form new projects. It is therefore only just that those who are forced to obey are more ingenious than those who command. *(He comes out of the pavilion and finds himself face to face with* ISUF.*)*

ISUF: Halt!

RAYMOND *(aside):* The rascal has surprised me.

ISUF *(astutely):* Where are you off to so fast?

RAYMOND *(aside):* Let's put him on the wrong scent. *(Aloud.)* I was coming to find you, my Lord.

ISUF *(aside):* I don't believe it. *(Aloud.)* But you were not unaware that we left this morning for the hunt.

RAYMOND *(astutely and with mirth):* Pooh!

ISUF: What do you mean, pooh?

RAYMOND *(as before)*: Nonsense!

ISUF *(ready to take offense):* Well?

RAYMOND: This morning! . . . You? . . . Ah! Ah! *(He bursts out laughing.)*

ISUF: Are you done?

RAYMOND: That is to say, you pretended to leave so as to give Jafar and the Princess total liberty, thanks to which we shall be able to discover their secret relationship with greater certainty. Isn't that it?

ISUF *(laughing):* That's true.

RAYMOND: If nature has endowed you with a rare sagacity, then believe, my Lord Isuf, that she has been no less generous in my case; were that not so, would we understand each other so well?

ISUF: You are right. *(Aside.)* I think he's deceiving me.

RAYMOND *(aside):* Let us see if he has found out. *(Aloud.)* So, what progress have you made? What have you learned?

ISUF: Why . . . not much.

RAYMOND: Yes, as usual . . . conjectures?

ISUF *(forgetting himself)*: Better than that.

RAYMOND *(aside):* He saw us. Let's give away one half of our secret the better to protect the other. *(Aloud, mysteriously.)* I know everything.

ISUF: Ah! Dear Raymond, how obliged I am! Inform me quickly . . .

RAYMOND: This pavilion was not built without design.

ISUF *(with seeming credulousness):* Of course. This romantic site, the picturesque view of that vast plane which stretches from the Tigris to the Euphrates, these splendid ruins of proud Babylon . . .

RAYMOND: You're far from the mark. It has nothing to do with the Euphrates or with proud Babylon.

ISUF: What then? I cannot guess . . .

RAYMOND: Nor do you know why the Princess comes here to walk almost every day?

ISUF: To take up music, reading, poetry and other frivolous pursuits, to which she, like her brother, attaches a truly ridiculous importance.

RAYMOND: You're far from the mark.

ISUF: How so?

RAYMOND: I admit what you say; that's just the pretext.

ISUF: The pretext?

RAYMOND: She comes here only to see her husband in secret.

ISUF: He has been absent for close to a year.

RAYMOND: It would have been a mistake for him to lose the habit.

ISUF: Zaida never goes out unless accompanied by a full retinue.

RAYMOND: True enough, to come from the seraglio and cross the forest. But once she has arrived . . .

ISUF *(feigning great surprise)*: You have opened my eyes. Yes, this affected desire always to be alone; this order to the people in her retinue to remain one hundred paces from the kiosk . . .

RAYMOND: So as not to be interrupted.

ISUF *(with considerable astuteness)*: But how can Barmecide get in here without being recognized? This same guard, which surrounds the pavilion, is an obstacle . . .

RAYMOND: Exactly . . .

ISUF *(aside)*: Let's see if he's being sincere.

RAYMOND *(aside)*: That's what you won't find out. *(Aloud.)* That's what I'll discover before long.

ISUF: Before long! Keep in mind that Harun will have my head cut off this evening.

RAYMOND: That's perfect!

ISUF: What!

RAYMOND: Fear nothing. *(Confidentially.)* I surprised Jafar.

ISUF: You surprised him?

RAYMOND: He was here when I came.

ISUF: Is that true? But what was your aim in coming here?

RAYMOND: To find out everything I didn't know, and, thank heaven, I have nothing more to learn.

ISUF *(aside):* Nor do I.

RAYMOND: I confess, my Lord Isuf, you've won me over. Before our conversation yesterday, I scarcely liked you; but your engaging manners, your persuasive tone, have captivated me.

ISUF: Rogue! And more than all that, the twenty million sequins.

RAYMOND: Listen, that's only natural. In short, I feel for you an affection so extraordinary that I should like to know your most secret thoughts, not leave you for a moment, follow you everywhere, see you . . . *(Aside.)* sent to the devil!

ISUF: I thank you.

RAYMOND: Really, you can't imagine all that I feel for you. I came here intending to serve you, and my expectation has not been disappointed. As you advised me, I displayed a great deal of interest in the Vizier, I appeared to be ashamed of my ingratitude; he was touched by my remorse which he believed to be sincere, and I have no doubt but that he will take me into his full confidence almost immediately. He has already confirmed my suspicions by telling me that he arranged a rendezvous with Zaida and that she is to come here when prayers are over. *(Aside.)* I shall be able to keep her from coming.

ISUF: Where is Jafar now?

RAYMOND: He has gone to meet her.

ISUF: Is that all you know?

RAYMOND: There is still something more. . . A surprise that I'm arranging for you.

ISUF: Tell me right now.

RAYMOND: No. Later, when I'm in possession of all the facts. I think I've told you a great deal . . . *(Aside.)* Too much! *(Aloud.)* Now you know almost everything.

ISUF *(aside):* More than you think! *(Aloud, extending his hand to* RAYMOND.) Well done. Carry on as before.

RAYMOND: I ask for nothing better. *(Aside.)* An easy dupe!

ISUF *(aside)*: He thinks he's deceived me! . . . Harun isn't coming.

RAYMOND: I'm going back to the seraglio. You wait at a distance from this pavilion for the husband and wife to arrive here. *(Aside.)* You'll wait for a long time.

ISUF *(aside):* Depend upon it.

RAYMOND *(aside):* Let's run to warn them. *(Aloud.)* Farewell!

ISUF *(holding him back):* Just a moment! Since you have so great an affection for me, why this haste to leave me? Stay.

RAYMOND *(aside):* I have a formidable opponent to deal with.

ISUF: The Caliph is coming just now.

RAYMOND: The Caliph? Ah! So much the better. *(Aside.)* Trouble upon trouble! *(Aloud.)* But no, now I think about it; his presence will upset everything. He must be kept away, otherwise the rendezvous won't take place.

ISUF: Set your mind at rest. *(Aside.)* To ward off the blow I'm aiming at you, you would have to be extremely clever.

Enter HARUN, *followed by his* EUNUCHS *and* SOLDIERS. RAYMOND *bounds toward the* CALIPH *and prostrates himself.*

HARUN: So you're here, Raymond?

RAYMOND: Always ready to obey Your Highness's orders.

ISUF *goes over to the* CALIPH *and speaks to him in an undertone;* HARUN's *face suddenly expresses indignation and anger.*

RAYMOND *(aside):* What secret is so urgent?

HARUN *(barely containing himself):* Is it possible?

ISUF *(whispering):* Order him to sing, you'll have the proof.

RAYMOND *(aside):* His brow darkens, beware the storm. *(Aloud.)* Commander of the Faithful, deign to excuse the boldness of your loyal servant, if he dares to show you his surprise at your returning so soon, especially when he thinks he notices in your features an alteration . . .

HARUN: It is true; I feel a secret uneasiness . . . I am plunged into anxiety . . . You could not have appeared more opportunely. I am going to rest for a few moments in this pavilion; perhaps you will succeed in distracting me. *(Hassocks are brought in, on which* HARUN *sits down.)*

RAYMOND: Command me, my Lord. Does your Highness wish me to give a diverting reading, to entertain him by a droll dance, or to recite for him one of those tales that give him such great pleasure?

HARUN: No, I prefer that you sing.

RAYMOND *(aside):* Isuf knows all! Let's brazen it out. *(Aloud.)* I'm in despair that I cannot satisfy your Highness. By what fatality must he ask of me the sole thing I am unable to do?

HARUN *(gradually working himself into a rage):* What's stopping you?

RAYMOND: An insurmountable obstacle, unfortunately too common among singers. *(He coughs.)*

HARUN: Wretch!

RAYMOND *(very gaily):* I admit that it is hard for a sovereign who can make millions of men stir at his slightest wish, and whose power extends over a vast area of the globe, to experience in the execution of his desires a check occasioned by so slight a cause; but, carried away by my zeal during the festivities I directed yesterday, the coolness of the night . . .

HARUN: Anyone but you would already have paid with his head for his audacious temerity.

RAYMOND: I shall be so bold as to convince your Highness that this would not be the way to help me regain my voice.

HARUN *(putting his hand on his poignard):* Were it not for the respect that our religion decrees for all the insane . . . *(With severity.)* Sing, I wish it.

RAYMOND *(aside):* I can do it without danger provided they don't hear any accompaniment. *(Aloud.)* Since your Majesty demands it, I am going to obey you; but I can assure you that you will not be pleased with me. *(He hums faking a cough.)*

ISUF *(in an undertone to HARUN):* Command him to accompany himself on his lute.

HARUN: Where is your lute?

RAYMOND: In the palace, my Lord; I'll run get it. *(Aside.)* I won't come back.

ISUF *(stopping him):* No need to; the Princess's lute is right here. *(He opens a cupboard cut in the base of a column and pulls out a lute.)*

RAYMOND *(aside):* We are all lost.

ISUF *(presenting the lute to RAYMOND)*: Here it is.

RAYMOND: In what condition! . . . The damp has made the strings snap.

HARUN *(turning toward the GUARDS, in a menacing voice)*: That's going too far . . . Off with him . . . *(The EUNUCHS all raise their scimitars.)*

RAYMOND: No, no . . . Don't bother; I'm going to sing. Your Highness has such engaging manners that nothing can be denied you. But I still must have time to choose a song that will please you.

HARUN: I don't care, as long as you obey me.

RAYMOND *(aside):* I'm going to compose one. *(In an undertone to ISUF.)* Lord Isuf, here's the surprise I was saving for you; you're not the one I would like to deceive. Jafar's son is hidden very close to this pavilion; order the soldiers to watch carefully what happens outside while I'm singing; because it is the signal at which he is to appear.

ISUF: I had great trouble prying that secret out of you.

He places the EUNUCHS in a menacing stance at each of the openings and around the pavilion; they all have raised scimitars and turn their backs to RAYMOND. ISUF comes back close to the CALIPH, to whom he speaks in an undertone, then he goes back upstage to watch outside. HARUN is seated to the right, in the downstage area.

RAYMOND *(standing, to the left, facing the* CALIPH. *He sings the following stanza, accompanying himself on his lute)*:

First Stanza

Laden with perfume and incense sweet,
Treasures of happy Arabian lands,
Hundreds of camels on delicate feet,
Followed the route onto Syrian strands.

AGIB *slowly lifts up the flagstone.* NAIR*'s head can now be seen peeping out;* RAYMOND *moves upstage without any emotional display, but showing the most marked terror, whenever* HARUN *takes his eyes off him.*

Suddenly Bedouins errant and fleet,
Pounce on their booty with furious hands . . .

He leaps upon the flagstone and closes it, singing with great energy the following two lines of verse.

Stop where you are, from that spot do not stray;
Move and you risk facing death right away!

ISUF *and the* EUNUCHS *execute a half-turn to the right, and by a very quick movement, come down toward* RAYMOND *threatening him with their scimitars.* HARUN *gets up.*

RAYMOND *(with a great deal of self-possession)*: What is it? What's bothering you? . . . Ah! Ah! *(He roars with laughter.)* What, don't you understand, these are the words that the sheik of the Arabs, in a terrible voice, addresses to the driver of the caravan?

He keeps on singing while dancing, but without moving off the flagstone.

And tra, la, la, tra, la, la, la.
Tra, la, la, tra, la, la, la.

There's the first couplet. *(In an undertone to* ISUF.*)* Return to your post, or else they could escape quite easily.

ISUF *(goes back to the entrance to the pavilion, but he comes back down very quickly and says to the* CALIPH *in a whisper)*: I've just seen the Princess's cortege.

RAYMOND *(who has overheard, pretends to sing very loudly)*:

Second Stanza

Distance yourself just as fast as you can,
Whispered the driver. . .

HARUN: Enough.

RAYMOND: A shame! The most interesting part comes next.

HARUN: I only wanted proof of your obedience.

RAYMOND: Now I've regained my voice, I could sing till morning. *(He sings.)*

HARUN: Be quiet. *(To* ISUF.*)* Have everyone leave. Undoubtedly, Jafar will not delay in coming to the side of his guilty spouse; as soon as they are reunited, you will have the pavilion surrounded to prevent them from escaping. *(To* RAYMOND.*)* Follow me.

RAYMOND *(aside)*: Villainous Isuf! Your wickedness prevails.

The CALIPH *and his retinue leave by the right.* ISUF *withdraws only when he hears* ZAIDA's *voice.*

Enter ZAIDA *and* JAFAR *disguised as a* MUTE, *as in Act One.*

ZAIDA *(to the* EUNUCHS *and the* WOMEN *who accompany her)*: Stay back at the same distance as usual, and do not let anyone approach. *(To* JAFAR.*)* You remain at the door to take my orders. *(The* EUNUCHS *disperse in the forest,* JAFAR *keeps his eye on them; when they have all withdrawn, he takes off his mask, comes* *back quickly to* ZAIDA *and they fly into each other's arms.)* Oh, Barmecide!

JAFAR: Dear light of my life! Now I have the proof that perfect happiness is not an idle dream.

ZAIDA: But this happy moment has been bought at the cost of how much torment and anxiety?

JAFAR: Pressing in my arms an adored wife I forget all we have endured. *(They embrace again.)*

ZAIDA: Oh! Jafar, the days of absence have been so long and painful!

JAFAR: It is true. But at least we were assured of a reciprocal tenderness, and however unhappy it may be, a mutual love suffuses the whole of life with a delicious charm that fills all the empty moments and that nothing can ever equal.

ZAIDA: Happier than Zaida, you had your son with you; our dear Nair at each moment provided you with the image of his mother; whereas, forced to give him up, immediately after his birth to alien hands, I could not cherish his first smile, so sweet a recompense for maternal cares. For five years I have not been able to enjoy for one single day his innocent caresses nor to shower him with mine. Oh! let me see that son so dear to me, I beg you, do not defer my happiness any longer. (JAFAR *goes to get* ZAIDA's *lute, which* ISUF *put back in its place.)* I do not ask you if you have taken all the precautions dictated by prudence; your tenderness is for me a sure guarantee.

JAFAR: Your slaves protect us from any surprise, and at a further remove, our friend, the gallant Raymond, is also watchful of our safety. Only the Caliph would have the right to enter here; but he is at the hunt.

ZAIDA: Let us carefully hide our secret from him. If he could suspect the existence of our son, you know his unbending severity, he would exact a vengeance on us that would be no less barbarous than insane.

JAFAR: Set your heart at rest.

ZAIDA: Keep in mind that we must deceive the jealousy of a woman whom you have disdained. She is most unhappy, that I understand, Barmecide; a heart that loses you, after imagining it possessed you, must be implacable in its hate.

JAFAR: Raymond's ingenuity will thwart all their schemes. Here, take this lute and you yourself give the signal at which your son is to appear.

ZAIDA *takes the lute and plays.*

JAFAR *(who, meanwhile, has made the rounds of the outside of the pavilion, comes back and knocks on the flagstone)*: Open, you may do so without fear; it is Jafar.

The flagstone rises. AGIB *appears first, sees* JAFAR *and lifts out the child who runs to his father's arms.* AGIB *closes the underground vault.*

NAIR *(appears afraid on seeing* ZAIDA*)*: Someone's with you?

JAFAR: Have no fear, my son; this lady is the kind Zaida I told you about so often.

NAIR: How she looks at me! As though she knows me.

JAFAR: She is your mother.

ZAIDA: Come here.

NAIR *(going timidly toward* ZAIDA, *who holds out her arms to him)*: She is calling me!

JAFAR: Draw close.

ZAIDA *(moving toward* NAIR, *whom* JAFAR *presents to her and whom she hugs repeatedly):* Come here, dear child!

NAIR: Do you really love me?

ZAIDA: Do I really love you? To ask his mother such a question.

NAIR *(caressing her):* I love you too.

ZAIDA: Dear Nair! Call me by the sweet name of mother; you have never given me that name.

NAIR: My mother! *(He rushes into the* PRINCESS's *arms; she covers him with kisses and takes him on her knees.)*

ZAIDA: Once more.

NAIR: My mother!

ZAIDA: How I like to hear that! Say it often, always . . . never give me any other name.

JAFAR: If you knew how much I trembled for his life, and what frightful dangers we have run! But I have triumphed over everything; I had promised to give him to you.

ZAIDA: How many times, thinking of the difficulties of this more than reckless undertaking, have I not repented for having wrested that promise from your love!

JAFAR: I had not met the slightest obstacle in going to Mecca; but scarcely had I left that city to return to my camp, when I chanced upon a party of Bedouins. Alone and burdened with this precious charge, resistance seemed destined to hasten my doom, when the horrifying thought of your despair on learning of our deplorable demise inspired me with extraordinary courage and audacity. My scimitar in one hand and your son in the other, I sprang in the midst of those barbarians. Without pity I immolated all that stood in my way. Their leader himself,

Abulcasem, fell under my blows and owed his life solely to my generosity. But soon my exhausted arm letting fall my weapon, I saw around me nothing but certain death. Suddenly the Prophet, or rather the desire to preserve our son, gave me the idea of throwing my enemies an open purse stuffed full of gold. They outdid one another in chasing after their prize, and, thanks to the agility of my steed, I made off across the desert and in an instant found myself sheltered from their pursuit.

ZAIDA: I shudder with all my heart!

JAFAR: But I had only extricated myself from that danger to fall into another that was far crueler. The ardor of my flight had carried me far from the road; soon the mid-day wind violently stirring up the burning waves of that sea of sand effaced even the slightest traces that had been imprinted there. For two days and two nights I wandered in that immense solitude, without finding a spring, without coming upon any shelter against the blazing sky. In the struggle I had lost the provisions I intended for my son, and I was pressing the flanks of my steed in the hopes of discovering a hospitable roof, when that faithful companion fell itself worn out by hunger and fatigue.

ZAIDA (*with all the solicitude of a mother*): Dear God!

JAFAR: I took my son in my arms. Clutching him against my heart, I sought to convey to him the residue of strength that remained to me, and in this fashion dragged myself along during the entire night. Finally, at the break of day, I discovered my camp. But to get there it was still necessary to cover a distance of twelve miles, and exhausted nature was unable to rise to this new effort. A devouring thirst had desiccated the springs of our life; stretched out upon the sands, we were going to perish . . . when I saw at my feet the fruit of a palm tree. I seized it ecstatically, I squeezed the juice out of it and let it fall drop by drop onto the lips of my beloved Nair . . . He was dying; this beneficent liquor brought him back to life . . . He opened his eyes . . . He recognized me . . . He smiled a fleeting smile at me . . . He was saved! We both were reborn, I carried him, and I successfully reached the goal of this perilous trip.

ZAIDA (falling on her knees): Lord of the Faithful! . . . Accept my expressions of gratitude for so great a favor. By preserving my husband and my son, you have given me more than life.

HARUN (off-stage): Follow me.

ZAIDA (terrified): My brother!

JAFAR (striking the flagstone with his foot): Agib! Agib! . . . (He comes back toward ZAIDA and tries to lead off his son.)

ZAIDA (beside herself): It is too late! . . . Here he is! . . . Make your escape, it is my wish.

JAFAR puts his mask back on and keeps to the side. ZAIDA hides her son in the closet where her lute was kept, then she comes back quickly to sit down on the flagstones to the left. She holds her instrument as though she were playing it; but fear has so unsettled her that she moves her fingers without touching the strings.

After the CALIPH makes his entrance, JAFAR stations himself to the right among the EUNUCHS; he is always in view.

HARUN (in a terrible voice, after having considered for a moment the pantomime enacted by his sister): Zaida, what is the source of this agitation?

ZAIDA (distraught, aside): I see nothing but death. Just heaven, spare my son.

JAFAR (aside): Oh, heartrending plight!

HARUN: Answer, Zaida, you were not alone.

ZAIDA (trembling): My Lord . . .

HARUN: Jafar was here.

ZAIDA: No, my Lord, it was not him.

HARUN: Who else would dare? . . . *(To his retinue.)* Look everywhere. Inspect those places. *(Several EUNUCHS go out and look outside the pavilion.)*

NAIR *(terrified by the noise he hears, opens the closet and cries out):* My mother! . . .

HARUN: His mother? . . . *(General astonishment.)*

ZAIDA *(rushing toward NAIR, whom she snatches out of ISUF's arms):* My son!

HARUN: So it's true! . . . You have deceived me! . . . Tremble traitors! . . . The more the culprits were dear to me, the more their punishment will be terrible. I want your chastisement, etched forever in human memory, to make posterity shudder and serve as an example to anyone who would dare conceive the guilty thought of disobeying me. *(To ISUF.)* Seize that child.

ZAIDA: Never.

NAIR *(struggles to resist ISUF's efforts, and seeks refuge next to JAFAR):* My fa . . . *(JAFAR puts his hand over his mouth.)*

HARUN *(to ZAIDA):* He'll be put to death before your very eyes . . . *(To JAFAR, as he presents him with his dagger.)* Slave, take this blade and plunge it in the breast of that child. *(JAFAR presses his son tightly against his own heart and embraces him repeatedly.)* Take it, I tell you. *(JAFAR falls on his knees and begs the CALIPH to spare this innocent creature.)* You dare resist me! *(He turns furiously to his GUARDS.)* Soldiers, cut off this slave's head. *(The EUNUCHS advance with their scimitars raised.)*

ZAIDA *(emits a piercing cry and falls fainting at JAFAR's feet, saying in a dying voice):* Spare Jafar!

RAYMOND *summons the* PRINCESS's SLAVES, *who revive her along with her son and give her aid.*

HARUN: Jafar! *(The* EUNUCHS *move back respectfully.   General tableau.)*

JAFAR *(taking off his mask):* Yes, cruel master, behold your friend, behold the upholder of your empire, which your barbarous capriciousness has reduced to the most wretched condition; behold the man who has hundreds of times spilled his blood to defend your glory and your realm, and yet you try to force him to shed the blood of his son, of your sister's son!

HARUN: Ah! Do not recall the wrong you have done me.

JAFAR: What have we done, but disobey an inhuman, an impossible order?

HARUN: In offering you Zaida's hand, I explained to you the political reasons that made it imperative your union not result in the birth of a child whose claims to the throne could, after my death, disturb the peace of this empire, by creating a dangerous rivalry between him and my son. Besides, I could not permit the blood of the Alis to be sullied by marriage with an outsider. My own law prohibited it. So I imposed a difficult condition on you, it is true; but before accepting it, before binding yourself by terrible oaths, you should have made sure of the strength of your virtue. "May I," you told me, your hand on the Koran, "May I call down on my head your vengeance and that of the Prophet, if I break my word." You violated this solemn oath, and your crime will be punished by death. Zaida who participated in the crime will share in your punishment.

JAFAR: Ah! My Lord, revoke this barbarous decree. Invent tortures to punish me, but spare Zaida. I alone am guilty, I seduced her; I alone betrayed you. In the name of our friendship . . .

HARUN: I renounce it.

JAFAR: Of my services . . .

HARUN: I have forgotten them.

JAFAR: Of your glory . . .

HARUN: I would tarnish it by not punishing a perjurer.

JAFAR: Spare your sister.

HARUN: She is nothing to me any more. Let them drag her to the seraglio, let them strip her of her rich garments and cover her with rags, and in this state let her be exposed to the gaze of the people and then be driven out of the palace. May Jafar, his son, all that bears the name of Barmecide disappear from the earth; before the end of the day, let them all be immolated.

RAYMOND: My Lord!

HARUN: Go, leave Baghdad within the hour; I banish you from my realm. *(To* ISUF *and the* GUARDS.*)* Go; the slightest delay in carrying out my orders will be punished by an exemplary chastisement. *(The* EUNUCHS, *the* SLAVES *and the* WOMEN *prostrate themselves at the* CALIPH's *feet and ask for forgiveness.)* Rash fools! Anyone who dares say a word to me in favor of these traitors will feel the weight of my just anger.

He leaves, his bearing full of menace. General tableau. RAYMOND *and* JAFAR *support the* PRINCESS, *who despite her swooning, has not let herself become separated from her son.*

End of the Second Act

Act Three

The stage shows the part of the ruins of Babylon that lies toward the Tigris. To the right, upstage, the walls of a stronghold, in which there is a small hidden door facing the audience. On the same side, quite close to the proscenium, a hut covered with palm leaves.

At the rise of the curtain, ABULCASEM, MORABEK, *and the* BEDOUINS *are seen at a halting-place; packs, camels, slaves, draperies thrown over palm branches, etc.*

MORABEK: Behold, we stand amidst the shards of glorious Babylon; over there lies all that remains of that ancient city, once the queen of the world, and today serving only to give shelter to a troop of Bedouins. For my part, I thank you, brave Abulcasem, for having led us to these ruins. We are all weary from the long and painful march we have just made; this is a convenient place for us to rest; if you take my advice, we shall prolong our halt until dusk. While your slaves, released from their chains, endeavor to charm your leisure hours, I shall go visit those famous monuments built by Nemrod and Semiramis.

ABULCASEM: I give my consent.

MORABEK: Slaves, the valiant Abulcasem, your conqueror and your master, permits you to divert him.

He goes off to stroll amid the ruins. Dances and games executed by ABULCASEM's *captives. This divertissement should be short and lively.*

ABULCASEM: Enough. Prepare for our departure.

MORABEK: Already? We just arrived. Why leave so soon?

ABULCASEM: We are too close to Baghdad. Do you think I wish to grace Jafar's victory? As much an intrepid warrior as an able minister, he has promised to drive the Bedouins completely out of Harun's realm. I would fly to meet him if we could fight on equal terms; but I have no wish to expose my comrades to the blows of a victorious army. His presence has forced us to leave the desert; now that he has departed, we can return. We shall cross the Euphrates again, and seek out some rich caravan, with a well-armed escort, whose capture will cover me with glory and enrich you.

MORABEK: Yes, you pursue idle dreams; while I accept as real only gold.

ABULCASEM: We each ply our respective trades.

MORABEK: Since you are so jealous of that vain title of glory, why have you not sought to redress the wrong you have received at his hands?

ABULCASEM: You call it a wrong? The chances of war are uncertain and erratic. Victor today, one can suffer defeat tomorrow. I fought against Barmecide; the victory, long unresolved, belonged to him. With a blow of his scimitar he could have cut short my days; he chose not to do so. That surprises you, while I understand it well. The death of an enemy adds nothing to the honor of having conquered him.

MORABEK: We are not of the same mind.

ABULCASEM: That is bound to be.

MORABEK: In such cases, the generosity of the victor adds to the shame of letting oneself be conquered.

ABULCASEM: That suffices, I say; on this point, we are unable to come to an understanding. *(To his followers.)* Begin the march.

MORABEK *(aside):* Woe to Jafar or to his clan if ever they fall into my hands; I shall soon avenge the outrage done to the Bedouins in the person of one of their Sheiks.

The tents are folded, the draperies removed, the entire camp is astir, and the small army of BEDOUINS *marches through the ruins with their baggage, their booty, their slaves, etc.*

ABULCASEM *(leaving):* Morabek!

MORABEK *(peevishly):* I'm coming. The proximity of a rich, mercantile city could provide us with frequent occasions to display both our daring and our skill . . . We must pull back and wait, in the midst of the burning sands of the desert, until chance wills it . . . *(Muttering, he prepares to join the army. A* BEDOUIN, *who has stayed behind, comes over and taps him on the shoulder, indicating to him to look to the left.)* What is it? . . . A Mussulman is drawing near from that side . . . What do we risk by waiting for him? Perhaps what the Prophet is sending us is a treasure. Let us draw aside and lower our visors so as not to be recognized and punished by Abulcasem if he should learn of this infraction of the discipline he is attempting to instill in us. *(He withdraws to one side.)*

ISUF *(arriving from the left and looking about on all sides):* I was told that a party of Bedouins had made their way into these ruins, and I was delighted to hear it; but it appears I was misled. According to the rumor that has been going around, I left Baghdad to come look among these covetous men for hearts closed to all human feelings, and to whom I could entrust the execution of my master's orders. Jafar's services and the recent glory with which he has covered himself have invested him with such prestige that even the Caliph himself would perhaps not find in all his realm an arm dedicated to his vengeance, except for mine. But my cautiousness opposes what my courage would favor. The army already mutters and resolutely demands back its leader. I must also fear Harun's inconstancy and not allow him the time to repent. I know that the same object can alternately excite his wrath and his pity. I therefore have not a moment to lose if I do not wish to see the results of ten years of plotting and trickery snatched away from me. The Bedouins, natural enemies of Barmecide, will not have the slightest scruple in serving me. Besides I am furnished with irresistible arguments. As soon as I see them, I will take a purse in each hand, and boldly advancing . . . *(He holds a purse in each hand.)* by means of these harbingers of peace I shall say to them: Welcome! I was looking for you. I suppose you like gold?

MORABEK *and the other* BEDOUIN [ABULCASEM] *step forward without making a sound; having come alongside* ISUF, *the one on the right, the other on the left, they simultaneously take hold of the two purses presented by* ISUF. *Then they go on the defensive.*

MORABEK: Tremendously.

ISUF *(at first a little disconcerted, dissimulates his uneasiness, then he affects a cheerful manner and great assurance):* Ah! Ah!

At this moment a man wrapped in an ample cloth robe, in the Arab style, mysteriously crosses the ruins, stops on seeing ISUF, *and disappears behind the walls of the fortress.*

MORABEK: That's what you wanted to know, isn't it?

ISUF: The answer is positive; only I find it a bit brusque.

MORABEK: We're not obliged to be polite.

ISUF: I can see that. But let's forego the formalities. That's only a paltry advance on the lavish reward I intend to give you, if you consent to what I've come to propose.

MORABEK: Speak, we are ready to satisfy you.

ISUF: I need not ask you if you are sensitive?

MORABEK *(ironically):* Arabs! Get to the point, what's this all about?

ISUF *(joyfully):* The Caliph has just condemned to death Barmecide and his whole family.

MORABEK: Ah! So much the better.

ISUF: So you hate him?

MORABEK: As much as you do.

ISUF: Who told you? . . .

MORABEK: Your eyes. In fact, you want to commission us to execute . . . (ISUF *makes an affirmative gesture.)* With pleasure.

ISUF: Harun may possibly revoke this sentence pronounced in a moment of anger; I shan't oppose it, quite the contrary, as long as it strikes down Jafar and his son.

MORABEK: Excellent. We each take one. *(Pointing to his comrade and himself.)* Where are they?

ISUF: First I had to make sure of your consent. This order from the Caliph *(He displays a scroll.)* authorizes me to remove the prisoners and have them sent wherever I see fit. So I am going to take them one after the other and bring them here, on the pretext of putting them in this stronghold, where Harun's son is being brought up. They will be kept out of view here and protected from surprise attack. *(With irony.)* On the way here, we are attacked by Bedouins . . .

MORABEK: According to what you say. Jafar and his son die in the skirmish.

ISUF: I was saved only by a miracle.

MORABEK: No, by running away, it's more natural if you know how to run.

ISUF *(aside):* And if by any chance the Caliph belatedly reverts to clemency, I am rid of my enemies, without its being possible to impute the odium of their death to me.

MORABEK: I see through you.   Ah! What talent! I'm not surprised you've come a long way. Go, we're waiting for you . . . Hurry up, because we've got to rejoin our little army.

ISUF: I shan't be long.

MORABEK: You'll find us here, or in the vicinity. Anyhow, you'll call us.

ISUF: Well, then, I can count on you? You are men of honor?

MORABEK: Like you.

ISUF: So long.

MORABEK (*affectedly*): So long, comrade.

ISUF (*aside, peevishly and as he's leaving*): Hunh! Comrade!

MORABEK: While we're waiting for that old rascal to return, let's visit the outworks of this fortress, where, we've been told, Harun's son is being brought up. Perhaps we'll have another lucky meeting. (*They go off to the right.*)

ZAIDA (*appears upstage. She comes forward slowly; her walk is uncertain and shaky. She stops at each step on piles of rubble. Her disordered clothes are those of a woman of the people. She is pale and worn out by exhaustion and need*): I have no more strength left . . . May my sufferings finally come to an end here! (*She falls at the foot of a palm tree.*) Has there ever been a more deplorable destiny than mine? Oh! No, certainly not; no misfortune can be compared to mine. Yesterday, seated next to the throne, intoxicated by the incense that burned for Jafar, certain of his love and of the existence of my dear Nair, I was the happiest of wives and mothers. Today, reduced to the most wretched state, shamefully driven out of Baghdad, as the vilest of creatures . . . forever separated from a husband and a son who were massacred almost before my eyes . . . ; without sanctuary, without support, without hope! . . . What have I left to do in this world? . . . Dear God! Do not prolong this painful agony; lose no time in reuniting me with those whom I have lost. Do not imitate the unbending severity of Harun. Barbarous brother! . . . May you never experience for that son whom you cherish so tenderly the cruel anguish to which you, without pity, consign the heart of the unhappy Zaida. *(She is overcome by her suffering.)*

HASSAN *(opening the little door of the castle)*:   I thought I heard moaning . . . and groaning . . . *(He looks about.)* Ah! It is a woman! *(He comes down and runs over to ZAIDA.)* The poor unfortunate creature . . . Good heavens! She is dying . . . It must be the heat . . . Let us lose no time in helping her . . . *(He goes back into the castle.)*

ZAIDA *(raising herself up with difficulty)*: What are these sweet tones that reach my ears? *(She looks all about sorrowfully.)* Ah! It is only an illusion! Is there someone in the universe who could take an interest in my fate?

HASSAN *(bringing water in an urn made of coconut)*: Here I am, poor woman, here I am; I have brought you water.

ZAIDA *(stretching her arms out)*: Oh! my need is great.

HASSAN: Here, drink. *(He pours water into her mouth.)*

ZAIDA: Thank you! Kind young man.

HASSAN: Now, some fresh dates. *(He presents her with a rattan basket which he holds in his hand.)*

ZAIDA: Who is this guardian angel sent me by heaven?

HASSAN: Take it, while waiting for me to bring you a serving of pilaf. I am going to ask my tutor to give you some. Although he expressly forbade me to step outside the walls of the castle, I hope he'll forgive my disobeying him considering the reason. If he won't let me come back, I'll send you . . .

ZAIDA: Stay, I beg you. This light succor is enough for me. *(She gets up.)* Tell me, kind young man, to whom I should render thanks.

HASSAN: What can it matter to you? Among the virtues, the taste for and the practice of which have been instilled in me since my childhood, I have above all been exhorted never to overlook an opportunity to help the unfortunate; but secretly, without ostentation, without any other recompense than that which one finds in one's own heart and which today I feel is the sweetest reward one can receive.

ZAIDA: What a noble soul!

HASSAN: But you who appear so unhappy, who can cause your pain?

ZAIDA: A cruel tyrant who has robbed me of my husband and my son.

HASSAN: You have been robbed of your son! Oh! That must be the greatest of misfortunes, if I judge by the suffering I experience in being separated from my father. See, the mere thought of it makes my tears flow. Poor mother, how I pity you! . . . But have courage, the God of the Prophet is all powerful . . . You will find them again.

ZAIDA: Never. In this moment, death . . . *(Tears prevent her from finishing.)*

HASSAN: Both of them?

ZAIDA: Both of them.

HASSAN *(timidly):* Perhaps . . . they were guilty.

ZAIDA: My loved ones guilty! . . . The truth is known to you, oh, heaven!!

HASSAN: What sort of a barbarian has sullied his name by this criminal act?

ZAIDA: Alas!

HASSAN (ardently): The Caliph certainly does not know about it, because he has never allowed anyone in his realm to commit an injustice or crime with impunity. Listen, good woman, he comes to see me almost every day; if you want, I shall tell him your misfortunes. But, no; rather go throw yourself at his feet . . . you will tell him that you have seen his son . . .

ZAIDA (aside): His son!

HASSAN: And that it was his son who took you in and sends you to him to request the protection he never refuses to anyone, even the lowest of his subjects. He is good, sensitive, generous; he will take revenge for you on your enemies, on those evil-doers who make your tears flow, and when you have obtained from him the justice that you demand, you will come find me again so that I can rejoice with you.

ZAIDA (aside): So he is the son of Almaide, our cruel enemy? . . . He is the cause, or at least the pretext of our being persecuted!

HASSAN: What is distressing you? You draw away from me! You look away from me! Have I hurt you without knowing it? Ah! I should be very angry with myself if I had, and I sincerely ask your pardon.

ZAIDA (aside): The impulse that I feel is unjust, I must repress it. Let us hide from this young man Harun's cruelty. Let us spare a son the frightful torture of having to blush for his father. (Aloud and in an affectionate tone.) I thank you, kind young man, for the advice your heart has suggested; but I cannot follow it. It is perhaps no longer within the power of the Caliph to repair the harm that the cruel . . . (She stops herself.) that has been done me.

I no longer wish for anything but to go far away from these parts. The sole favor that I ask heaven for is soon to terminate days forever blighted by misfortune and tears. *(She makes a move to leave.)*

HASSAN *(holding her back)*: You shall not leave in such appalling destitution. Entry into the castle is strictly forbidden to your sex, I therefore cannot ask you to accompany me; but while awaiting my return, you can rest in this hut that you see, over there . . . close by, covered with palm leaves. I shall soon come back to bring you some provisions and a little gold, which I receive thanks to Harun's benevolence.

ZAIDA: I shall accept with gratitude what comes from you alone. As for the gold, I refuse it.

HASSAN: Why?

ZAIDA *(concealing her real thoughts)*: It would be of no use to me.

HASSAN: Come, let me take you. *(He supports her and leads her to the entrance of the hut.)* At least you will be sheltered from the sun. Don't be impatient; I shall come back as soon as I can. God of the Faithful! May you thus adorn each of the days that you allot me! *(He returns to the castle.)*

Enter NAIR *and* ISUF.

NAIR *(to ISUF, who leads him by the hand)*: Where are you taking me?

ISUF: That's what you're going to find out.

NAIR: Is it close to my mother?

ISUF *(with cruel irony)*: Yes . . . Yes . . . you soon will be reunited.

NAIR: You're being kind to me. I thought you were wicked; but I see that I was mistaken.

ISUF: *(going upstage and looking for the* BEDOUINS): Where are they? Good, I see them . . . *(He makes signs off-stage.)*

NAIR: Who are you calling?

ISUF: You're too curious.

NAIR: Take me quickly to my mother.

ISUF: You're in a great hurry.

NAIR: You promised me.

ISUF: Be patient!

Enter MORABEK *and a* BEDOUIN.

MORABEK: Here we are.

ISUF: All right, here's the son first.

MORABEK: Why didn't you bring them both?

ISUF: I left the father about a half-mile away, closely guarded by a reliable escort. I feared his wrath if we made him a witness to . . .

MORABEK: Very prudent. One after the other, it all comes out the same. *(To his companion.)* Take care of that one, he's too small for me. *(The* BEDOUIN *draws his scimitar and bears down on the child with a determined air.)*

NAIR *(seeking refuge close to* ISUF): Protect me, I beg you, from that rascally man.

ISUF *(pushing him roughly toward the* BEDOUIN): Bedouin, do your duty.

NAIR: Don't kill me, I beg you. *(He raises his clasped hands toward the*

BEDOUIN, *who appears to hesitate and lowers his weapon.)*

ISUF: You hesitate? . . . Well, then! *I* shall strike him. *(He draws his scimitar and advances on* NAIR; *but by moving more rapidly than a bolt of lightning, the* BEDOUIN, *with his left hand, hides the child behind his shield, and covers him with his body, while with his right hand he lifts the upper part of his helmet and holds his scimitar over the head of* ISUF, *who recognizes* RAYMOND.) What, is it you?

RAYMOND: Yes, it's me.

ISUF: So I'll find you everywhere?

RAYMOND: Everywhere. I'll pursue you to the gates of hell. Hidden in these ruins, I heard everything. I wanted to see how far your savagery would go. Scoundrel! . . . What, not even the tears of this innocent creature were able to move you? Oh! It is time to strike that obdurate heart.

MORABEK *(coldly)*: Better not, it could blunt your scimitar.

NAIR *(to* RAYMOND): Don't kill him, I beg you.

ZAIDA *(coming out of the hut)*: Do my ears deceive me? That voice . . . *(She rushes toward* NAIR *whom* RAYMOND *hands over to her.)*

NAIR: My mother.

RAYMOND: Princess, embrace your son.

ISUF: Oh, rage!

MORABEK *(to* ISUF, *with irony)*: Things aren't going so well.

ISUF: You too? In violation of our agreement . . .

MORABEK: What do you expect? He tied my hands. *(Pointing to* RAYMOND.) You gave me only one purse to do evil, he gave me six to do good. Listen; conscience aside, Arabs know how to count. 500% profit is not to be sneezed at. Ask whomever you please.

ZAIDA: Dear Raymond, where is Jafar? Can you bring him back to me?

RAYMOND: I hope so, Madame.

ZAIDA: Ah! Even if you succeed, how will we escape Harun's vengeance? His hatred will pursue us everywhere.

MORABEK (to RAYMOND): You don't need me any more; I am going to rejoin Abulcasem.

RAYMOND: Did you say Abulcasem?

MORABEK: That is the name of the Sheik of my tribe.

RAYMOND: I've heard of him. Is he far from here?

MORABEK: A mile at the very most.

RAYMOND: Wait. (Pointing to ISUF.) Watch him. (He pulls off a palm leaf and marks letters on it with the tip of his dagger, writing from top to bottom.) "Gallant Abulcasem! . . . (As he writes, he utters words without any apparent connection.) "Jafar . . . In the desert . . . Help him out . . . You will find the Caliph there . . . As a first reward, I am sending you a slave whom you can make into an excellent camel driver." (To MORABEK.) You are going to take him this rascal. (Pointing to ISUF. Then he continues writing.) "One hundred blows with a stick well applied every morning will soon bring him into line . . ."

MORABEK: Don't worry, it will be done, I make it my responsibility.

ISUF (aside): Cursed traitor!

MORABEK: Keep quiet, or I'll start the beating.

RAYMOND: Don't fail to. He is lazy and evil; without such chastisement you won't ever make anything out of him.

MORABEK: Night and day if need be.

RAYMOND *(to* MORABEK*)* Go, hasten to bring this written document to Abulcasem, and take this wretch with you.

ISUF *(to* RAYMOND*)*: Mercy, my dear Raymond.

RAYMOND: Have you shown any to this child or to that unhappy mother?

ISUF: We'll share, as I promised you.

RAYMOND: No sharing between us! You alone will have the shame and the opprobrium; and I the pleasure and the honor of having thwarted your criminal designs; we shall each be rewarded according to our merits. *(To* MORABEK.*)* Rid us of this evil-doer.

MORABEK: A propos; he is the bearer of an order of the Caliph which puts the prisoners at his disposition. *(He takes the scroll from* ISUF*'s belt and gives it to* RAYMOND.*)* Take it, and use it to your own advantage.

RAYMOND: Thanks. Proceed with dispatch.

ISUF *(in a mournful tone)*: Farewell my twenty thousand sequins.

MORABEK: Forward, march. *(He leads him upstage through the ruins.)*

RAYMOND: You, Princess, stay here with your son. I am going to meet Jafar. I shall by turn use persuasion and force to get him away from that traitor's henchmen.

ZAIDA: Alas! What can you alone do against all of them?

RAYMOND: His danger and my friendship have magnified one hundredfold my powers. *(With great energy.)* I shall fight to deliver Jafar to you as long as a single drop of blood runs in my veins.

ZAIDA: Generous friend! . . . Raymond! . . . Raymond! . . . Ah! Let me follow you. (ZAIDA *and* NAIR *follow* RAYMOND *and disappear on the same side as he has taken.)*

Enter HASSAN *and* HARUN *in disguise. They both come out through the little door to the castle;* HASSAN *appears first. He begs the* CALIPH *to come down quickly.*

HASSAN: You are going to see her; she is resting in that hut. Oh! She is so unhappy. You won't be able to resist taking the same interest in her that she inspired in me. I promised her that you would protect her.

HARUN: It is the duty of a sovereign.

HASSAN: And that you would avenge her against her persecutors.

HARUN: Certainly, if she has not merited her fate.

HASSAN: I'll venture to answer you for her. One must be truly wicked to subject to such tortures a poor woman, whose every feature betokens candor and innocence. You are going to judge for yourself. *(He goes near the hut.)* Come, good woman. Well now! Come out. *(He enters.)* She's no longer there. Where is she then? Because I had told her to wait for me. *(He runs up and down the ruins.)* Where are you, good woman, come . . . Ah! I see her. *(To his father.)* I am going to bring her to you; but I shall not tell her that you are the Caliph; your presence might intimidate her. *(He disappears for a moment.)*

HARUN: Kind Hassan! Oh, my dear son! Henceforth for me you will take the place for all those whom I have lost. Absenting myself from Baghdad, to avoid witnessing the execution of the harsh orders I have given, where could I find sweeter and more restorative consolations than those I imbibe from your excellent character and from those virtues that assure me your name will someday become the splendor and glory of the Orient?

Enter NAIR, ZAIDA, *and* HASSAN. ZAIDA, *seeing* HARUN, *hides her son with a gesture of terror.*

HARUN *(shaken, averting his gaze)*: You here!

HASSAN *(joyfully)*: So you know her? Ah! So much the better.

HARUN: Can it be Harun's sister who affronts my eyes in such a state of destitution?

HASSAN *(aside)*: His sister!

ZAIDA: Yes, it is she. Despite the abasement to which you wished to reduce her, her proud and independent spirit has not changed one iota. The unfortunate Zaida is still alive, but she no longer has a brother.

HARUN: No longer?

ZAIDA: No. The great, the magnanimous Harun no longer exists.

HARUN: You are right, I am no longer anyone other than your judge.

ZAIDA: It is true; but God will be yours.

HASSAN *(in an undertone to* ZAIDA*)*: You are going to drive him into a rage.

HARUN: Was it to defy me that you sought a face-to-face meeting?

ZAIDA: Far from desiring it, your son will tell you that I wished to flee from you. How can I tolerate the sight of the murderer of my husband and of all his family?

HARUN: Who gave you back your son?

ZAIDA: Heaven, less unbending than you, wished to leave me at least some consolations in my misfortune.

HARUN: I can take him away from you.

HASSAN *(throwing himself at his father's knees)*: Harun, my father! I know not by what great crime she has merited your anger; but, whatever it may be, is she not too severely punished by the loss of your friendship, by the misery in which you see her plunged? I implore you, do not separate her from her son. If some barbarian deprived you of yours, if I were taken away from your love . . .

HARUN: Ah!

HASSAN: Judge her sorrow by what you would feel. You promised me to protect and defend her. If you have been deceived; if she is innocent, to do so is a duty, that is what you told me. If she is guilty, well, then! It is an act of goodness and clemency, and you owe me an example of each of the virtues.

HARUN: Do you know for whom you are pleading? This child, whose life you are begging me to preserve, will become your cruelest enemy.

HASSAN: This child? *(He takes NAIR in his arms.)* You will never hate me, will you?

NAIR: Never.

HARUN: Some day his claims to the throne will stir up interminable wars in your realm.

HASSAN: And I would be the cause of that frightful sacrifice! . . . Ah! Far from wishing blood to be spilled, I want no throne at all if it must cost innocence a single tear. Zaida, and you, weak creature, embrace Harun's knees, raise your suppliant arms to him . . . Pardon! Oh, my father! . . . Pardon . . .

ZAIDA *and* NAIR *(at* HARUN's *knees)*: Pardon! . . .

HARUN *(deeply affected, raises them up, and says with great emotion)*: Well, then! . . . If there is still time . . .

Enter one of the CALIPH's GUARDS.

GUARD: Commander of the Faithful, a frightful sedition has just broken out. The escort that was conducting Jafar, charmed by Raymond's arguments, has just taken the Vizier back to his camp. The army has received its leader with transports of joy bordering on delirium. The soldiers openly call him their master. Flee, my Lord, or you have everything to fear from the audacity of the insurgents.

HARUN: Harun flee! I shall go confront them. My presence will soon recall them to their duty.

MORABEK *(off-stage)*: Follow me! . . . Let us rush in on this side. *(He comes in from the rear, at the head of a sizable number of his troops.)*

HARUN: Bedouins!

MORABEK *(to* HARUN, *whom he takes for a common soldier)*: Where is the Caliph?

HARUN: You are going to find out. *(He climbs up the staircase which leads to the castle, crying.)* To my side! . . .

MORABEK: You're calling for help? *(He springs at the* CALIPH *who is defended by* HASSAN, ZAIDA, *and* NAIR.)

HARUN: Soldiers, obey the voice of your master.

HARUN *draws back and reaches the left side of the stage.*

ABULCASEM *(appearing on the threshold of the door)*: Ah! So you're the master. I thank you for letting me know; because you're the one I'm looking for, and I would not have recognized you in that disguise.

HARUN: What do you want?

ABULCASEM: To make you my prisoner.

HARUN: Harun, prisoner of a Bedouin!

ABULCASEM: Why not, when the Bedouin is cleverer or stronger than Harun?

HARUN: Never.

ABULCASEM: Come now. . . without any more ado, give me your scimitar.

HARUN *(adopting a defensive stance)*: Come get it.

ABULCASEM: All resistance is futile. The garrison of the fort has been disarmed and taken captive.

HARUN: The cowards!

ABULCASEM: Surrender with good grace.

HARUN: No.

ABULCASEM: So you prefer to fight with me? I consent; I won't be put out by trying my strength against so noble an adversary.

HARUN *(falling back to the left and adopting the en garde stance)*: Come close, if you dare.

ABULCASEM: Why not? *(A single combat takes place between* ABULCASEM *and the* CALIPH, *who is soon disarmed.)*

JAFAR *(running in)*: Stop, Abulcasem!

ALL: Jafar!

ABULCASEM: So it's you, Barmecide? Welcome. You gave me a gift of my life in the desert; I was informed of your danger, and I hastened to pay off my debt to you.

JAFAR: I thank you. My faithful companions in arms have seen to my revenge.

ZAIDA: *(going in front of* JAFAR *and frightened by the state of agitation she sees him in)*: Jafar, I implore you, silence your too just resentment.

HASSAN *(as before)*: Spare my father!

JAFAR *(pushing them both away)*: Leave me. *(Turning with nobility and pride toward the* CALIPH.) You see now, Harun, your situation offers no hope of escape; your guards are committed to me; the Bedouins are your enemies; here you are alone amidst the most frightful dangers, and you no longer have in your defense the upholder of your crown, your most zealous friend, Jafar. You forced him to abandon your cause both by your injustice and by your cruelty. Recognize at last how dangerous it is to surrender to the violence of the passions. He who governs a great people owes his subjects great examples. If, repressing a blind frenzy, you had listened only to the voice of justice, by preserving a wife and a son for the loyal subject who had just saved your realm, you would not have in a single day tarnished your glory, outraged friendship, slighted nature and compromised the supreme rank.

HARUN *(with bitterness)*: Crafty politician, take advantage of my wrongs to satisfy your ambition.

JAFAR: You said it, Harun. I confess, the opportunity is too good to miss. Abulcasem, and you, trusty soldiers, do you promise to serve me?

ALL: Yes.

ABULCASEM: Ask of me all that you will.

HASSAN *(aside)*: I tremble!

ZAIDA *(aside)*: Could I have misjudged Jafar?

JAFAR: All of you swear by Mohamet to obey me blindly.

ALL: We swear it.

JAFAR *(energetically)*: Well, now, do as I do. *(He raises his scimitar. The SOLDIERS and the BEDOUINS do the same.)* All of you fall at the feet of your legitimate Sovereign. *(They all lay down their weapons and prostrate themselves before the CALIPH. The SLAVES of the BEDOUINS have run in and line the ruins. General tableau.)*

HARUN: Ah! Jafar! . . . How unjust I was, and how noble your vengeance is! *(He raises up JAFAR and holds out his arms. JAFAR rushes into them.)* Zaida, Nair, Hassan, Raymond, all of you come to my arms.

JAFAR: Oh, my master! *(The curtain falls.)*

End of *The Ruins of Babylon*

The Dog of Montargis

or

The Forest of Bondy

Anonymous Translation
1816

Foreword

Although horses had already appeared in theatrical performances at the Cirque Olympique (including the celebrated *Accusing Horse* who solved a crime by producing a piece of the culprit's jacket), Guilbert de Pixérécourt's *The Forest of Bondy, or The Dog of Montargis* was the first and most famous of a long line of plays with a dog hero. In an enthusiastic review of the premiere at the Théâtre de la Gaîté in 1814, Charles Nodier urged his readers to hurry to see *The Forest of Bondy* before its canine star was hired away by some clever provincial manager. According to Nodier, *The Dog of Montargis* enjoyed great success with fashionable society as well as with the usual followers of melodrama. For many weeks, after the conventional greeting, "How are you today?" the question asked by all Parisians was, "Have you seen the Dog?"

In Pixérécourt's text, the villain Macaire kills Dragon offstage in the second act of the play. The anonymous English version of 1816, which nicely captures the period flavor of the work, greatly expands the role of the dog, who is onstage in only a few scenes in the original. In the adaptation, not only is Dragon allowed to live, but he also pursues the villain to his death in the final scene — the only denouement possible for a dog-loving Anglo-Saxon audience.

At the first performance in Paris in 1814, Pixérécourt's "Historical Note," giving the authentic biography of the dog hero, was distributed to the audience. The story of the Chevalier d'Aubri was well known at the time, and historians debated whether his dog was a barbet or a greyhound; the Théâtre de la Gaîté opted for the former. The lead in *The Forest of Bondy* was actually split between Dragon and the mute boy Eloi, originally played by beautiful dancer and mime Mlle Dumouchel. In both the London and New York productions of the 1816 English adaptation, this character (called Florio) was played by actresses, but in the original 1814 Covent Garden version, the role was acted by the famous equestrian, tightrope artist, and pantomimist, Andrew Ducrow.

The Dog of Montargis was considered by Nodier as Pixérécourt's masterpiece. The original French Dragon was signed to a long contract and became a celebrity, along with such other animal stars as the stags Coco and Azor and the elephants Baba and Kiouny.

Daniel Gerould

René-Charles Guilbert de Pixérécourt: "Historical Note"

Aubri de Mont-didier, traveling alone through the forest of Bondy, is murdered and buried at the foot of a tree. His dog remains for several days on his grave and leaves it only when compelled to do so by hunger. He comes to Paris, to the house of a close friend of the unfortunate Aubri and, by his mournful howling, seems to announce to him the loss that they have both suffered. After eating, the dog starts his moaning again, goes to the door, turns his head around to see if he is being followed, comes back to his master's friend, and pulls him by the coat to tell him to come with him. The strangeness of all the movements made by this dog—his coming without his master whom he never left, the sudden disappearance of the master, and the allotment of justice and events that scarcely allows crimes to remain undetected for very long—all of these things cause Aubri's friend to follow the dog. As soon as he reaches the foot of the tree, the dog redoubles his wailing, scratching the ground to tell him to search in this spot: the friend digs there, and finds the body of the unfortunate Aubri.

Some time thereafter, the dog sees, quite by chance, the murderer, whom all the historians name as the chevalier Macaire; he jumps at his throat, and it is exceedingly difficult to make him let go. Whenever the dog meets Macaire, he attacks him and chases him with the same fury. The animosity of this dog, directed only against this man, begins to strike people as something extraordinary; they recall the affection he had for his master, and at the same time several occasions where this chevalier Macaire had given proofs of his hatred and envy toward Aubri de Mont-didier. A few other circumstances augment these suspicions. The king, informed of all the things that people are saying, sends for the dog, who appears calm until the moment, when seeing Macaire in the middle of a score of courtiers, he turns around, barks, and tries to jump at him.

In those days, single combat between the accuser and the accused was decreed when the proofs of the crime were not sufficient. These sorts of combats were called *God's judgment*, because people were persuaded that the heavens would have performed a miracle rather than let innocence go down to defeat.

The king, struck by all the evidence that was mounting against

Macaire, judged that it was high time for the testimony of battle, that is to say, he decreed a duel between the chevalier and the dog. The lists were marked in the Ile Saint-Louis, which at that time was only an uninhabited wasteland. Macaire was armed with a heavy club; the dog had an opened cask where he could retreat and from which to make his forays. The dog is let loose; immediately he runs out, circles around his adversary, dodges his blows, threatens him first on one side, then on the other, wears him down, and finally springs up, seizes him by the throat, knocks him down and forces him to confess to his crime in the presence of the king and of all his court. The memory of this dog has been thought worthy of being preserved by a statue that still can be seen, within the last few years, on the mantelpiece in the great hall of the Chateau of Montargis.

It is this fact, unbelievable no doubt if it were not recorded in our old chronicles and reported by historians worthy of credit, who place it in the reign of Charles V, nicknamed *the Wise,* that I have attempted to put on the stage.

Such temerity finds its justification in the moral goal that the author has set himself. Indeed, how can we help but admire such a prodigy and not recognize in this the all-powerful hand of the deity? How could we not be touched by an example of loyalty so rare among men, above all if the author has been able to embody it with some skill and embellish it with forms ever so slightly dramatic. This task presented great difficulties, but the author receives for his labor very sweet recompense every night in the flattering eagerness with which the public comes in throngs to the performances of this work, in the enthusiastic applause that it receives, and above all in the tears that his work causes to be shed.

Authors who report this anecdote and upon whose authority it was thought fit to draw include:

Olivier de la Marche, *Traité des Duels.* (He was alive in 1487.)

Jules Scaliger, *De Exercitatione.* fo. 272, edition of 1557.

Belleforest, in his book *Histoires prodigieuses.*

Claude Expilly, in his *Plaidoyer sur l'Edit des Duels,* p. 343.

Bernard de Montfaucon, *Monuments de la Monarchie française.* vol. 3, p. 70.

Marc de Vulson, Sieur de la Colombière, in *Le Vrai Théâtre d'honneur et de chevalerie,* edition of 1648, vol. 2, p. 300.

Saint-Foix, *Essais historiques sur Paris,* edition of 1778, vol. 3, p. 181.

Sainte Palaye, *Mémoires sur l'ancienne Chevalerie,* vol. 3, p. 398.

THE DOG OF MONTARGIS

or

THE FOREST OF BONDY

An Historical Melodrama in Three Acts

by

René-Charles Guilbert de Pixérécourt

Music by Alexandre Piccini

Presented for the first time in Paris at
the Théâtre de la Gaîté on 18 June 1814

CAST OF CHARACTERS

DRAGON, Captain Aubri's Dog

COLONEL GONTRAM, Captain of a company of Archers

AUBRI DE MONT-DIDIER

MACAIRE   } Archers in this company

LANDRY, friend of Macaire

SENESCHAL, Judge of the County

GERTRUDE, innkeeper

LUCILLE, little servant at the inn, Dame Gertrude's goddaughter

FLORIO, mute page at the inn

BLAISE, lackey at the inn

GUARDS

PEASANTS

SERVANTS

The action takes place in Bondy, near Paris, in the Fifteenth century.

Act One

Scene: a large Gothic hall, which is used for the county meetings and public ceremonies. The back is quite open to the country. Music. Dame GERTRUDE, *without.*

GERTRUDE: Stop a bit! Stop a bit! Don't be in such a hurry! (*The* THREE PEASANTS *and* WILLIAM *enter, bowing to Dame* GERTRUDE.) So, the Seneschal is to give me the meeting here. What can he want with me? Something of prodigious importance, I dare say.

WILLIAM: Yes, I dare say it is, for I heard him say it was summit about the great lodger-folk, as are returning from the wars. But here is the Seneschal. He'll tell you better than I can.

Enter the SENESCHAL *and* FOUR SERVANTS.

SENESCHAL: Well, Dame Gertrude, every hour I am in expectation of the arrival of the regiment of the guards, commanded by Colonel Gontram, at our village of Bondy. Heroes with their brows encircled with laurels ever receive our heartiest welcome. It is for that purpose I have consulted with you, landlady of the first inn of the village, how we might show them the greatest respect. This hall will be decorated with the trophies of my armory, and with the embellishments of your tasteful fancy, it will, I think, in every respect answer our purpose.

GERTRUDE: I am sure, Mr. Seneschal, Dame Gertrude is always proud to obey your honor's commands. My inn, though I say it, is a capital inn. It is the only inn in the place, to be sure, but it has excellent accommodations, and all that it contains is not too good for those veterans, who have fought so bravely for their country.

SENESCHAL: Nobly spoken, Mrs. Gertrude. Have you provided a

repast to be brought here, to refresh the soldiers after their weary march?

GERTRUDE: I have, Mr. Seneschal, and the lads and lasses, with garlands and streamers, are ready to meet and welcome them.

BLAISE *enters, making a great noise with his sabots, and crying.*

BLAISE: Missus! Missus! *(Aside.)* Dash me! If there bean't Mr. Seneschal himself. I must off with my stumpers. *(Takes off his sabots.)* I ax a thousand stumps—pardons, I do mean, sir, but I have got a little private business with missus here.

GERTRUDE: Private business with me, dolt! Speak out directly, I insist upon it. I've no private business with anybody.

BLAISE: Don't you be angry, missus, but that chap as slept last night in our loft, that little wee pockfretten man, with a hump on one shoulder he brought his donkey with 'un, you do know no offence to you, I do hope, sir, but it was his donkey for all that.

SENESCHAL: Go on, friend.

BLAISE: Patience, sir, patience. Well, then, dang me, missus, if I can get either of them 'ere two beasts to pay their reckoning.

GERTRUDE: You can't?

BLAISE: No, neither stumpy nor donkey. And when I told 'em that warn't manners, he as could speak best of the two, called I a baboon. Now missus, if that be genteel, I know nought of good breeding.

GERTRUDE: Booby, let the fellow go, and do you run to my granddaughter, Lucille, and to her cousin, Florio, and tell them to come here directly—here in the town hall.

BLAISE: What for?

GERTRUDE: What's that to you? Tell them to bring our carpets and garlands, that were trimmed up so smart.

BLAISE: Carpets and garlands! Now what the dickens can you want with them there?

GERTRUDE: Hoity, toity! Do as you're bid, and hold your tongue, Mr. Impertinence.

BLAISE: I wool—she's mad wi' I. I be always timbersome when she do say hoity toity.

SENESCHAL: Go, and take these men with you, and bring hither some of the coats of mail. I shall give a feast tonight.

BLAISE: No, shall ye though? I'll go directly. A feast tonight! His armory! I'll comparison myself up like King Pepping. Come along, Gregory, come, Peter, come, Jonathan. *(Exit, with* FOUR PEASANTS.*)*

SENESCHAL: While I give the necessary directions to my people, you will see to the decorations of the hall. We have no time to lose, for young Captain Aubri tells me the regiment may be hourly expected.

GERTRUDE: Aye, that young Captain Aubri knows all about it. He was born in this village, and has been waiting here some days to join this very regiment on his return from Paris, where he has been to present the colors taken from the enemy, to the king.

SENESCHAL: Which preference, they say, has caused much jealousy among some of the officers of the regiment.

GERTRUDE: Psha! Jealousy! Merit always makes jealousy. That is the reason Dame Growley is always so jealous of me.

LUCILLE *(without)*: Come, cousin Florio, come along.

GERTRUDE: But see, our young folks are coming already with some of the fine crinkum crankums.

SENESCHAL: Farewell then, Mrs. Gertrude. I know I may depend on you.

GERTRUDE: That you may, Mr. Seneschal. Your servant.

Exit SENESCHAL *and* FOUR SERVANTS. *Music. Enter* LUCILLE, *carrying a basket.*

LUCILLE: Come along, Florio.

GERTRUDE: Well done, my child. Lucille, here is a job you will like. Arrange these garlands, and dispose of these carpets to the best advantage. There will be a festival this evening in the hail.

LUCILLE: Yes, grandmama. A festival! Florio! Florio!

Enter FLORIO. *Music.*

GERTRUDE: I shall leave it all to you and your cousin Florio.

LUCILLE: Oh, yes! Florio will be of great assistance to me.

GERTRUDE: Aye, aye, I know how it is. Florio is a prodigious favorite.

LUCILLE: He is good, and he's unfortunate.

GERTRUDE: Yes, he's unfortunate. He lost his parents when young, and his speech by an accident. Though dumb, he is not deaf, I'm sure, for he obeys every word you say.

LUCILLE: Yes, we understand each other, don't we, Florio? (*Music.* FLORIO *nods assent.*)

GERTRUDE: Well, well, be always a good boy, Florio, and I will never forsake you.

Music. FLORIO *kisses* GERTRUDE's *hand.*

I must now go and give orders for a good supper for our glorious defenders. Children, make the best use of your time in my absence.

LUCILLE: We will, grandmama.
  (Exit GERTRUDE. *Enter* TWO GIRLS *with the decorations. Music.)*
  Come, my dear Florio, help me to arrange this.
  (Exeunt girls. FLORIO *signifies he will do it willingly.)*
  How beautiful it will be! There, twine these garlands round the windows. Place these carpets and flowers on the balustrades. What think you, Florio?
  (FLORIO makes signs that he approves, takes the garlands, forms festoons round the windows and doors, places the carpets and flowers, etc. Music.)
  Is not that pretty, my dear Florio?
  (FLORIO signifies that everything must be pretty that comes from her mouth. Music.)
  Flatterer! You say that I am pretty. But it is not me, but my age that is pretty. Who is not pretty at sixteen? I am good, too, good as well as I can be. But that's nothing—all women are so.
  (FLORIO signifies not all. Music.)
  Or ought to be.
  (FLORIO consents. Music.)
  I love you, Florio, as my brother, and Florio loves Lucille as his sister.
  (FLORIO signifies not so. Music.)
  He feels such gratitude toward her.
  (FLORIO signifies not so. Music.)
  How, Mr. Florio? You do not love me as your sister? You do not feel gratitude towards Lucille, who so much pities your misfortune, and who takes such lively interest in all that concerns you? Fie, Florio, fie! I did not think you could be so ungrateful.
  (FLORIO answers by the most expressive pantomime that it is not gratitude, but love, the most passionate, he feels for LUCILLE. Music.)
  Don't talk to me of love, but mind your work.

(FLORIO, *attentive to the last wish of* LUCILLE, *runs to the other window, jumps on the balustrade, and begins to decorate it, like the first, when he loses his balance and is near falling, but is saved by* LUCILLE, *who gives a loud shriek. While* LUCILLE *is supporting* FLORIO, *their faces are quite close to each other, and* FLORIO *snatches a kiss.* LUCILLE *immediately disengages herself and retires a short distance with a pouting air, wiping her cheek with her apron.*)
That is very wrong, Florio, indeed! I don't like it.
(FLORIO *follows and sues for pardon. Music.*)
No, sir, I will not forgive you, ever. (FLORIO *kneels.*) No, sir, I won't. I am very angry, very angry indeed! To dare to rob me of a kiss.
(FLORIO *assures her that he is in despair for having displeased her, and that he is ready to return the kiss he has stolen. Music.*)
Restore the kiss you have stolen! A likely matter!
(FLORIO *protests he could put it back in the same place. Music.*)
You could put it back in the same place! That I defy you.
(FLORIO *insists that he could. Music.*)
Well, now, just for curiosity, let's see how you could manage that.
(FLORIO *approaches her with much timidity and kisses her again. Music.*)
I declare he has hit it. The same place exactly.

Enter BLAISE, *in a coat of mail, a breastplate, a helmet with plumes, his visor down, and a truncheon.*

BLAISE: Caitiffs! Desist.

LUCILLE *(runs away and screams):* Oh, Lord! What's that?

BLAISE: King Pepping. *(Lifts up his visor when* FLORIO *catches hold of him.)* Why, don't you know me? I'm Blaise.

LUCILLE: No . . . yes . . . why, it is that fool, Blaise, sure enough. And how came you trussed up in that fashion?

BLAISE: Seneschal sent I to the armory. All the headpieces, and breast-platters, and jeon pairs of breeches to be stuck up here for a merrymaking. Ecod, it puzzled I, at first, how to put 'em on. I run my left leg into King Pepping's right arm, and rammed my head so tight down a field marshal's stomach, it stripped the skin off my ears to get 'em out again. Here do come t'other lads. Somehow they weren't so awkward-like at it as I was.

PEASANTS *enter with pieces of armor, which* LUCILLE *makes them arrange about the room. Music.*

LUCILLE *(instructing the peasants)*: There now, one here, another there. Well done! That's mighty tasty. Come, Florio, let's you and I go and ask grandmother what's next to be done.

Music. Exeunt FLORIO *and peasants.*

BLAISE *(detaining* LUCILLE*)*: Stay, miss, stay a bit. Now, just tell me if it bean't a burning shame for a pretty girl like you to look so sweet upon Dumby there, when there's such a nice young fellow as I stands at your elbow?

LUCILLE: You!

BLAISE: Yes. I have all my senses about me, and that's more nor he can say for himself.

LUCILLE: But he has common sense, and that's more than you can say for yourself.

BLAISE: There now! That's the way you be always snubbing a body.

LUCILLE: 'Tis your own fault. Why don't you leave me alone? I have told you a thousand times, I love Florio, because he is unfortunate, because my grandmother loves him — because everybody loves him — because, poor fellow, he has nothing in the world, and I have nothing either.

BLAISE. Put nought and nought together, and what does that make?

LUCILLE. Why, something, perhaps. In six years hence, what with industry and good managing, we may have saved up a little money. Then I shall be twenty-two and Florio twenty-five, and that's a nice age for us both to be married, you know.

BLAISE: Yes, Dumby will make a right proper husband for you, I do take it.

LUCILLE: You take it so, do you?

BLAISE: Yes, I do take it.

LUCILLE: Then take that along with it. *(Gives him a sound box on the ear.)* And never speak to me again, you ugly monkey, you!

BLAISE: Dang her little fistesses. But here be Captain Aubri coming. He be the Seneschal's favorite, and your grandmother's favorite, too, and . . .

LUCILLE: Yes, he's everybody's favorite in this place.

BLAISE: Well, then, I have a great mind to tell he of you, that's what I have.

Enter AUBRI.

AUBRI: Ah! My pretty Lucille, where is the Seneschal?

LUCILLE: Not here, captain. But if you'll have the goodness to wait a little bit, he'll not be long, I dare say.

BLAISE *(mimicking her)*: "He'll not be long, I dare say." She be soft now as mother's milk. Who'd think the little toad could hit so plaguey hard?

AUBRI: Why, Blaise, Lucille! My pretty girl, you were quarreling when I came in.

BLAISE: Noa, captain, noa. She was only just pummacking me a little bit.

AUBRI: Why, one would think you had both been married for a year at least.

LUCILLE: I married to him! I'm sure, I'd rather . . . yes, I'd rather never be married.

BLAISE: Aye, that be always the way. Now, sir, be that treating I like a Christian? (AUBRI *smiles.*) By the by, captain, talking of Christians, how do your dog do? This is the first time I ever see'd you without him. He do ne'er pop his snout in the village, but folks do say, "There be Captain Aubri coming."

AUBRI: I have just let him range about the forest for a time. He'll pick up something to eat there, I warrant.

BLAISE: I be glad he do pick up there, 'cause most days he do pick it off my plate. Sartain your dog Dragon be a beast of uncommon satigasity.

LUCILLE: That be more than you are, though you do both dine off the same plate.

Military band heard at a distance.

AUBRI: Hark! My regiment is arrived. Now, then, to put on my sword and belt, and present myself to my commander.

LUCILLE: The soldiers coming in! Oh, captain! Captain! Do take me with you, to see them march into the village.

AUBRI: Allons, then, my little Lucille. *(Exeunt, arm in arm.)*

BLAISE: To see the soldiers! Ah, she be true woman, fond of all sorts, silent and noisy. Dang me if I do know which she'd follow soonest, the dumb or the drum, for my part.

Exit. To a grand military march, the regiment of guards is seen to defile down the mountains. They come forward, preceded by peasants, male and female, with streamers. GERTRUDE, LUCILLE, BLAISE, *and* FLORIO *mix with the group. When the guards are all drawn up by* MACAIRE *and* LANDRY, *the* SENESCHAL *enters with* COLONEL GONTRAM.

SENESCHAL: Colonel Gontram, I esteem it the most honorable and agreeable part of my office to receive and welcome, in the name of the whole country, an officer the fame of whose exploits has been borne even to the extremities of the empire.

GONTRAM: For my brave companions in arms, I thank you, Mr. Seneschal. Your flattering tribute of praise is theirs, and I hasten to restore it. To the general may belong the merit of the plan, but the soldiers' is the hard task of its execution. Let them then share the full measure of glory whose valor has insured the success.

*Loud flourish of drums and trumpets. Branches of palm are raised, which form an avenue for the tables, which are arranged at the bottom of the stage—*GERTRUDE, LUCILLE, FLORIO, *etc., busy in preparing them. Music.*

BLAISE: There! Now, what does your generalship think of that? All my doings.

GERTRUDE: Hold your fool's tongue, do. *(She stops his mouth and puts him out.)*

Enter AUBRI.

GONTRAM: Ha! My dear Aubri!

MACAIRE *(aside, and spitefully to* LANDRY*)*: His dear Aubri!

GONTRAM *(to* AUBRI*)*: Has your mission proved favorable?

AUBRI: More so than I dared to hope, my colonel. Admitted to an audience, I presented to the king the colors our regiment took from the enemy. His Majesty, having read your letter, addressed me in these obliging terms: "Aubri, we are satisfied with the account Colonel Gontram gives of your valor. We nominate you captain of the company now vacant, and give *our* consent to your marriage with his daughter."

MACAIRE (*low to* LANDRY): Landry, did you hear? Captain of a company, and husband to Clotilde!

LANDRY: Too well I heard.

GONTRAM: I suppose you did not long delay carrying this pleasing intelligence to your good mother, and to my daughter, Clotilde.

AUBRI: Profiting by your permission to join you here, I flew to offer to my lovely Clotilde the homage of a heart whose love was sanctioned by the sovereign and approved by her father, and before my departure from Paris I had the happiness of passing two days with my mother.

GONTRAM: I congratulate you, my dear friend, in having made such good use of your absence, and I am certain there is not one of your comrades who is not pleased with your good fortune.

LANDRY: Certainly. (*Aside to* MACAIRE.) Why don't you speak?

MACAIRE (*with suppressed jealousy*): You interpret well our sentiments, Colonel. We know that the reward granted by the king to an individual in the regiment is an honor done to us all. Perhaps, however, we may each be allowed to feel some portion of regret that he himself was not the fortunate person.

The SENESCHAL *approaches.*

SENESCHAL: Will Colonel Gontram and his brave companions deign to partake of our rural cheer?

GONTRAM: Willingly.

The trumpets sound, and the whole party disperse themselves, the officers at a circular table in front, the soldiers at the back. Music.

BALLET

After the ballet the whole party rise from table.

SENESCHAL: Will Colonel Gontram permit me to show him the apartments which are prepared for him?

GONTRAM: I am ready to attend you. But before I seek repose, some confidential person must bear this letter to the governor at Laigny. It is of the utmost importance and requires an immediate answer.

MACAIRE *(comes forward)*: Colonel, I am at your service.

GONTRAM: No, Macaire, you must be fatigued with your long march. It is fair that Aubri, who has rested while he waited for us, should have the preference.

MACAIRE *(aside* to LANDRY): The preference! How that cursed word torments me!

AUBRI: Colonel, I was about to observe the same. *(Taking the letter.)* Tomorrow, at your hour of rising, I will bring you an answer. *(Drum rolls, a march. Exeunt all but* MACAIRE, LANDRY, AUBRI, *and* GERTRUDE.)

GERTRUDE *(advances)*: Gentlemen—Lieutenants Macaire and Landry, I hear you called—your beds are prepared at my house. Captain Aubri will show you the way.

MACAIRE *and* LANDRY *retire up.*

AUBRI: No, dame, I shall not be your lodger for tonight. I have business at Laigny.

GERTRUDE: What? Pass through our forest of Bondy so late! St. Denis forbid! Why, there's hardly a week but we hear of some horrid murder.

AUBRI: Fear not! My dog, Dragon, will be my companion.

GERTRUDE: He might be of some service to warn you of danger, but Dragon is not strong enough to defend you from assassins.

AUBRI: Such fears affright not a soldier.

GERTRUDE: Well, heaven protect thee! You soldiers will have your own way. Gentlemen, shall I show you my house?

MACAIRE: We will follow you anon, dame.

GERTRUDE: You'll easily find it, it's the only inn in the place. And such accommodation! But I'm not given to boasting, so I'll say no more till you come. Farewell, Captain Aubri. I wish you was safe back again with all my heart.

AUBRI: Never fear. Goodnight, dame. I shall take an early breakfast with you. *(Exit Dame* GERTRUDE.) Farewell comrades, till we meet again.

MACAIRE *(stops him)*: Aubri, ere we part, I must have some discourse with you. Before you came into the regiment, I was happy. I was honored. Happy in the possession of the confidence of my colonel, I looked forward to a marriage with his daughter, and the expectation of the next vacant company. You have blasted all my hopes, supplanted me in my love and my ambition. My hate, therefore, my most deadly hate, is yours.

AUBRI: I have long seen with regret, Macaire, that the most unjust suspicions have excited your animosity against me, and I have carefully refrained from provoking a temper naturally violent. I cannot but pity you.

MACAIRE: Pity me! Heavens! Do I live to be an object of pity to Aubri?

AUBRI: He must ever be an object of pity who is a prey to his unruly passions.

MACAIRE: Spare morality, and answer me at once. Will you give up your pretensions to Clotilde and resign your commission in this regiment?

AUBRI: When did you ever know me guilty of a base and dishonorable action? Give up a distinction conferred upon me by my sovereign? Resign the hand of Clotilde, the stimulus to all my actions, the sweet reward of all my labors? Never but with life.

MACAIRE: With life then defend them. Will you accept my challenge?

AUBRI: My courage is as well known as my abhorrence of dueling.

MACAIRE: You have your choice.

LANDRY: Why should two valuable lives be sacrificed? Surely one should suffice. You are both so skilled in arms that to have the first fire is to have the other's life at command. Let fortune, then, the soldier's fate, decide in his favor, who throws the highest.

MACAIRE: I consent.

AUBRI: I cannot turn assassin, or impiously throw away that life which belongs not to me.

LANDRY: If you agree not to these conditions, Captain Aubri, your courage must be suspected.

AUBRI: He who dares suspect shall have sufficient proofs.

MACAIRE: *I* dare! Give *me* your proofs.

AUBRI: Thus urged, the laws of honor must be obeyed.

LANDRY: You consent, then?

AUBRI: I do.

LANDRY: The lot shall then be Macaire's.

MACAIRE: Soon we will return with the means of vengeance. Till then, farewell.

Exeunt MACAIRE *and* LANDRY.

AUBRI *(alone)*: To what a dreadful extremity am I reduced! Renounce the dearest object of my wishes, at the moment I have attained them, or commit an act my soul abhors! Become a duelist! Yet should I refuse, to have my fair name disgraced! To be branded as a coward! How shall I decide?

Enter LUCILLE.

LUCILLE: Oh, Captain Aubri, I'm so glad I've found you! My grand-mother is so uneasy at your passing the forest with no arms but your saber, and no companion but your dog, poor Dragon, that she has sent your pistols. Not by me, but by Florio, for I could not touch them for the world.

AUBRI: Thanks, my pretty Lucille. Wear this ring for my sake.

LUCILLE: That I will, but there is no occasion for a keepsake to make me remember Captain Aubri. Here is Florio with the pistols. So good-night, and a safe return. *(Exit* LUCILLE.*)*

FLORIO *enters and gives the pistols to* AUBRI. *Music.*

AUBRI: The kindness of these peasants quite overpowers me. *(To* LUCILLE.*)* Goodnight. *(To* FLORIO.*)* Florio, you appear faithful and discreet. Can I entrust you with a commission?
(Music. FLORIO *signifies that he would do anything for him.)*
The journey I am about to take may be longer than I expect. Should I not return by tomorrow morning at eight o'clock, will you promise to bear this purse and pocket book to my mother? You know the street where she lives.
(Music. FLORIO *expresses surprise, but promises to obey his orders.)*
And take these pieces of gold for yourself.

(FLORIO *refuses.*)
Nay, take them. Aubri requests you will.
(FLORIO *takes them. Aside.*)
It may be his last request. They are here. *(To* FLORIO.) Florio, goodnight. Remember.

Exit FLORIO. *Music.* MACAIRE *and* LANDRY *enter.* LANDRY *places a table in the center.*

MACAIRE: There is a pistol, well loaded. *(Putting it on the table.)* Landry is our mutual friend.

LANDRY: And there is a dice-box. Now, whoever throws the highest is to have the first fire, at eight paces. Macaire, I'll throw for you. *(Aside.)* I'm sure of my throw. *(He throws twelve.)* Twelve! *(Showing the dice.)* That's an unlucky throw for you, Captain Aubri. Here, Macaire. *(Giving him the pistol from the table.)*

MACAIRE: Not yet. 'Tis Captain Aubri's turn.

LANDRY: He has no great chance. *(He changes the dice.* AUBRI *throws twelve.)* Twelve! 'Tis wonderful! We must begin again. *(He is about to throw.)*

MACAIRE *(snatches the box)*: Let me throw.

LANDRY *(aside)*: Imprudent man! He has got the wrong dice, (MACAIRE *throws ten.*) Ten! Come, not so bad. (AUBRI *throws eleven.*) Eleven! *(Aside.)* Nay, then, Macaire is lost! His own rashness has destroyed him.

MACAIRE *(gives the pistol to* AUBRI): My life is in your hands. I am ready to follow you.

AUBRI: Not a step! Here, on this spot, will I take my revenge. (MACAIRE *places himself to receive the fire of* AUBRI, *who seems to take aim at him.*)

MACAIRE: I am ready. Take your ground.

AUBRI: Now, Macaire, 'tis thus that Aubri is revenged. (*Turning suddenly, he fires the pistol through the window.*) Comrade! Comrade! I had the courage to expose my own life, but not to take yours. Henceforth let us be friends.

MACAIRE (*gloomy, aside*): Again! In every way my conqueror!

VOICES (*calling without*): Follow! Follow!

LANDRY: Ah! The report of the pistol has alarmed the village. The colonel is here. What excuse can be found?

AUBRI: I will answer for all.

Enter the SENESCHAL, COLONEL GONTRAM, GERTRUDE, LUCILLE, *and* FLORIO, *etc. Music.*

GONTRAM: What means this tumult?

AUBRI: I am in fault, my colonel. Dame Gertrude, in her careful attention to my safety, sent me my pistols to guard me through the forest. Thinking that the loading might be damp, I discharged this through the casement, and humbly crave your pardon for my disturbance.

SENESCHAL: I am glad it is nothing worse. I am often awakened by the noise of firearms in the forest which do not end so peaceably.

GONTRAM: Aubri, again farewell. Tomorrow morning I shall expect you. Let the watch be set.

AUBRI: Tomorrow, colonel, at an early hour.

MACAIRE (*aside*): That morrow you shall never see.

They separate according to their different quarters, MACAIRE *threatening* AUBRI *as* MACAIRE *passes through arch.*

End of the First Act

Act Two

Scene: the portico of the inn, supported by rustic pillars. On the left is the door and two windows; the windows are on the first and second wings, the door is on the third. Farther on the same side is the stable. On the right is a staircase which leads to the chamber of LUCILLE, *under which* FLORIO *is discovered asleep. At the back is seen a yard with a palisade, the forest in the distance. A lamp is suspended from the roof. The entrance to the yard is supposed to be at the back to the right.*

The clock strikes four. The dog, DRAGON, *is heard to bark at the back for some time. At length he comes on and scratches at the door of the inn. Finding it not open, he tries to get in by putting his paws upon the latch. At last he jumps up and seizes the handle of the bell, and keeps pulling and ringing till Dame* GERTRUDE *opens the window.*

GERTRUDE: Hey-day! Who is this ringing so early in the morning? *(The dog barks.)* What, Dragon, is it you? And all alone! Oh, heaven defend us! Something dreadful has happened to your master, Captain Aubri. I'll come down and open the door. *(She comes out with a lantern.* DRAGON *barks and pulls her by the gown, as if to invite her to follow him.)* He seems to try to draw me from the house. Ah, poor Captain Aubri, some accident has surely befallen him. He may be close to the house, mayhap. *(The dog barks.)* Well, Dragon, I will follow you. If I find him hurt, I can return for assistance. *(She places the lantern on the stage while she shuts the door.* DRAGON *takes it up in his mouth and runs off with it, looking behind to invite her to follow him.)* Well, Dragon, I'm coming! I'm coming!

Exeunt. Apposite music at intervals. Enter MACAIRE *and* LANDRY *by an opening which they make by removing some of the paling, and which they replace.* LANDRY *puts a spade which he has brought with him against the paling. Music agitated.*

LANDRY: There. The spade is replaced on the spot whence we took it.

MACAIRE (*wild and distracted*): Did no one perceive us? Are you sure? No one?

LANDRY (*his sangfroid contrasted with the agitation of* MACAIRE): The owl or the raven might have looked on. What other witness could have been abroad such a night as this?

MACAIRE: Has every precaution been taken for concealment?

LANDRY: The thicket and the earth are sufficient concealment of the body, and we went out and returned without a soul's perceiving us.

MACAIRE: Hush! Landry, hush!

LANDRY: What now?

MACAIRE: Did you hear no footsteps?

LANDRY: All silent as the grave.

MACAIRE: I thought we were pursued.

LANDRY: Vain terrors!

MACAIRE: Oh, they are too real! First and dreadful terrors of conscious guilt.

LANDRY: Let us retire to rest.

MACAIRE: To rest! Rest for me! Ha, no, no!

LANDRY: Have you not rid yourself of a hateful object? One who, like your evil genius, seemed to mar all your happiness?

MACAIRE: True. Yet had I a right to take his life?

LANDRY: Yes, the right of hatred and thy interest. But useless now are these reflections. Let us retire. We have already stayed too long. *(Seeing* FLORIO.) Some one lies there.

MACAIRE *(all agitation)*: How! Where!

LANDRY: Beneath that staircase.

MACAIRE: Wh—at? Who?

LANDRY *(approaches the staircase)*: 'Tis a boy asleep.

MACAIRE *(a little reassured)*: Or feigns to sleep.

LANDRY: If I thought that. . . *(Puts his hand on his dagger.)*

MACAIRE: Another murder! Oh, no, no. *(Restraining* LANDRY.) Landry, you shall not! No more, I conjure thee! Come, let us go in! Ah, when again will these eyes be closed in peaceful rest?

Music. LANDRY *goes to* FLORIO *to see if he is really asleep, and signifies to* MACAIRE *that it would be more prudent to put him out of the way, and draws his dagger.* MACAIRE *holds his arm and forces him into the chamber by a window on the ground floor, which they had left open.* BLAISE *is heard in the stable speaking to the horses.*

BLAISE: So ho, there, Smiter! Whoy ho, Captain! *(He enters with a quarter-sieve in his hand.)* Dang the horses! How they do whinney for their breakfast. They do know what it be o'clock, just like I, and they do always ha' their corn at 4 o'clock i' th' morning. *(He fills a small basket at the corn bin with the quarter measure, singing while he does it):*
> Oh, Bondy's forest's dark with leaves.
> Oh, Bondy's forest's full of thieves!
> They hold your bridle, take your cash,
> And then they give your throat a gash.
> Ira lara la *(et cetera)*!
> All in the forest of Bondy!

LUCILLE (*looking out at the casement*): Aren't you ashamed, Blaise, to be making such a noise? Why, 'tis but four o'clock, and you'll wake every guest in the house.

BLAISE: Wake 'em! How can that be, foolish? It be what I sings every night to put myself to sleep. Ira lara la. (*Singing the burthen.*)

LUCILLE: Hush, I tell you! Remember who's here—officers, gentlefolks, that belong to no less than the king!

BLAISE: Hee, hee! It bean't about them, Sissy, that you be in such a fantigue. It be for your own dear dumby, young Mr. Mumchance, who be asnooring there under the staircase, to be nearer your chamber.

LUCILLE: Well, suppose he is. What then?

BLAISE: What then! Why, he might sleep in the stable, as I do. I gave him an invitation, for stable bean't a single bedded room. There be snug lodging for single men under every manger. But no, he mun quarter here, forsooth. As house be full of military, Mr. Dumby be your advanced guard, I do suppose.

LUCILLE: Well, and suppose that too. It is no reason why you should keep plaguing him.

BLAISE: I don't plague 'un, not I. I do sing because I ha' got it in my natur, just like a nightingirl. (*Sings.*)

> A duke did through the forest push,
> A robber jumped out of a bush;
> Your money quick, lord duke, he said,
> Or, please your grace, I'll shoot you dead.
> Ira lara la (*et cetera*)!
> All in the forest of Bondy.

(*He goes into the stable with the corn.*)

LUCILLE (*coming out of the chamber*): He does it on purpose to spite me. But I'll be quits with you, Mr. Grumps. I'll teach you to be a spy upon people, that's what I will. (*She hides behind the pillars on seeing* BLAISE.)

BLAISE: The poor beastesses be munching away for dear life! Why, Louis! I say, odd rot it, awake man! Awake! It be peep o' day, so I'll put out the lamp. (*He lets down the lamp, which is fastened by a string cord to the roof on a pulley.*) Miss be gone in again. She do fancy *I* can see nought, but can see pretty plain what she be ater. (*Blows out lamp.*) Yes, yes, I can see clear enough how she ha' made up her mind. (*He puts the lamp near the staircase.*)

LUCILLE *appears at the back and seems to be watching for some opportunity to play him a trick.*

Dumby do sleep plaguey sound. I can't rouse 'un yet, though I ha' tried hard. It's my notion he don't care much for miss ater all, else he'd never snore. Your true lovers, I ha' heard, do never snore. I'll ha' tother touch at him. (*Going nearer to* FLORIO *and increasing his voice.*)

> Fat Friar John the forest paced;
> A cord was tied about his waist.

While BLAISE *is singing,* LUCILLE *comes gently behind and hooks the cord, which has suspended the lamp, to his girdle. She then beckons* LOUIS *from the stable, and they pull the cord with all their force, and* BLAISE *is taken off his legs.*

BLAISE (*crying out violently*): Murder! Help! Help! Murder!

FLORIO, *who is awakened by the noise, comes up to him and releases him.* MACAIRE *rushes in, followed by* LANDRY. *Music.*

MACAIRE (*his looks distracted*): Who calls me? What would you?

LANDRY: Silence, silence, my friend!

BLAISE: Lawk, sir, I do want nought of you, not I. But, when folks will hang up in the air, I must bawl out.

LUCILLE: It was only a little trick of mine, sir. I am very sorry it has disturbed you.

BLAISE: A trick of yours, was it? Now, I'll tell your grandmother of you, that's what I will. She shall give it you for hanging up I by the hips, for all the world like a haunch of venison.

LUCILLE: Well, go and tell, do now. And I'll go with you, and so shall Florio. So, come along.

BLAISE: Ah! Do take Dumby now with you, to bear false witness. But he can't speak nought against I, that be one comfort.

Exit LUCILLE, FLORIO, *and* BLAISE.

LANDRY: It was fortunate for us that we had not to encounter more penetration. You would have discovered all. What could you be thinking of?

MACAIRE: Exhausted by fatigue, I had fallen into a restless slumber. The most horrible dreams tormented me. I saw my victim, heard his groans and his last heart-rending words. "Can you murder me, Macaire?" Tortured by remorse, I thought I was flying through the forest, when I was awakened by the dreadful cry of "Murder!" Without knowing what I did, I rushed, as I thought, to meet my accuser.

GERTRUDE *without.*

GERTRUDE: Holloo! Blaise! Florio! Lucille!

MACAIRE (*violently agitated*): Hark! What noise is that? Someone called from without!

GERTRUDE (*without*): Quick! Rise! Get up!

MACAIRE: We are discovered!

LANDRY: 'Tis impossible!

They exeunt into chamber. Enter Dame GERTRUDE, *speaking as she enters.*

GERTRUDE: Blaise! Florio! William! Rise! Rise!

LUCILLE, BLAISE, FLORIO, *and six other domestics come out of the inn, the* SENESCHAL *and* COLONEL GONTRAM *from their apartments,* MACAIRE *and* LANDRY *from theirs. The* SENESCHAL *and* COLONEL *are attended by* SERVANTS.

GERTRUDE: Oh, run, run to the entrance of the forest! There you will find the body of the unfortunate Captain Aubri! The moaning of his dog will guide you to the spot.

MACAIRE *(aside to* LANDRY*)*: What, did you not dispose of the dog?

LANDRY: I thought I had done it effectually.

SENESCHAL *(to the* SERVANTS*)*: Come, follow! *(Exit with* BLAISE, FLORIO, LUCILLE, *and* TWO SERVANTS *and* FOUR PEASANTS.*)*

LANDRY *(aside to* MACAIRE*)*: Now, Macaire, be firm, or we are lost. *(Aloud, with a confident manner and apparent solicitude.)* How, Dame Gertrude, what said you? Our companion Aubri!

GERTRUDE: Has fallen by the hand of an assassin.

GONTRAM: How came you to the knowledge of this dreadful calamity?

GERTRUDE: I will tell you, Colonel. I'll tell you, if my fright will permit. I had risen very early to make preparations—It was just four o'clock—when I heard a noise at the door. The bell rang violently. I opened the casement, looked out, and saw Captain Aubri's dog, Dragon. On my opening the door, he barked and drew me by the gown, as if he meant to say his master was in danger. Trembling and astonished, I followed him to the entrance of the forest, where he stopped, and, plunging into a thicket, he began to scratch the earth, which had been freshly turned up. He never rested till he had exposed to my view — oh, piteous sight! — the body of his murdered master!

GONTRAM: Dear unfortunate Aubri! I was then the innocent cause of your death. Let us now avenge it, comrades! Let us search the forest. The murderer shall not escape. (Takes the hand of MACAIRE.) To you, Macaire, to you in particular I entrust this charge. I know you loved not Aubri in his life, but I see grief depicted on your countenance at his death.

MACAIRE (confused): You cannot imagine . . .

GONTRAM: Yes, I can guess what passes in your mind. You now feel the injustices of your conduct towards that youth. This does you honor, Macaire.

MACAIRE (still confused): Oh, Colonel!

GONTRAM: Your own feelings will prompt you to seek and bring to condign punishment the author of this horrid murder.

LANDRY (to GERTRUDE): But where is the faithful and attached companion of our lamented Aubri?

GERTRUDE: Lying upon the body of his master. Neither by caresses nor menaces could he be induced to quit it.

Enter BLAISE, flurried and out of breath.

BLAISE: Well, if it bean't the most surprisingest, most unaccountablest! Who would ha' thought that.

GERTRUDE: Speak! Thought what?

BLAISE: Thought that — I'm quite out of breath — oh, missus!

GERTRUDE: What has happened?

BLAISE: E'en a'most an impossibility. They ha' gotten wicked wretch as ha' swassinated Mister Aubri.

GERTRUDE: What, in custody?

BLAISE: Yes, nabbed. Taken up.

GERTRUDE: So much the better.

LANDRY (aside to MACAIRE): For us it is.

BLAISE: They ha' nabbed 'Un, that be a sure thing, for they ha' found both cash and pocketbook as belonged to the dead body, on parson o' barbarous malefactor.

GERTRUDE: How?

BLAISE: How? Why, all through Dragon. Dang me if that 'ere dog bean't a magicianer.

GERTRUDE: Did the poor, faithful dog then . . .

BLAISE: Lord love you! He be as sensible . . . aye, as sensible as I. We had scarce gotten to the thicket where 'a lay, then he began to sniff, sniff, sniff at murderer's pocket, and by and by 'a pops snout right into 't.

GERTRUDE: Well?

BLAISE: Says Seneschal, who be almost as deep as Dragon hissel, says he, sarch that 'ere young fellow, when ecod, out comed poor Mr. Aubri's purse and pocket book. Now that, as Seneschal did say, was strong proof consumptive.

GONTRAM: 'Tis most extraordinary.

GERTRUDE: And who is this wretch? Do you know him?

BLAISE: Know 'un! Would be odd if I didn't. Why, it be Dumby.

GERTRUDE: Florio!

BLAISE: Yes, yours and Miss Lucille's darling.

GERTRUDE: It can't be. You must be out of your senses to say so.

MACAIRE *(apart to* LANDRY): This mistake is most fortunate.

GERTRUDE *(to* GONTRAM): Oh, sir, it is impossible! Florio is a poor orphan, deprived of speech. I have sheltered him, brought him up in innocence — I have, poor boy! Everybody that knows him, pities him, loves him, and . . .

BLAISE: What I do tell thee be true, though, and here Seneschal do come wi' 'un. How innocent he do look i' the face! Oh, there be no trusting to the phizmahogony. *(Retires up, talking with* GERTRUDE.*)*

LANDRY *(apart to* MACAIRE): Let us go away as soon as possible.

MACAIRE: Colonel, our presence here is useless. We hasten to execute your orders.

GONTRAM: Nay, now your search is unnecessary. The culprit is in custody.

MACAIRE: Let me hope, then, you will honor me with the dispatches entrusted to the unhappy Aubri.

GONTRAM: True, to the governor at Laigny. In this confusion they had escaped me. Wait in my apartment, and I will bring you your instructions.

Exeunt MACAIRE *and* LANDRY. *Music. The* SENESCHAL *enters with* FLORIO, LUCILLE, GUARDS, PEASANTS, *etc.*

LUCILLE *(in great distress)*: Oh, Seneschal! Grandmother! Good gentle folks! Pray, do not put my poor dear Florio in prison.

GONTRAM: Who has a right to stay the cause of justice? The judge must be as impartial as the law of which he is the organ.

GERTRUDE: That youth, Mr. Seneschal, is innocent.

SENESCHAL: I wish he may prove so.

GERTRUDE: With my life I'll answer for it.

LUCILLE: See how he weeps. (FLORIO *in tears.*) My dear Florio, do not take on so! They cannot be so wicked as to harm you.

SENESCHAL: Can he write?

GERTRUDE: No, Mr. Seneschal.

SENESCHAL *(to* LUCILLE*)*: Then you, who seem so familiar with his language, you must interpret from his actions the answers I cannot understand.

Music. FLORIO *throws himself on his knees to the* SENESCHAL *and weeps.*

SENESCHAL: Your tears are interesting. Your age, your misfortune, and the seeming goodness of your life, till now, plead strongly in your favor. But the heavy charge now brought against you can only be refuted by your innocence.

FLORIO *calls heaven to witness his innocence. Music.*

LUCILLE: He relies on providence and the equity of his judge for his preservation.

SENESCHAL: Florio, have you so soon forgotten the instructions of your youth, and the virtuous examples around you, as to take away the life of a fellow creature?

Music. FLORIO, *in despair, shrinks with horror at the idea, and throws himself into the arms of* LUCILLE.

LUCILLE: He says his soul shrinks with horror at such a thought.

SENESCHAL: Is there therefore any proof that this purse and pocketbook belonged to Captain Aubri?

GONTRAM: There is. The one was the work of my daughter, the other a present from me.

SENESCHAL: That is strong proof indeed!

GERTRUDE: Florio, do you acknowledge that these belonged to Captain Aubri?
(FLORIO *assents.*)
Unhappy boy! He is his own accuser!

SENESCHAL: How came they in your possession?

FLORIO *endeavors to explain that* AUBRI *gave them to him to carry to Paris. Music.*

LUCILLE: He says that they were given to him by Captain Aubri to carry to . . .

SENESCHAL: Whither?

Music. FLORIO *points to the side of Paris.*

LUCILLE: To Paris.

SENESCHAL: And for whom?
(FLORIO *makes every effort to explain but is unable.*)
 Was it for a friend?
(FLORIO *shakes his head.*)

GONTRAM: For my daughter, perhaps?
(FLORIO *again shakes his head.*)

LUCILLE: Was it for his mother?
(FLORIO *signifies that it was.*)

GONTRAM: For his mother! That is most improbable! Aubri had passed two days with his mother in this very week. And, far from receiving pecuniary aid from her son, she, on the contrary, added to his income. Besides, why deprive himself of his pocketbook? Every circumstance but adds proof—alas! too positive—that Florio is the perpetrator of this most horrid deed.

SENESCHAL: How did you reenter the inn?
(FLORIO *assures him he never went out. Music.*)

LUCILLE: He assures you that he never went out.

SENESCHAL: Where does he, in general, sleep?

GERTRUDE: In a room upstairs. But last night I was obliged to remove him for the accommodation of my customers.

SENESCHAL: Where did he lie last night?

GERTRUDE: In the stable with Blaise.

BLAISE: I axes a thousand pardons, missus, for gainsaying you. It be true, he was to ha' slept in that stable, and I had put two bundles of nice clean straw under manger for 'un, but he did not like it and chuse to turn in there all alone underneath the staircase.

GONTRAM: This is most material, Mr. Seneschal. Why should he choose that uncomfortable situation, but for the facility it affords of going out and coming in without noise, by passing over that paling?

LUCILLE: No indeed, Mr. Seneschal, that was not his motive. If I must speak the truth, it was out of love for me that he lay there. He was so happy to watch over me and be my guard! Ah, my poor, dear Florio! Who could have thought that your love for me would have put your life in danger?

GERTRUDE: He is innocent. Dame Gertrude pledges herself he is innocent. Appearances are against him, but appearances are often deceitful. The principles of honesty and religion I have taught him since his childhood could not in any instant be destroyed. No, the first crime a youth commits is never murder. Look at his calm and open countenance. Is that like guilt? Let full time be granted, I'll to the village and seek some clue to find the real assassin! Courage, my dear child. Heaven will never abandon the innocent.

Music. She rushes out. All go up the stage to took at Dame GERTRUDE *as she goes out.*

GONTRAM *(perceiving the spade against the paling)*: Whose spade is this?
(Music. FLORIO *signifies that it is his.)*

SENESCHAL: Did you place it here?
(Music. FLORIO *assents.)*

LUCILLE: He did.

GONTRAM: This is the strongest evidence of all. The spade is his. He placed it here, he owns it. Look, Mr. Seneschal. See? It is covered with fresh earth.

All the spectators come forward to look at it, and express conviction. Music.

SENESCHAL: Florio, what answer can you make to that?
*(*FLORIO *appears confounded.)*

GONTRAM: Mr. Seneschal, what need there further proof? Either pass judgment on this wretched youth, or at the foot of the throne I will seek that justice you refuse.

SENESCHAL: Florio, every circumstance conspires to convince of your guilt. Your crime is but too evident. Let him be conducted to the court. There before the assembled people I must pronounce the dreadful sentence of the law!

All in the utmost consternation. LUCILLE *utters a piercing cry.* FLORIO, *with his hands crossed upon his breast and his eyes raised to heaven, seems to meet his fate with resignation. The soldiers advance to bear him away:* LUCILLE *throws herself on her knees to prevent them. The spectators, the* COLONEL, *and the* SENESCHAL *appear much affected. Music agitated.*

End of the Second Act

Act Three

Scene One

A large hall of the inn. It is opened at the back and terminated by a balcony which projects on the outside and looks upon a garden, at the end of which is a woody eminence. This balcony extends to the whole breadth of the stage. There is a window on the left and a door on the right. LUCILLE is looking out on the balcony.

LUCILLE: Blaise returns not. I sent him to the prison to see my dear unhappy Florio, to give him all the consolation in his power. Alas! They cruelly refused to admit *me* to him. This barbarous judgment is another murder. Could my Florio, ever so kind, so gentle, become at once . . . Oh, never, never! Soon they will find out his innocence, but perhaps too late. *(Weeps.)*

BLAISE *is seen at the back. He enters crying.*

BLAISE: Oh, miss! 'Twill soon be all over! Already I seed all from up yonder. Poor Dumby and I didn't well agree *(Sobbing.)*, but now he is going to be hanged, I . . . Oh! *(Roars.)*

LUCILLE: Oh, Blaise, have you then seen my poor Florio?

BLAISE *(blubbering at intervals)*: Yes, miss, they let I bid 'un good-bye. I handed to 'un bottle o' wine you sent to comfort 'un. He took but one tiny sup, so I drank the rest to comfort *me*. He do send his cornplim . . . I do mean his long last, last love to 'ee. He do vow he be innocent. And, poor soul, 'a lifted up his two hands to clouds, and—oh! But come, miss *(Wiping his eyes.)*, while there be life, there be a little hope still. Where be Seneschal?

LUCILLE: In the next room writing to the king an account of the whole affair.

BLAISE: To the king! Dang it, if the king do take it in hands, who knows? I do think now he'll say, "This here affair, my lords, be but a blindish-like business, and it be my notion, my lords, that when I come to sift the bottom on 't, things mought seem to be what they mought be, my lords. And, if 't be as how . . . " Yes, I'd lay ten to one, the king will say just so, in my very words. So, cheer up a bit, do 'ee now.

Drum rolls. A mournful march.

LUCILLE: What do I hear?

BLAISE *(looking out)*: Mercy on us! They be a-taking 'un to the place o' execution! They be to pass under this very balcony! What can I say to poor miss? *(To LUCILLE.)* Oh, I . . . I'll go see, miss . . . oh, dang it! I can stand it no longer. *(Exit BLAISE.)*

LUCILLE *(alone)*: The noise approaches this way. Oh, should it be him! *(Goes upon the balcony.)* 'Tis he, my Florio! My poor Florio! They are dragging him to execution.

The procession, leading FLORIO to execution, is seen to pass over the eminence at the back. He casts the most piteous looks toward LUCILLE, who faints at the sight of him. The door at the right opens with a sudden noise, and BLAISE and Dame GERTRUDE enter. Music.

GERTRUDE *(with violent agitation)*: Lucille! Revive! Look up! Look up!

LUCILLE *(revives)*: Is it you, grandmother? Have they killed him?

GERTRUDE: Killed him! No. I hope to save him.

LUCILLE: Do you, grandmother? Do you indeed? *(Throws herself on GERTRUDE's neck.)*

GERTRUDE: Is the Seneschal at home?

LUCILLE: I believe he is, grandmother.

GERTRUDE *(knocks at door)*: Mr. Seneschal! Mr. Colonel!

Music. The SENESCHAL *and* COLONEL, *and* SERVANTS, *come out of chamber.*

Give instant orders that the execution may be stopped.

SENESCHAL: On what grounds?

GERTRUDE: First, stop the execution. The unhappy culprit is on the scaffold. The information that I bring may lead to his acquittal.

SENESCHAL: Go, and from me direct . . .

LUCILLE: Oh, let me fly! But will they believe . . . *(Going.)*

SENESCHAL *(to a SERVANT)*: Do you follow her.

LUCILLE: Dearest Florio! Oh, that I may arrive in time! Stop! Stop! Oh, stop! *(Exit, followed by the SERVANT and BLAISE.)*

SENESCHAL: Now, Dame Gertrude, what information have you to give?

GERTRUDE: As Florio has been condemned by circumstances, fresh evidence may perhaps preserve him. Mr. Macaire, in going to Laigny, was obliged to pass near the cottage where lay the body of the unfortunate Aubri. His dog, Dragon, who had never quitted it for a moment, no sooner perceived him than with the most frightful howl he rushed upon Macaire. His comrades surrounded him, but in vain they opposed their resistance. Dragon, with his eye flashing fire and his mouth foaming with rage, seemed to point out the murderer and to long to revenge the death of his master.

GONTRAM: And so you think that this slight accusation . . . ?

GERTRUDE: It is not slight. Remember how Mr. Macaire hated the young Aubri. This passion . . .

SENESCHAL: Hold! Such groundless assertion is offensive to justice.

GERTRUDE: Forgive me, Mr. Seneschal, if my anxious zeal to save an orphan's life should make me speak too free. But look! See!

MACAIRE *is seen running from the eminence at the back, pursued by* DRAGON. *The* SENESCHAL *and the* COLONEL *go up the stage with* GERTRUDE. *Music.* MACAIRE, *pale, with his hair disheveled and in the greatest disorder, enters from the right. He shuts the door with every sign of fear, then crosses the stage and goes into the apartment on the left without observing those who are at the back.*

GERTRUDE: Now with your own eyes you have seen the truth of what I told you.

SENESCHAL: It is very extraordinary.

GONTRAM: But it proves nothing but that Macaire, otherwise very brave, dares not expose himself to the fury of this animal.

GERTRUDE: Hear me to the end! You know how Dragon discovered by his scent his master's purse and pocketbook on the person of Florio. But you know not what the bystanders are ready to declare upon oath, that he afterwards fawned upon this poor Florio and repeatedly licked his hands. Now, let me ask you, would he have fawned upon the assassin of his master? Oppose these marks of kindness to the rage and fury he shows on seeing Macaire, and say who is most likely to have been the murderer.

SENESCHAL: Colonel Gontram, this evidence is strong and cannot be dismissed without further examination.

GONTRAM: Vengeance on the murderer of my friend is all that I desire. Should Macaire be guilty, let his punishment be equal to his crime. I will give instant orders for his company to be drawn up; meanwhile, do you assemble the villagers. His accusation will be public, and his defense unprepared. The secret workings of his soul will be seen upon his countenance.

SENESCHAL: They will. Your instructions shall be punctually obeyed. Dame Gertrude, follow me.

Exeunt. MACAIRE *comes out of his apartment. Music.*

MACAIRE: Did I not hear the sound of voices in this hall, and my name pronounced aloud? No person was here when I came in. I must have deceived myself. No, no, it was another phantom of my troubled brain. Am I in a frightful dream, or is it real? Has this arm, which till now was terrible only to my country's foes, been raised to murder my companion, my friend? Torn by anguish and remorse, life's a burden! Oh, Aubri! Oh, my friend! *(He falls upon a bench quite overcome.)*

LANDRY *is seen on the eminence. He endeavors to draw the attention of* MACAIRE, *who is too much absorbed to observe his signs.* LANDRY, *having first seen that he is not observed, draws from his belt a roll of parchment, undoes the belt and makes a packet of it, then throws them over the balcony.* MACAIRE, *roused by the noise, sees* LANDRY, *who motions him to pick up the packet, and disappears.* MACAIRE *rises, picks up the packet, and reads.*

MACAIRE: "You shall be freed from the danger that threatens you. The animal whose sagacity was so much to be dreaded shall be disposed of." Ah! Then I breathe again! *(Reads.)* "I have given you *my* belt, which wear instead of yours that was left in the forest. I have got leave of absence and shall not require it. Be collected! And above all, heed not the scruples of your conscience, then all will go well." How easy to give such advice, how difficult to follow it. Landry is in the right. My belt wanting, that alone might have convicted me. In my terror I had forgotten it. *(Puts on the belt.)* Someone approaches. Now, Macaire, be firm!

Your life depends on your conquering your feelings. *(Enter the* SENESCHAL *and the* COLONEL, *followed by* GERTRUDE, *who stands apart.)*

SENESCHAL: Well, Lieutenant Macaire, have you recovered from your alarm?

MACAIRE: Alarm! What alarm?

SENESCHAL: Why, the alarm occasioned by . . .

MACAIRE *(with forced gaiety)*: True, true! I have, Mr. Seneschal, and trust that the valor or the honor of a soldier is not compromised by avoiding the attack of a furious animal, whose master had taught it to be gentle only to himself — as the colonel knows.

GONTRAM: I do, and am perfectly ready to think, Macaire, that what happened proceeds from that natural cause. There are some, however, who think otherwise, and upon such a trifling circumstance dare to suspect that you are no stranger to the murder of Aubri.

MACAIRE: I, my colonel! I! Who dares? I am ready to submit any proof, sir, you may require.

SENESCHAL: The execution of Florio has been respited, and the whole village demands that both you and he should be confronted.

MACAIRE: This proposal is strange, but if it be your wish, sir, I am ready.

GONTRAM: Go, Macaire. Return hither at the head of your company, and with the bold front of conscious innocence, confound the malice of your accusers.

MACAIRE: I go, my colonel. *(Aside.)* May my courage support me in this most dreadful trial! *(Exit.)*

SENESCHAL: Now, Dame Gertrude, were not your suspicions of Macaire unfounded?

GERTRUDE: Well, I say nothing, but . . .

BLAISE, *at the threshold of the door, beckons and makes signs to* GERTRUDE.

BLAISE: Missus! Hist! Only a couple of words!

GERTRUDE: Presently, presently.

BLAISE: Nay, it mun be directly, else 't won't do.

GERTRUDE: Well, be quick. *(Bringing him forward.)*

BLAISE *(whispering)*: I ha' gotten th' murderer this time in good earnest.

GERTRUDE: Where?

BLAISE: I' my pocket.

GERTRUDE: Idiot!

BLAISE: If 't bean't himsel, it be what will find him out. His belt! Mum! Nought more nor less. Hush!

GERTRUDE: Hush indeed! No, no. Come forward and tell these gentlemen all you know directly. *(Puts BLAISE over to COLONEL.)*

BLAISE: Why, mun I though?

GERTRUDE: Yes, everything.

BLAISE: Hem! Well then, missus, you do know little Annette, blacksmith's daughter, o' our village here? She were out making a faggots i' th' forest this morning, when she came to a thicket, as mought be three foot high like.

GERTRUDE: Well?

BLAISE: Patience! Well, what should be in middle of thicket but this here belt, all smeared with blood? She makes me but three hops to skirt o' wood and fell a-bawling for her dear life. When we came up, she had th' belt in her hand. Now, you mun observe that thicket where she found un ware but twenty paces from where Mr. Aubri, poor soul, ware killed.

SENESCHAL: Indeed! Well, proceed in your story.

BLAISE: I ha' nigh done 't, sir. Well, we all began a-putting this and that together, and, says I—I ware spokesman, sir—that belt ha' been used to assassinating purpose, 'cause there be blood on 't, and, says I, belt do belong to one o' the guards as marched yesterday into our village, so, it be one o' guards who ha' done the job, so Dumby be no guard, so it can't be Dumby. So I brought th' belt here. So, when I came to missus, I said, I—oh, you do know that, so that is all.

SENESCHAL: All the guards have belts alike. We cannot then discern to which of them it belongs.

BLAISE: Axing your pardon, sir, they ha' but one belt apiece, and any blockhead that is not blind may see one o' them han't gotten his own.

GERTRUDE: Hold your tongue. (Putting him across.)

GONTRAM: Thy reflection is just, my friend. At length I hope to hit upon a method of discovering the real assassin. Give me the belt.

BLAISE: There 'a be, and much good it may do you, sir. (Music. Enter LUCILLE with FLORIO in haste.)

LUCILLE: But a few minutes later, and this poor sufferer would have been no more.

SENESCHAL: He is not yet acquitted, but strong circumstances have lately arisen in his favor.

FLORIO *expresses his thanks to the* SENESCHAL. *From the rising ground the company of guards, with* MACAIRE *at their head, march down and are drawn up in the hall. The* COLONEL *passes in review the whole company, examining their accoutrements minutely. He finds nothing wanting, and all stand unconcerned. At length he says with a solemn voice:*

GONTRAM: The murderer of Aubri is amongst you! The stain of blood upon his belt has discovered him.

The soldiers look at each other — all but MACAIRE, *who by an impulse quickly bends his head and looks with terror on his belt.*

MACAIRE *(forgetting himself)*: On the belt!

GONTRAM: Macaire! Why such terror? Is there any stain of blood on you?

MACAIRE *(violently agitated)*: On me, my colonel?

GONTRAM: Give me your belt!

MACAIRE *trembles so he can scarcely unclasp it.*

How! This is not yours. 'Tis Landry's. Here is his name! *(Showing it written on in the inside.)* Where is yours?

MACAIRE *(in the deepest confusion)*: My belt, Colonel? I've lost it in the forest. No! Not in the forest!

GONTRAM *(coming closer to him and holding the belt before his eyes)*: No, 'tis here! Stained with the blood of the murdered Aubri!

MACAIRE *(shudders and puts his hands before his eyes)*: Aubri's blood! Oh, hide it from my sight! It calls for vengeance! I can bear it no longer. I confess my crime! That youth is innocent!

FLORIO *utters an exclamation of joy.*

I murdered Aubri in the forest of Bondy.

GONTRAM: Horrible confession! Bear him hence! And let the most ignominious death . . .

MACAIRE *(drawing a pistol)*: No, this shall prevent . . . *(He is about to shoot himself when two guards wrest the pistol from him.)*

GONTRAM: Bear him to instant execution!

Exeunt all but MACAIRE *and two guards. They are leading him away when, in a frenzy of despair, he breaks from his guards, and, seeing no other way to escape, he leaps through the window. One of the guards fires his pistol after him.*

GUARD: Curse on the pistol! He has escaped unhurt! *(Reenter* COLONEL GONTRAM.*)*

GONTRAM: Now, what's the matter?

GUARD: Macaire has escaped!

GONTRAM: Escaped!

GUARD: He will reach the waterfalls.

GONTRAM: He must not! Go round by the bridge! There you may intercept his flight! Sound the alarm!

Exeunt COLONEL *and* GUARDS. *Alarm bell, drums, etc. . . .*

End of the First Scene

Scene Two

Extensive view of rocks and waterfalls. Across the stream, from rock to rock, an alpine bridge. Music. MACAIRE *is seen to cross it, followed by* DRAGON. MACAIRE *then descends a sloping rock and comes on the stage.*

MACAIRE: Why should I fly? 'Tis not to preserve this wretched life, but to avoid a base and ignominious death!

BLAISE *(without)*: Holloo! Holloo!

GUARD *(without)*: Holloo! Holloo!

MACAIRE *(starts)*: They are here! On every side I am beset! Then for my last and desperate attempt!

GUARD *enters.*

GUARD *(to MACAIRE)*: Wretch! Yield your forfeit life!

MACAIRE: Never will I surrender to those I have been accustomed to command!

The GUARD *rushes on* MACAIRE. *They struggle.* MACAIRE *overcomes him and exits. The dog is heard, without, and* MACAIRE *is seen to fly up the rocks, and appears on a high one that overhangs the waterfall.* GUARD *sounds his bugle, and all the hills are covered with* SOLDIERS *and* PEASANTS.

GUARD *(to SOLDIERS)*: Present! Fire!

The soldiers point their muskets and are about to fire when MACAIRE *leaps from the point of the rock into the stream, and the curtain drops amidst the huzzahs of the peasantry that the murderer has at last met with his merited fate.*

End of *The Dog of Montargis*

Christopher Columbus

or

The Discovery of the New World

Translated by Marvin Carlson

THE AUTHOR TO THE PUBLIC

Human genius has never conceived anything more astonishing, nor executed anything bolder, than the discovery of America. Christopher Columbus has always been the object of my admiration. History offers not a single example of firmer character, more heroic courage. This is not to speak of his knowledge, which was astonishing for the century in which he lived. If it were possible to add further to the interest that the very name of this famous navigator inspires, it would be the dangers that he faced, the persecutions that he suffered, the revolting injustices of which he was the victim. Some have gone so far as to challenge his glory of having enriched the earth with a new world. A Florentine adventurer named Amerigo Vespucci, a mere companion of that Alonzo Ojeda, who reached Santo Domingo only after the Admiral's third voyage, and who landed there only to be shamefully chased away, dared upon his return to publish a narrative of his travels that he claimed to be discoveries. His work, copied from the journal that Columbus placed in the hands of the Minister, being the first printed about this interesting land, was studied around the world, avidly read, and was convincing. The imposter had the glory of giving his name to the new continent, and the little island of Saint Christophe is the only monument that brings back to the world the memory of Columbus!

Ever since I became concerned with literature I have constantly desired to put this extraordinary man on the stage. Some twelve years ago I sketched out the play that I am offering today to the public. I planned it for the Théâtre de la Porte St.-Martin, and there were even several meetings held to discuss how it was to be staged. The closing of the theatre, which occurred five times in six years, forced me to give up on this work for a certain time. However, I decided to finish it for the Théâtre de la Gaîté when M. Lemercier presented his "Shakespearian" comedy entitled *Christopher Columbus* at the Odéon in 1809. I here declare, with the frankness that is basic to my character, that I owe much to this distinguished author. For the first time I had, like him, transgressed the dramatic rules and created an irregular play. Since the beautiful poetry and the very great talent of M. Lemercier did not bring the

French spectators to accept him, I felt I should not risk the same, after him, with much inferior means.   There was nothing to legitimize my boldness.   Enlightened by experience, I therefore made major changes in my drama and managed, not without much difficulty, to maintain at least the unity of time and of action; my play lasts only twenty-four hours.   If I did not have it presented earlier, it is because I wanted an interval of several years to pass between two works bearing the same title.   On the other hand, if I had not thought it proper to hold the play back still longer, that is because I did not want anyone to think for a moment that I had the intention of imitating Jean Bart, which my officious friends would certainly have said.   For seventeen years I have often suffered, as is the custom, from ingratitude, but I have never borrowed from anyone, at least not in my own country.   The only idea in my title was to provide the necessity of setting a scene on a ship, since one could not discover America without crossing the ocean.

I did not labor to establish some machinist's reputation.   My ship is simple and of a nature that it could be constructed almost without expense on the smallest stages, but I was strongly attached to keeping the technical terms, and to depict what might be called the "mores of a ship."   I devoted similar care to the third act, imitating the habits, customs, and characteristic gestures of the savages.   Everything is strictly according to truth.   I looked for the elements of these results in the story of Columbus,[1] in the writings of missionaries,[2] in the numerous narratives by voyagers,[3] and particularly in the critical situation of my hero.

None of the works I have written has required more research

---

[1] *La Vie de Christophe Colomb*, written by his son, Fernand Colombus and translated into French by Cotolendy. Paris, Barbin, 1681.

Colomb dans les fers, Epitre by the Chevalier de Langeac. Paris, Didot Aîné, 1782.

[2] *Histoire générale des Antilles*, by P. Dutertre. Paris, 1667.

Moeurs des Sauvages Américains, by P. Lafitau. Paris, 1724.

[3] *Abrégé de l'Histoire des Voyages*, by de La Harpe and others. Paris, 1780.

Collection des Voyages anciens et modernes autour du Monde, by Bancarel. Paris, 1808.

and encountered greater obstacles; this was more than three months in rehearsals. But at the end it matters little. The dramatic author has the obligation first and foremost to please, no matter by what means. If he fails, nothing else he does matters, and he has no right to complain.

The public will no doubt think, as I do, that it would be completely ridiculous to use our own language, even corrupted, for men who are seeing Europeans for the first time. Fully confident that my innovation could not fail to be approved by persons of taste, I made the inhabitants of Guanahani speak the language of the Antilles, which I have taken from the *Dictionnaire Caraïbe* created by R.P. Raymond Breton and published at Auxerre in 1665. Within the play will be found the translation of all those words which I felt, in any case, I ought to use in moderation.

Letter from M. E. de Vaulabelle to M. de Pixérécourt

Paris, 9 March 1842

Here, my dear friend, is the little work that you requested of me. I am fearful that I have not fulfilled your expectations in a suitable manner. But whenever I write upon whatever subject, I have never been able to make myself master of my pen, which has the detestable and perpetual habit of taking me wherever it wants to go.

I wanted to write about Pinçon, since you have sent me the history of Dieppe for that purpose, a history that I have read along with everything that concerns the said Pinçon. Well, I don't know how it happened, but this damned Pinçon never emerged a single time from my pen. This is not for lack of knowledge, or lack of will, but, I repeat, I do not always say what I want to say, and a good part of the obscurity that I suffer as a writer is precisely due to this, to this infirmity of my poor will. I am never able to do anything of value.

Perhaps I was also obsessed with the idea that you required five or six octavo pages, and in the fear of not fulfilling my task, I flung myself headlong into digressions that all too often took me away from your play.

Be that as it may, I hope that you will not be too unhappy with me; otherwise I would be most troubled.

If it would be possible for you to send me proofs, I would be much obliged to you. I nearly die of fear every time something of mine is printed. My own errors are numerous enough, God knows, without the editors coming along to add others of their own invention. One hundred sixty errors in the second edition of my latest novel removed, some eight years ago, any desire or strength in me to publish anything else. Add to that that this is the second time in my life that I have given my name to the public aside from my stories for children. Do not make this second time my last. I fear printing more than fire; it has always seemed to me that a man in print is a man dead. You whose experience at this moment is quite the contrary will laugh at my fears, but what can you expect? This is the way I am made.

Farewell, my dear and excellent friend. I thank you for having thought that I could do something good for you, and I am a thousand times grateful to you for having provided me with the occasion to demonstrate to you how deeply I hold you in my heart.

El. de Vaulabelle

Note on *Christopher Columbus*

This melodrama enjoyed a great, but brief success. After a hundred and seventeen performances in Paris and in the provinces, *Christopher Columbus* disappeared from the stage. It is difficult to explain why a work so boldly conceived and so skillfully executed did not survive the length of a thousand or fifteen hundred performances, as have most of the excellent works of this author.

Perhaps the brevity of the dramatic career of *Christopher Columbus* was due to the lack of sympathy the rabble has for those superhuman men who, like our hero, act under the influence of a kind of metaphysical passion, such as, for example, the love of glory. To leave an immortal name after oneself is and will always be a perfectly foolish if not incomprehensible thing to a public that lives from day to day without thinking of yesterday or concerning itself with tomorrow and who are less interested in a navigator who set off to discover a new world at the end of the sea than they would be in someone who went no further than from the Boulevard St.-Martin to the Observatory to discover a new star at the end of a telescope.

Be that as it may, we understand why M. Pixérécourt was strongly tempted to put on the stage this adventurous spirit who set out in search of another hemisphere. There is a certain sympathy between the boldness of the sailor's expedition and the daring of the conceptions of the dramatic author. One discovered America, the other created Melodrama, and both, keeping in mind their proportions, discovered a World.

Moreover, what noble heart would not be seized with admiration and pity for that great man, that demigod, whose crown of glory was also a crown of thorns! First he had to beg for a ship, from sea to sea, which the Kings of the Ocean refused him, not because they were lacking in ships, but because they were lacking in faith in his genius. He is a madman, they said. And the more he spoke reason to them, science at hand, the more they thought him ignorant or demented.

"But just listen to me, you Christian kings!" Columbus would cry. "Over there men who are your brothers and women who are your sisters are living under threat of eternal damnation. And only a ship is needed for the salvation of all these men and all these women!"

The Christian kings remained deaf.

"Over there also are fertile valleys and rich mountains. All these valleys and mountains can be yours for a ship!"

The kings remained silent.

"Over there also," he added, "are immense rivers which contain diamonds and pearls. All these diamonds and pearls can be yours for a ship!"

One queen understood him. "Let him be given three ships," she said.

So Columbus knelt before Isabella, weeping and praying, praying God to bless this great queen who had not doubted him and weeping over this poor woman who was sending him over there to seek pearls for her.

Thus he is on the sea, in the middle of the ocean, with three large ships, but, dear heaven! drinking with gusto salt water, sailing through tempests and going always, always straight ahead like a man who knew his way, like a good proprietor on the road to his castle.

And yet his companions never ceased to demand of him news of this new world that they did not see approaching. "I see it well enough," he would reply. "And just where?" "Here." And he would point to his own forehead.

Sailors are not content with gestures, especially hungry sailors. Lacking the means of life they lost heart. A conspiracy was formed. Columbus was declared a traitor and sentenced to death. As the sharks were awaiting their prey, however, a south-west wind sprang up to calm these angry spirits. This wind bore the scent of flowers, the flowers of America.

Columbus was proclaimed king. But alas, his royalty was that of genius. Unhappy he who displays it during his lifetime!

He inspired envy; he had enemies. New voyages and new discoveries by adding to his fame stimulated further the hatred of his contemporaries. His glory was challenged, he was stripped of his honors, his new world was stolen from him and soon, treated as the least of men, he lived out in misery and shame the remainder of a life which had enriched Spain and immortalized its king.

It is known that Christopher Columbus died at Valladolid May 20, 1506, fourteen years after having discovered America. But where was he born? This is not known. Some assert that he was born in 1441 in the state of Genoa. But where? In Genoa itself say the Genoese, in Savona say the inhabitants of that village, among us, respond the villagers of Corogéo and Succao. Not at all, reply the citizens of Nervi, it was within our walls that Christopher Columbus was born. Amid all these diverse claims, it is difficult to know what to think.

Yet others had the idea of making him a Corsican. Doubtless it seemed ingenious to them to give the same birthplace to Napoleon and to Columbus, to the greatest leader of modern times and to the greatest navigator of olden times. According to them, Calvi was the real homeland of Columbus. M. Giubéga, the former prefect of Corsica, consulting the registers of this town, found there the birth certificate of the illustrious sailor.

Very well. But why has there been such a delay in making public a fact of such great importance? It will soon be a year since the *Revue de Paris* gave us this news and since then nothing from M. Giubéga, no more news given in the *Revue de Paris*, nothing on this question anywhere, not even perhaps in Calvi.

Could it be perhaps that suddenly the noble rivalries of all these towns, communities and villages that have claimed Columbus as their child will finally be silenced by an estimable Italian scholar, M. Isnardi, who declared the other day, evidence in his hand, that Christopher Columbus was certainly born in Cogoloto, in the state of Genoa?

It is true that the proofs brought forward by M. Isnardi in support of his thesis brook no contradiction; they are four authentic documents, dated 1586, 1590, 1595, and 1602, in which is stated in the clearest terms: "Columbus of Cogoloto, so famous in Spain . . ."

It is also true that the evidence furnished by Genoa, Savone, Nervi, Succaro, Corogéo, and especially by Calvi will not be able to be questioned and that these towns and villages will establish in an equally authentic manner their right to be proclaimed, each one in particular and all together, as the sole mothers and nurses of the immortal navigator.

What is to be concluded from all this? I do not know. But I very much fear that the biographers have taken more pains to discover the corner of the earth where Columbus was born than he himself took to discover America.

But let us return to the M. de Pixérécourt's drama.

What struck me the most in this work was not the originality of an exposition that begins before the rising of the curtain, nor the novelty of a plot that is developed on the high seas, nor the calm majesty of character of Columbus himself, nor the verisimilitude of the base features of the conspirators with whom the painter surrounds the noble portrait of his hero, nor the naturalness of a dialogue unheard-of on the stage before now, where the language of sailors never went beyond the "hard-a-starbords!" and the "hard-a-ports!" of the traditional theatre.

What particularly struck me, I must say, was to encounter there, on that ship, among the conspirators and in the midst of the storm, the purest emotions of the soul, the holy affections of the family.

And in my opinion, this is not among the least reasons for the great and legitimate success gained by M. de Pixérécourt, the large part that he has given to family feelings in each of his dramas. Memories of the cradle, filial and paternal embraces, all that sublime tenderness that works so powerfully on our theatre audiences almost always occupy a prominent place in his compositions, because they also occupy a prominent place in his heart. "I have kept all my life a profound respect for my parents, filled with fear," says M. de Pixérécourt on page xxiv of his *Souvenirs du jeune âge*.

Perhaps this would be the proper place to say in what circumstances I had the precious blessing to be counted among the friends of M. de Pixérécourt. For a long time I had only a very immature and unreasonable critical reaction to this skillful author, incorrectly and wrongly appreciating dramas in the *Figaro* and elsewhere, plays about which my inexperience of theatre did not allow me to understand very much. However, M. de Pixérécourt, a learned lover of books and an indulgent author, pardoned my journalist's errors in consideration of my taste for old books. Our relationship was already amicable; it would soon become intimate.

I came to publish, with which press I no longer remember, a novel written in haste, in less than six weeks, the last volume of it particularly having been written, as they say, straight from the heart. Family love played a great role in it. I sent this novel to M. de Pixérécourt. He, who has made so many tears flow, circulated it in his turn and from that time on he loved and esteemed me to such an extent that even after ten years this friendship and esteem have lost nothing of their power. The greatest and most cherished proof that he could give me of this I have received in obtaining from him the honor of pairing my name with his and of signing at the bottom of this page.

El. de Vaulabelle

CHRISTOPHER COLUMBUS

or

THE DISCOVERY OF THE NEW WORLD

An Historical Melodrama in Three Acts

by

René-Charles Guilbert de Pixérécourt

Music by M. Darondeau

Presented for the first time in Paris at
the Théâtre de la Gaîté on 8 September 1815

CAST OF CHARACTERS

CHRISTOPHER COLUMBUS, Genovese navigator and scientist

DIÈGUE, his son, going by the name of Pédrille

VINCENT PINSON, captain of the Niña, one of Columbus's ships

ROLDAN, crewmaster of the Santa Maria, Columbus's flagship

MARGARITA, boatswain on the same ship

INIGO, a Portugese peasant, godson of Columbus

ORANKO, cacique of the island of Guanahani

AZAKIA, young savage, son of Oranko

KARAKA, old savage

KEREBEK, her son, engaged to Azakia

Two SAVAGES

SAVAGES, inhabitants of the island

Spanish SAILORS

The Scene of the first two acts is COLUMBUS's *flagship, the Santa Maria. The third act takes place on the island of Guanahani, one of the Lucayes.*

The action takes place in 1492. It begins October 11, toward noon, and ends at approximately the same hour the following day, October 12, the day of the discovery of the New World.

Act One

The stage is divided into two horizontal parts. The upper part represents the front of the ship sailed by COLUMBUS, *from the mizzenmast to the prow. The lower part represents the room called the Council Chamber. This entirely enclosed room takes up scarcely a third of the stage depth; it is narrow and the ceiling is low. Within it are several rope chairs, a table, barrels, a chest, some stools. Two stairways lead to the bridge. Both go up to the second level and are provided with banisters. They are facing away from the prow, that is to say someone descending them has his back to the audience. The space beneath these staircases forms a kind of sentry-box facing the audience. Closets have been built into it. The rear of the room is provided with small windows through which the sea can been seen. Downstage on each side is a porthole.*

During the overture, which first suggests a violent storm, orders are heard behind the curtain given in a loud voice by ROLDAN, *the crewmaster, always preceded by a whistle.*

ROLDAN: Strike the main sail! Strike the foresail! Strike the mizzen! . . . (*Thunder, rain, hail, wind, the roaring of waves, all combine to fix the attention of the spectator and to transport him in imagination into this scene of horror. A moment of calm, followed immediately by a fearful crash.*) We're going aground! (*Two cannon shots are fired.*) All hands on deck! (*Indeed the noise is heard of the entire crew rushing from the rear to the front of the ship.* MARGARITA, *the boatswain cries out in fear.*)

MARGARITA: Man the pumps! Shipwright to the hold! We're taking on water! (*Gradually calm weather succeeds this violent tempest, its return expressed by the orchestra. The orders of the crewmaster are heard one after the other.*)

ROLDAN: Hoist the outer jib! Trim the mizzen! Right the helm! . . . (*As the curtain rises,* INIGO *is seen tied to the mizzenmast which traverses the floor of the bridge.*)

INIGO (*he unstops his ears*): God-a-mercy. Good weather, again. (*He unties the bonds which hold him and advances timidly.*) Yes, I can still stand up . . . that shows the sea's calm and the ship on course. It's God's truth, I thought my hour was up! What a ruckus! I never felt the like! These sailors say that there is nothing to beat a good tempest. Well, the fun's all theirs! It's the first I ever saw, but if God asks me, I'll tell him to make it the last. Merciful God. Not to have a hole to stick your head in, not a bit of a corner to hide. I was sittin' on a bench there in steerage, when bang! A wave threw me headlong, and smashed my nose. I jest got up when wham! The boat started what they call pitchin' and I fell slap on the side farthest from my nose. I hobbled up to the bridge and got there just in time to be downed by a wave. Finally I hid down here in the Admiral's cabin where I got the bright idea to tie myself up to this piece of wood so that I could stay on my feet and give up my soul to God in peace. Ah! Why did I have to follow Signor Columbus instead of staying in Portugal with my mother? "Go on, Inigo," that good woman told me. "Go offer your services to your godfather, the Admiral. Young men are improved by travel, and you could not do better than to set sail with this brilliant seaman, who is going to another world. Who knows? Perhaps you will make a fortune there. He who risks nothing gets nothing. You don't possess a *maravedis*, so you are not risking much. And then you will gain the gratitude of this fine man. While I was suckling his son by his first wife, he taught you to read. As for me, I gave you the little knowledge I possessed. You know a bit about cooking, you can mend a doublet nicely. Indeed you know a little about everything, so you should be able to make yourself useful on board. Farewell. Be honest and good. Wait, I will give you . . . my blessing, and so, be gone." I left for Cordova, offered myself to the Admiral. He received me well and promised me six piastres upon our return. We set sail and so far it hasn't been too bad, although it was forty-two days, more or less, that we've seen nothing but sky and water before this damned tempest came along to freeze my blood.

COLUMBUS (*coming down the right stairway*): What are you doing down here?

INIGO: Nothing, Admiral, Sir.

COLUMBUS: Who brought you here?

INIGO: Fear.

COLUMBUS: Fear! Do you dare to make such a confession to me?

INIGO: It's not that I wanted to, Admiral, Sir, it's just that . . . you see . . . I'm not used to such a ruckus . . . I never seen death that close. It's not much fun to die without getting sick . . . really, it's not nice at all. My heart nearly exploded! And I wasn't the only one, either. Every man on the ship was saying his prayers, even you, Sir Admiral, when I had the honor of meeting you on the bridge, you were quite pale . . . for whatever reason.

COLUMBUS: That's enough. I forgive your fear; it was natural enough. But the crew is relying on you to restore its strength. Hurry up and distribute provisions.

INIGO: I'm running, Admiral, Sir. (*He kisses his hand and climbs back up onto the bridge.*)

COLUMBUS: I love that young man. He is faithful, affectionate, zealous. His presence reminds me of those happy days I spent in Portugal, in the bosom of a dearly beloved family. It reminds me above all of my older son, the good Diègue, who went with me on several voyages, but whom I could not expose to the dangers of an excursion whose end is so uncertain. Ardent, impetuous, as I was at his age, he desperately wanted to come with me. For the first time I had to use my authority to force him to remain in Spain. How strongly I have congratulated myself for my prudence, today especially . . . If, as I thought at one point, my ship had gone down in this tempest, the most violent that I have experienced during the forty years that I have roamed the seas, we would both have perished. Then what support would have remained for my wife and my two younger sons? None at all. And beyond that, envious souls would not have been lacking to attack my memory, to depict me as an adventurer; my name would have been blackened in the future. But, what am I saying? What fearful thoughts are these to dampen my spirits! If I were shipwrecked before discovering this new continent, the object of all my dreams, of my ardent explorations, or my long meditations, I would nevertheless be accused of having lied to the court, of having seduced innocent citizens to make them victims of my own imprudence! And yet it exists, this new hemisphere; yes . . . it is out there . . . to the west lies a world unknown to the Europeans . . . I have the deepest conviction of it. I would have landed there this very night if this cursed storm had not carried me off God knows where. I have made a sounding, and touched bottom at 128 fathoms, which I am sure indicates that we are approaching land. The day before yesterday, the sailors pulled in with the grappling hooks a newly cut piece of wood, the bark of which seemed to us of a new species. And finally, yesterday, in the morning, the whole crew saw a dove swooping down on the main mast. Now, according to my calculations we must be twelve hundred leagues from Teneriffe. This bird could not have been able to make so long a flight as that without pausing to rest. When it left, it flew off toward the south-west. Yes, all these signs are more than enough to convince me that this unknown continent exists and that I am close to it. If I am not fortunate enough to set foot on it, I wish at least that no one be allowed to deny me the glory of having shown the way. I would have done enough for my contemporaries.

INIGO (*from the top of the right staircase*): M. Columbus. May I have a word with you?

COLUMBUS: Come down.

INIGO: Y'see. I'm in a real fix. The storm left everything higglety-pigglety in the kitchen. Nothing's left in place. The ham's in the jam, the crackers are in the compote, the water's in everything. It's like Noah's flood. As God is my witness, I put aside a bit of soup for you that I had sealed up. I can't see how it happened but we jounced around so much that I couldn't swallow a drop of it. It's as salty as sea water.

COLUMBUS (*smiling*): Truly, it must resemble it a little. Go find the crewmaster, Roldan. Get from him the key to the hold where the provisions are kept. The damage will soon be righted.

INIGO: Dear godfather. If it's all the same to you, could you send somebody else?

COLUMBUS: Why? When I give you an order . . .

INIGO: It's just that I don't like to talk to this M. Roldan. He never says anything but Hou! Hou! Hou! (*He imitates the deep voice of the crewmaster.* COLUMBUS *laughs.*) Oh, dear lord, he's coming down right now!

He runs down before ROLDAN, *who comes down the left staircase.*

INIGO: Master . . .

ROLDAN (*always brusquely*): What?

INIGO: The Admiral, Sir, told me . . .

ROLDAN: Good.

INIGO: . . . to ask you . . .

ROLDAN: Wait for me on the bridge.

INIGO (*aside, upstage*): He's always so nice, our chief! He scares me to death! (*He imitates* ROLDAN.) Wait for me on the bridge.

ROLDAN: What's that? Haven't you gone yet?

INIGO: Keep cool.

ROLDAN: On the contrary, I've no time to waste.

INIGO *leaves, after a sign from* COLUMBUS.

COLUMBUS (*aside*): An excellent sailor, this Roldan, but a little strange. (*To* ROLDAN.) Well, Roldan, what news?

ROLDAN: Bad.

COLUMBUS: Bad. Is the ship leaking again?

ROLDAN: Not at all.

COLUMBUS: Has the wind changed?

ROLDAN: No.

COLUMBUS: It is still . . .

ROLDAN: Brisk. North-east.

COLUMBUS: Our speed is . . .

ROLDAN: Twelve knots.

COLUMBUS: And that's not so good, in your opinion?

ROLDAN: Very bad. For you.

COLUMBUS: What do you mean?

ROLDAN: That you are lost.

COLUMBUS: Lost?

ROLDAN: Hopelessly.

COLUMBUS: Come, explain yourself. A little more elaboration.

ROLDAN: I don't know how to turn a phrase.

COLUMBUS: True enough. On the other hand, you know your duties.

ROLDAN: That's what I'm paid for.

COLUMBUS: But you must say enough to be understood. What have I to fear?

ROLDAN: Everything.

COLUMBUS: Where are my enemies?

ROLDAN: Here, it seems.

COLUMBUS: You know them.

ROLDAN: Of course.

COLUMBUS: Who are they?

ROLDAN: The whole crew.

COLUMBUS (*taken aback*): The whole crew ? . . .

ROLDAN: Correct. Except me and that peasant, who doesn't count.

COLUMBUS: Why are they against me?

ROLDAN: They say that you have misled them.

COLUMBUS: And what do they propose to do about it?

ROLDAN: Throw you into the sea.

COLUMBUS: Into the sea!

ROLDAN: No doubt that's what will happen, if that's what they have decided.

COLUMBUS: No doubt?

ROLDAN: There are forty of them, and only two of us. How can we resist?

COLUMBUS: There is always a way open to the one who does not lack courage and keeps a cool head.

ROLDAN: I know that as well as you. We can perhaps kill half of them, ten apiece. That will be a good showing. But the other half will then throw us overboard, and that will be an end of it. At any rate if this misfortune occurs, keep cool and stay close to me. I can swim like a shark. When you get tired, rest on my back. If, as you believe, land is not far away, by heaven, I'll carry you there, even if I die on reaching the shore. If we die in mid-ocean, well, that will not be my fault, I will have served you until my last breath. You like empty phrases. There you have some. Are you satisfied?

COLUMBUS (*deeply moved*): Brave man! Let me embrace you!

ROLDAN: As you will. (COLUMBUS *holds out his arms to him.*)

MARGARITA (*outside*): Master!

COLUMBUS: It's the boatswain.

ROLDAN: Here. What's the matter?

MARGARITA (*coming down*): The lookout has just sighted a sail.

COLUMBUS: How far off?

MARGARITA: Some two leagues.

ROLDAN: I'll go have a look. (*Aside to* COLUMBUS, *indicating* MARGARITA, *who seems deferential when he is observed.*) Watch out for that hypocrite. He's the most dangerous of all.

COLUMBUS: I will heed your advice.

ROLDAN: You would do well. I admire you as a great genius, but if you get out of this alive, you will be in my opinion the greatest man in the world.

ROLDAN *exits up the left stairs and* MARGARITA *up the right. Before leaving, and as* ROLDAN *is speaking to* COLUMBUS, MARGARITA *makes menacing gestures.*

COLUMBUS: Roldan is right. It is impossible to stand alone against an entire crew in mutiny. Like him, I feel the danger of my situation, but I must remain true to myself. In undertaking this extremely daring enterprise I knew that I would run every sort of risk, would expose myself to infidelity, to caprice, to the fury of greedy men that were drawn to follow me by their lust for gold but who did not have, as I did, to support their courage or sustain them in defeat, the noble desire to carry out a great project and to render their name immortal. If I perish, as all signs indicate, let at least the fruit of my labors not be lost to the world. I will confide to the ocean this brief report of my hopes and my sufferings. Let us see if I have omitted anything. (*He takes from his desk a sheet of parchment and reads the following:*)[4] "Aboard the Spanish vessel the Santa-Maria, 11 October, 1492. Born in 1442, in the state of Genoa, of an honest family, but one reduced to poverty by the Lombard wars, I developed in my youth a taste for travel and made frequent trips to the Levant. Stirred by the Portugese discoveries, I undertook the study of astronomy, geometry, and especially cosmography. The result of my work, of my calculations, was the personal conviction that there existed another hemisphere. The authority of the ancients, and especially the round form of the earth together supported my opinion. But while my thought reached out to the ends of the world, poverty held me in captivity. Great sums were needed to carry out the plan that I had conceived. I wanted to give preference to my own country. I offered to the Genovese to go and discover this new continent for them. The senate regarded my project as the dream of a madman, and I received only a rejection. The bonds that I had formed in Portugal attached me

---

[4] All the details which follow are historic. [*Author's note.*]

to that realm. Adopted by my heart, it had a right to my services. I presented my plan to Don Juan, who welcomed it with interest, but my memorandum was passed on to a favorite who possessed the folly of presumption combined with the jealousy of ignorance. The noble design that he conceived was to profit from my knowledge to rob me and appropriate my glory. Revolted by this betrayal, I left Portugal and fixed my eyes and my hopes on Spain. After five years of disgust and of patience that only the love of glory could sustain, my proposition was rejected as impracticable. I was preparing to leave this country for ever and was going to take my indignation and my projects to London when Prior Jean Peres, the respected scholar, begged me to postpone my departure. He took me to the camp of Santa-Fe, and obtained for me the favor of being presented to Isabella and to explain my ideas to her in person. She adopted them. I was soon covered with regards and honors. The rulers of Spain deigned to sign an agreement with me in which I was named Admiral of the Seas, Viceroy of Terra-Ferma and all the islands that I discovered, with full power to install governors and judges. In her enthusiasm, the generous Isabella pawned her own jewelry to gain the necessary money. She gave me 18,000 piastres. I fitted out three caravals in the port of Palos and left this last third of August, with a crew of ninety men and provisions for a year. I set sail for the Canaries, which I reached August 12. I set sail again September 1 and steered always to the west, finding myself the following October 10 (yesterday), 12,000 leagues from the Island of Fer at 25 degrees north latitude. There, everything indicates that I am nearing the end of my voyage and the discovery I have so long desired. I have sounded bottom at 128 fathoms." (*A great noise is heard from the bridge.*) What an uproar! . . . What is the source of these confused cries? . . . Will these wretches not give me the time to leave this memorial to posterity? (*He replaces his writing in the drawer of the table.*)

ROLDAN (*very disturbed*): Summon your courage, Columbus.

COLUMBUS: It never leaves me.

ROLDAN: Our chances are lessening. They are now twenty-five to one.

COLUMBUS: What are you saying?

ROLDAN: That the enemy has received support.

COLUMBUS: This sail that they signaled? . . .

ROLDAN: It is the launch of the third ship, carrying Vincent Pinson and seven or eight of his men.

COLUMBUS: Do you know why they have come on board?

ROLDAN: They want to speak to you.

COLUMBUS: Tell them to wait. I will be on the bridge in five minutes.

ROLDAN: That's a long time. They appear anxious.

COLUMBUS: Go. I want to finish up here first . . .

ROLDAN: I am afraid . . . Here they are.

COLUMBUS: I will receive them

During this short scene an ever increasing clamor has been heard outside.

Enter INIGO, PÉDRILLE, PINSON, MARGARITA, SAILORS *noisily and in disorder. They have a menacing air.*

COLUMBUS: Who has given you permission to enter the Council Chamber without being summoned?

PINSON: I have.

COLUMBUS: I was not aware that a subaltern could give others the permission that he needed to seek himself.

PINSON: Now you know.

PÉDRILLE: Well?

COLUMBUS: What audacity! By what right . . .

PINSON: That of the stronger. Lower your voice, Columbus.

MARGARITA (*half aloud*): Yes.

INIGO (*aside*): Well! He's bold, that one.

PINSON: Listen, and consider well what I am going to say in the name of the three crews.

COLUMBUS: I could refuse to listen to you, for I am the sole commander here.

PINSON: Our rights are equal.

COLUMBUS: If you impose them.

PINSON: You command the Santa Maria, I, the Nina.

COLUMBUS: In fact you are trying to lead astray these brave men. Here are my letters-patent from the King and Queen of Spain. You have all acknowledged me as admiral of the fleet sent to discover the New World.

ROLDAN: That's true.

COLUMBUS: You have taken an oath to obey me.

ROLDAN: That's also true.

COLUMBUS: This title gives me unlimited authority . . .

PINSON: Which you are not able to execute without us or our consent.

COLUMBUS: Take care, you will soon be the proof of the contrary.

PINSON: My comrades will refuse to obey you.

ROLDAN: Not all.

COLUMBUS: I defy you.

ROLDAN: No, do not defy them.

COLUMBUS: Moreover, that Vincent Pinson, driven out of Dieppe three years ago . . .

PINSON: Driven out! . . .

COLUMBUS: Don't interrupt me. Yes, driven out, and declared by a ruling of the Admiralty unfit to serve on the ships of this city for having rejected the principles of subordination and good faith necessary to shipping and commerce.[5]

ROLDAN: That was honorable.

COLUMBUS: That this same Pinson, I say, conceived the guilty hope of corrupting faithful seamen and of getting them to rebel against their chief does not astonish me. It is the natural consequence of his previous conduct. I should have expected it.

ROLDAN: And refused his services . . .

COLUMBUS: And especially not believe in his repentance and his protestations. He is of an age when one no longer reforms vicious inclinations. But, even so, let him learn that I will never

[5] See the *Mémoires chronologiques pour servir à l'histoire de Dieppe et de la Navigation Française*, v. 2, p. 77. [*Author's note.*]

suffer the slightest infraction of the discipline that I have established on my ship.

ROLDAN: That is just.

COLUMBUS: The first one who defies it will be hanged from the yardarm.

INIGO (*aside*): For the first time.

ROLDAN (*aside*): Good. He is not afraid.

COLUMBUS: Now I will allow you to speak, not in your own name, but in that of the crews of the Pinta and the Nina. Although I would have preferred to hear their wishes by another organ than yours, if their demands are just, I will be quick to support them.

PINSON: On the faith of a usurped reputation and seduced by your glowing promises, we foolishly consented to go with you over these uncharted seas. A few days would be enough, you told us, to open up across the ocean the pathway to a still unknown world. And yet, nearly two and a half months have gone by since we left Palos. On September 1 we left the Canaries. Now it is October 11, and during forty-two days of continual sailing we have discovered nothing. Your dream has in no way been realized. The fearful storm that we have just undergone brought us to the end of our strength and our patience. We are perhaps five or six hundred leagues from Europe. We have risked our existence for too long without reward. I am therefore announcing to you that the three ships have resolved to set sail for Europe this very day.

COLUMBUS: Good. If I order it.

PINSON: Believe me, Columbus. Do not put your authority in jeopardy. It will fail.

COLUMBUS: Wretch! When you should be stimulating the courage of your men, you have instead incited them to revolt.

PINSON: We will not serve the insane projects of an ambitious man who seeks only to make a great name for himself at the expense of our gullibility.

ALL: Right.

COLUMBUS: I admit it. I had the noble ambition to bring myself fame by this glorious discovery, the most outstanding doubtless that man's genius has achieved. I never hid from you that we were going to experience a thousand dangers, risk running upon reefs, face tempests; but these dangers, these storms, was I not exposed to them along with you? If I succeed, will not every one of you, along with me, have a right to the gratitude of all civilized nations? Will you not share with me the rewards promised by the court of Spain?

PINSON: It is by speeches like that that you have blinded us. You have always shown us the favorable side of this mad expedition. We are more determined today than ever to see your conjectures as idle fancies, and to believe that this delusion, in short this new world, exists only in your mind.

COLUMBUS: It is true that it was upon conjectures that I founded my reasoning, but these conjectures were so powerful that they achieved in my eyes all the force of truth. As you know, Portugal owes to my father-in-law, Barthelemeo Perestrella, the discovery of Madiera and Porto-Sancto. That wise sailor told me a hundred times that the same success could be found in the West that he found in the South. In the Azores he saw on a beach a statue whose pedestal bore inscriptions in an unknown language. The figure, dressed in a savage costume, extended an arm toward the setting sun, and seemed to point that pathway to the boldest of sailors. It has been noted on these same islands that when the western winds have blown for a long time, the sea leaves on the coasts bits of strange wood, plants of an unknown type, and even dead bodies that by many signs were recognized to be neither Europeans nor Africans.[6] Have you not observed the same signs during our voyage? Have they not continued to accumulate, especially during the last few days? Are these not conclusive proofs? Yes, I swear in all the sincerity of my conscience that there is, to the West, an unknown land, and that we are not far from it.

PINSON: Very well, presumptuous adventurer. You can discover it by yourself. As for us, I say again, we set sail today for Spain.

COLUMBUS: I defy you to do so.

PINSON: Who then will prevent it?

COLUMBUS: I will. I who alone have directed the course, and who alone, in all the fleet, know exactly where we are.

ROLDAN (*aside*): That's it, then.

INIGO (*aside*): Trapped!

COLUMBUS: You think that we have only sailed five hundred leagues since our departure? Know then that in fear of frightening you, I have hidden from you each day more than half of the distance we have covered. Nearly fifteen hundred leagues now separate you from Spain. Now, return there; you have my permission.

MARGARITA: Villain!

MARGARITA *menaces* COLUMBUS *with a hatchet that he carries at his belt.* PINSON *threatens him with his sword, but is held back by* PÉDRILLE. *All the sailors are furious and follow the example of* MARGARITA. COLUMBUS *is in the greatest danger, yet he remains calm.*

ROLDAN (*holding* MARGARITA's *arm*): One moment. If you want to return to Spain, you must not kill him, since he alone can lead

---

[6] *Histoire de Saint-Domingue*, by P. Charlevoix, v. 1, p. 66. [*Author's note.*]

you back.

PÉDRILLE (*then all the other sailors, one after another*): He is right.

MARGARITA: Yes, the argument is unanswerable.

COLUMBUS (*thanks ROLDAN with a glance, then turns back toward the sailors*): At any other time I would have punished this mutinous behavior, but I understand your concerns and I want to set them at rest. If in three days we have not reached that foreign shore, I swear upon my word as an Admiral to take you back to Spain. Until then, support my efforts, redouble your enthusiasm and activity. Beside the thirty ecus of pension promised by the king of Spain I promise a special reward to whoever among you first sights land. I am going up on the bridge to take a sounding. I hope on my return to see every one of you at his post and everything put back in order.

ROLDAN (*aside*): He got out of it very well.

COLUMBUS: Follow me, Roldan.

He proudly walks through the crowd that was threatening him a moment before, and who, overwhelmed by the influence of the great man, open a clear passage for him, take off their hats, and bow. COLUMBUS *climbs up to the bridge by the left stairs.* ROLDAN *follows him.*

INIGO (*aside, while all the others exchange looks*): Really! You gotta admit that my godfather Christopher has a lot of guts. I'm shaking like a leaf, and he goes right on as if nothing had happened.

PÉDRILLE (*coarsening his voice*): What? . . . You were saying . . .

INIGO: I was saying that I wasn't saying anything, Sir . . . mustache. (*Indeed,* PÉDRILLE *has a very handsome black mustache.*) It's really remarkable . . . if it wasn't such a black . . . And worse . . . yet . . . oh! No . . .

PÉDRILLE: Are you staring at me? (*He pushes against* INIGO *rudely, throwing him to the ground.*)

INIGO: Why'd you do that? There's an old saying that says when a dog . . .

PÉDRILLE: Do you know who I am?

INIGO: Not at all. Not at all.

PÉDRILLE: I hear the scorn in your voice. Would you be sorry to find out who I am?

INIGO: That's not what I said. (*Aside.*) He's really got a chip on his shoulder! (*Aloud.*) I'm full of respect for you, and to prove it, I'm getting out. Dinner's coming up and the crew's waiting for me. (*Aside.*) Ugh! It's really nasty for a young man to be so crude. (*He escapes.*)

PINSON (*aside, entering with* MARGARITA *as* INIGO *climbs up*): The very existence of Columbus is an obstacle to my plans. Let us use his absence to get the mutiny started again. (*He posts two sailors on the right and left stairs to keep watch during the following scene.*)

PÉDRILLE (*pointing to* INIGO *as he disappears*): I frightened him to get rid of him. (*He reenters the scene.*) Well, Captain, what do you think of all this?

PINSON: That Columbus more and more abuses the power he has over us, or rather our weakness.

MARGARITA: Right, right.

PÉDRILLE: We certainly didn't show much spirit.

MARGARITA: Right, right. What should we have done?

PINSON: Killed him without mercy. That's the only way out of the critical situation he has gotten us into.

MARGARITA: Yes, the only way.

PINSON: What can we hope from this three-day delay? What will be the result of this new act of condescension? To find ourselves a hundred leagues further on, in even more unknown seas, and therefore even further dependent upon him. Inevitably another postponement will follow this one and meanwhile the supplies are running out and who can look forward without shuddering to the horrible extremity to which we may be reduced?

PÉDRILLE: That would be horrible. But what if, against all expectations, we do indeed find this new continent?

PINSON (*aside*): Exactly what I hope! With Columbus dead, I will claim credit for the discovery. (*Aloud.*) It is not possible.

MARGARITA: Right, right. It is not possible.

PINSON: Trust me. Let us free ourselves at once from this visionary and return, if we can, to our homeland.

PÉDRILLE: Who can guide us there now that this devil of a man has lead us so far?

PINSON: I will take on the task. As you know, Pédrille, and as you must attest to your comrades, I am no less familiar than Columbus with the compass and astrolabe. I will take responsibility to get us back to Spain, if indeed you want to return there.

PÉDRILLE, MARGARITA *and all the* SAILORS: Of course we want to. Of course!

PINSON (*in a subdued voice which he maintains until the end of this scene, when it becomes more spirited*): In that case, follow my instructions and destroy the only obstacle that stands in the way of the return that you want so much.

PÉDRILLE: I will follow the captain's instructions, but (since we must be ready for anything) what will we say when we arrive in Spain? How will we explain the absence of the Admiral?

PINSON: We will say we suppose he fell overboard while observing the stars.

PÉDRILLE: Very well.

MARGARITA: And for that supposition to be true, he must really be thrown overboard.

PÉDRILLE: No.

MARGARITA: Why not?

PÉDRILLE: He might be able . . . to swim to safety, to call for help, to attach himself to a cable, to follow the ship, who knows? And our story would be exposed.

PINSON: Pédrille is right . . . He must not survive.

PÉDRILLE: If my comrades wish to do me the honor . . .

MARGARITA: I claim it, first as your leader, since I am boatswain, and you are . . .

PÉDRILLE: Only a simple sailor.

MARGARITA: And further, because I have a personal score to settle with Columbus. He has mistreated me more than once on this voyage, and I have prayed to God daily for a chance to avenge myself. He finally dismissed me and I want to make use of the occasion. I am not capable of murder, but when the death of the Admiral is called for by all three crews it becomes in those circumstances an act of humanity since it serves to preserve the lives of eighty individuals who otherwise would certainly perish as victims of his ambition. My conscience therefore will give me no trouble in this matter, on the contrary . . .

PÉDRILLE: There's no question of conscience here.

PINSON: No, but of courage, and on that account I support Pédrille. He is perhaps the boldest man on my ship. He's a very devil.

PÉDRILLE: It is true. The captain doesn't exaggerate. Therefore I request to be teamed with the honest boatswain, who wishes to kill the Admiral. Two are better than one; I will support him if he falters.

PINSON: I see nothing wrong with that, and I will reward this mark of zeal in the future.

PÉDRILLE: Thank you, commander. I totally support this plan, as you see . . . I do not act out of self interest. In the meantime, it occurs to me that you should perhaps return to the Nina.

MARGARITA: My comrade is right. Surely when the Admiral knows you have gone he will be less on his guard. Therefore it will be easier . . .

PINSON: That makes sense. Let's go. If the supply chief gets in your way . . .

PÉDRILLE: He will follow his master.

PINSON: I don't care for that Roldan.

MARGARITA: Nor do I. He has a superior air.

PINSON: I suspect he supports Columbus.

PÉDRILLE: Don't worry. We will arrange all for the best. Make haste, they may return.

PINSON: I will keep constantly in view. As soon as the business is finished, raise the black flag and I will come to take command.

PÉDRILLE: Agreed.

MARGARITA: Very well, comrades! When do we begin?

PÉDRILLE: At once. I like to have things settled. No one will notice that the Captain has one man less in his party, but there is no doubt that the contrary will be true if I am observed here after he has returned to his ship. So our course is set. We are in the Admiral's chamber, and I will not leave it until my plan is executed.

PINSON (*to* MARGARITA): As I said, he is a demon . . . let's go, farewell. (*To the* SAILORS.) You, don't breathe a word.

PÉDRILLE and MARGARITA: Farewell, Captain.

PINSON *climbs up to the bridge. All the* SAILORS *follow him.*

MARGARITA: Let's organize our plans quickly. Now, how shall we proceed?

PÉDRILLE: Bravely.

MARGARITA: That's not what I mean. We must surprise the Admiral, attack him unexpectedly.

PÉDRILLE: How cowardly!

MARGARITA: It makes little difference how one defeats an enemy, provided that he is destroyed. The important thing is to run as little risk as possible. The closets built on either side of this room can hide us from his sight. We will wait there to strike him when he is asleep or absorbed in his calculations.

PÉDRILLE: Even if it angers you, since you are going to kill him, I cannot help saying that this way . . .

MARGARITA: Repulses you?

PÉDRILLE: Yes.

MARGARITA: All right, then leave. There is still time. See, Captain Pinson's boat is just setting sail. Do you want me to call him? (*He goes to the left porthole.*)

PÉDRILLE (*pushing him away brusquely*): No, no. I don't want that, You'd like for me to leave. I don't know what you're plotting, but I'm staying.

MARGARITA: Very well. There's no leaving now. I hear the Admiral.

PÉDRILLE: Luckily for you.

MARGARITA: Quickly, to your post. I to mine.

PÉDRILLE: Good . . . good . . . I don't need your advice. (*He enters the left closet,* MARGARITA *the one to the right.*)

COLUMBUS (*entering*): Pinson has gone. My crew seems calm, but the seeds of mutiny are still present. Except for Roldan, I have everything to fear from the men who surround me. Once one has passed beyond the bounds of duty, it is difficult to return. The slightest pretext can serve for these mutineers that my firm countenance intimidated this time, and if they are aroused again, I will perhaps be left without means to defend myself or time to finish this brief account. A few words will be enough to end it. I will await developments with greater peace of mind if I can be certain of leaving behind me an honorable and moving report. (*He sits, opens the drawer and reads again the concluding lines.*) "All these details are true, and they form a mass of irresistible proofs in favor of my theory. If I fail, may some other, more fortunate than I, profit by these insights and achieve this great discovery which will be the glory of the century in which it occurs!" (*He signs.*) Christopher Columbus.
In order to confide this precious document safely to the ocean, the only faithful friend that remains to me, I will wrap it in this piece of waxed canvas.[7] (*He opens a chest at the rear and pulls from it the waxed canvas.*) Stamp it on both ends . . . (*He puts a large piece of red wax on both ends which he stamps with his seal.*) And then

place it in this firmly sealed cask. (*He inserts his writing through a bunghole that he then seals with heavy blows of a hammer, then he writes on the cask with the point of a dagger.*) "To His Highness,[8] the King of Spain." Now go, and may the winds carry you to your destination! (*He throws the cask into the sea through the porthole to the left which he has opened. While* COLUMBUS *has his back turned and is leaning out,* MARGARITA *leaves his closet.*)

MARGARITA (*aside*): I could ask for nothing better. He is already halfway there. (*He advances on* COLUMBUS, *dagger raised, and prepares to stab him in the back.*)

PÉDRILLE *rushes from his hiding place, and stabs* MARGARITA *in the arm with a stiletto, causing him to drop his knife, then pushes him violently back into the closet, shutting the door behind him.*

COLUMBUS (*turning quickly*): What's that? . . . What do I see? . . .

PÉDRILLE (*removing his wig, his mustache, and falling at* COLUMBUS's *feet*): Your son.

COLUMBUS: My son!

DIÈGUE: Who begs your pardon for having desired, despite your prohibition, to share your glory and your risks.

COLUMBUS: You ask for pardon, when you have just saved my life! Come, my dear Diègue, come to the arms of your father.

ROLDAN (*rushing down from above. He has an arquebus slung across his shoulder, a sword at his side and an axe in his hand*): What the devil is going on here?

COLUMBUS: My son, dear Roldan.

---

[7] All the details that follow are historic. [*Author's note.*]

[8] The word "Majesty" was not yet in use. [*Author's note.*]

DIÈGUE (*to* ROLDAN): An assassin . . .

ROLDAN: Where is he?

DIÈGUE (*pointing to the closet*): In there.

ROLDAN (*He opens the closet, revealing* MARGARITA *on his knees, pointing to the wound on his arm.*): Margarita! . . . Villainous rogue! . . . I will finish you off. (*He raises the axe in both hands.*)

DIÈGUE (*stopping him*): No.

COLUMBUS: Let him live to witness my happiness.

ROLDAN: He will try again.

COLUMBUS: Let him live, I say. He is no longer a danger. We are now four and prepared to face the storm. (COLUMBUS *again embraces his son.* ROLDAN *threatens* MARGARITA. *The curtain falls.*)

End of the First Act

Act Two

The stage represents the open sea. Only sky and water are seen. The middle of the stage is filled, from left to right, by a cross-section of Columbus's ship, viewed from the port side, from the main mast to the mizzenmast. With the exception of the main sail and the mizzen sail, which are taken in, all the others are unfurled, but they cannot be seen. The stays of the two main masts serve as wings to the right and left, so that the middle of the bridge is open. This bridge, two wings deep, is not opened as in a modern construction. It is three-dimensional from one end to the other and in all directions. To the left, a few feet from the mizzenmast, is a capstan equipped with a small cable. The staircases by which one descends to the between decks are presumed to be out of sight on the forecastle and quarterdeck to the right and left. Eight portholes can be counted going across the stage. This structure is not equipped for war, carrying only two cannons in the rear for signaling, and they cannot be seen from this angle. The portholes serve only to light the rooms constructed in the between decks. An iron rail without bulwarks runs along the planking from port to starboard. Since the tackle of the two main masts is basically in alignment with the wings and the two large sails are furled and form a kind of ceiling, nothing hinders the view of the rear of the stage. The hull being almost entirely hidden, the vessel extends no more than five feet out of the water, so that the floor of the bridge is at most seven or eight feet above that of the stage. The artificial sea should come right up to the prompter's box. The more of it there is in front of the ship, the greater the illusion that will be produced. MARGARITA is on the bridge. INIGO has half of his body through porthole no. 6,[9] which is supposed to provide light for the kitchen. He holds an enormous piece of biscuit in one hand and in the other a line. There are also SAILORS.[10]

---

[9] The portholes are counted beginning on the left. [*Author's note.*]

[10] In general, except when otherwise indicated, this bridge is never empty. It is more or less filled with sailors who are working, coming and going. Therefore their presence is not usually noted. It is taken for granted. [*Author's note.*]

MARGARITA (*crossing the bridge from left to right, he stops near the middle and goes back*): All right, all right. I have figured you out, Columbus. Your pretended generosity doesn't fool me. It only makes me more eager to find the occasion to destroy you. Whenever we land you will not hesitate to revoke this pretended pardon that you have given me and to turn me over to justice. But I won't let myself be caught in that trap. The battle is on, and one of the two of us will go under today. (*He goes out to the right.*)

INIGO (*speaking with his mouth full*): I don't wanta brag, really, but there ain't nobody in this fleet more useful than me. Not only am I the cock of the galley . . . that's the funny name they give the cook . . . The cock! . . . not only am I the cock, I bake bread, I fix the food, I serve the Admiral, I am even the fishmonger. Really, it's easy to see that I couldn't do much more. Here I drop my line from the window of my kitchen . . . I catch fish with one hand and fry them with the other . . . I'm doin' the poor beast a favor, they hardly know what hit 'em. I don't even give 'em time to think. There's one now good as dead. I feel a nibble . . . (*He pulls gently on the line, at the end of which is a hook. DIÈGUE is seen on the starboard side.*)

DIÈGUE (*on the bridge, holding a line and passing from starbord to port*): Let's see if I'll be luckier on this side. (*He drops his line.*)

INIGO: Who's up there?

DIÈGUE: Me. Well! Inigo, any luck?

INIGO: Quiet! . . . I have one (*He pulls in the line again and finds nothing.*) Nobody home. Ah! It's infuriating.

DIÈGUE: I haven't waited long, myself! . . . There's a bite!

INIGO: Scusi! That one was on my line. He left me for you. No doubt about it, you've robbed me, just like a lot of other folk did before. I'd fix you for that if you weren't my blood brother.

DIÈGUE (*pulling out a fish with golden scales*): Just look.

INIGO: Oh! What a beauty! Look! He has gold scales! Oh! How sweet he is! (*As he looks up, a tuna appears at water level and seizes the biscuit that he holds in his left hand.*) What! What! . . . my biscuit . . . my biscuit . . . did you see that fish grab my biscuit?

DIÈGUE (*laughing*): It's a tuna.

INIGO: Wait, thief! . . . Rogue! . . . You'll get your biscuit! . . . Eat your friends and leave me my dinner!

INIGO's *cries attract members of the crew. In an instant the bridge is covered with* SAILORS *all of whom lean over the railing and look down on the port side.*

INIGO: There's enough beasts down there that you don't need to bother me . . . Are you listening? (*All laugh at him.*) Come back, here . . . I'm talkin' to you . . . and it's all your fault, Signor Diègue.

DIÈGUE (*still laughing*): And why is that?

INIGO: It's true . . . If you were over there . . . across from me, by the other porthole, I wouldn't have looked up, and that blasted fish wouldn't a had a chance to grab my biscuit. Please come down here, brother . . . right, it'd be good of you.

DIÈGUE: Very well. Hold my line . . . while I go down.

INIGO: Good. I'm much obliged.

DIÈGUE *disappears for an instant. The* SAILORS *return to their work.*

INIGO: I need to pull a little trick. Since he has all the luck, I'll snag his good fortune and give him my bad. (*He changes his line from one hand to the other.*) Just in fishin', you understand, since I'd rather go straight to the bottom of the sea than cause the littlest harm to my blood brother.

DIÈGUE *appears in porthole no. 5,* INIGO *remains in no. 6*

INIGO: There . . . that's much better for me, we can at least chat more cosy. (*He gives him a line.*) There must be a stool in that cabinet. Take a seat, signor my brother. I'll do the same, and we'll have a bit of gossip. I got a lot to tell you after our little separation! . . . You know its fourteen years since we saw each other?

DIÈGUE: And you call that a little separation?

INIGO: I could say that it wasn't even a separation at all, at least for me, since I never let a day go by without givin' a thought to you.

DIÈGUE (*holding out his hand*): It's true. We have always loved each other.

INIGO: As for that, I'm the one who loved you better.

DIÈGUE: You do me wrong.

INIGO: No, no, just cast your mind back, I was always beaten for you . . . Oh, excuse me, signor my brother, I oughta say, I was always beaten for you, signor!

DIÈGUE: Go on, go on, speak from the heart and your language will always be proper.

INIGO: You were a rogue, a little devil of a tease, bold as a lion. You still seem just the same.

DIÈGUE: On the contrary.

INIGO: A good thing, too, since there's a pack of rascals on this boat, they're almost all rogues. Except me and the Admiral, and then you and the crew chief Roldan, that brute who never speaks more than a couple of words. The rest aren't worth a *maravedis*.

DIÈGUE: I agree. I think my father was wrong to forgive the Boatswain.

INIGO: Wrong, was he? Here's what I think. Between us, Signor

Columbus is too soft. Since we set sail, these no-goods have made fools of themselves a hundred times, and he's never punished anyone. God spare him from paying for it some day.

DIÈGUE: It's all over. They won't dare try anything more now.

INIGO: Wish I could believe it.

DIÈGUE: There are four of us able to put up a good fight. By God, let them try it, and we'll see!

INIGO: Four? How do you figure that?

DIÈGUE: Wouldn't you stand up for yourself?

INIGO: Well, maybe not entirely. I'd do the best I could. I hope with time and teachin' I'll come up to the mark, but until things change I reckon you'd do better to count me as a half.

DIÈGUE: I have a higher opinion of you.

INIGO: That ain't the problem. If I was sure I was stronger than the other fellow, I'd fight like the devil. But tell me, how did you manage to come along so close to us over there on that rascal Pinson's ship without anybody suspecting?

DIÈGUE: I was incognito.

INIGO: Oh, I get it, you used another name, and even another face, 'cause that black mustache really made you ugly! You had a really evil mug!

DIÈGUE: Determined to share the glory or the dangers which would come to my father as the result of this great project, after having embraced him on his ship, I returned to land and his vessel set sail. The Pinta was to leave a half hour later, and so I had time to disguise myself as you have seen. My step-mother, who had resisted her husband's project with all her might, fearful of the enormous perils to which he was exposing himself, arranged for me to be hired on the crew of the Pinta under the assumed name of Pédrille. We both hoped that I could watch out for Columbus and that my aid would be of use to him. It was no doubt God who inspired us. He permitted, for the first time perhaps, an act of disobedience to become a meritorious act, since I had the honor to save my father's life.

INIGO: As for that, it's a sure thing that without you, my poor godfather would be dead at least. Hush! . . . Ah, finally, I feel something on my line . . . (*Aside.*) I knew I'd get good luck with his. (*Aloud.*) . . . Hullo! It's a bunch of thorns! . . . I got no use of stuff like that. (*He starts to throw it back into the sea.*)

DIÈGUE: (*stopping him and taking the branch, which has a few leaves and small red fruit*) Stop, my friend. This is better than you imagine. This branch seems in fact to belong to a spiny tree that I have never seen in Europe. You see it has recently been cut. This leaf, this red fruit, they are also unknown. This discovery will delight my father. I am going . . .

INIGO: Oh, please, signor my brother, don't rob me of the pleasure of doin' somethin' delightful for the good sir Columbus.

DIÈGUE: Your point is well taken, since it was you . . .

INIGO (*retracing his steps*): Where is Lord Columbus anyhow?

DIÈGUE: He was making a sounding when I went to look for him.

INIGO (*returning again*): You'll wait here for me, won't you. I'd like to keep fishin' with you till evening.

DIÈGUE: Yes. Go on, then. (INIGO *leaves.*) I fully share the concerns of this faithful servant. Pinson is clever and ambitious. He will not give the mutineers time to cool off, and I fear that before the three days requested by my father have passed, the traitor will organize some new rebellion. In any case, it is agreed between Roldan and myself that one or the other of us will accompany Columbus everywhere. The mutineers will get to him only over our dead bodies.

COLUMBUS (*from offstage left*): Margarita!

ROLDAN (*also offstage*): Boatswain!

MARGARITA (*offstage right*): What is it, Signor?

COLUMBUS: Call the crew to present arms on the bridge. (*He appears.*) Yesterday's storm prevented us from carrying out our customary drills; we must make up for lost time. (MARGARITA *appears briefly at the rear and immediately disappears again.*) That will do. (*A* SAILOR, *who preceeded* COLUMBUS, *crosses the bridge, carrying the sounding line.*)

INIGO (*running to meet* COLUMBUS *with the branch he fished up*): Look here, Signor Columbus. See what I fetched up with my line? A green bush!

COLUMBUS: Just cut! . . . Further support for my theories! (*To* ROLDAN.) You have touched on many foreign shores. Do you recognize this plant?

ROLDAN: No.

COLUMBUS: This bark?

ROLDAN: Not at all.

COLUMBUS: This fruit?

ROLDAN: Not that either.

COLUMBUS: Where did it come from?

ROLDAN: By heaven, I have no idea.

COLUMBUS: From the continent we are seeking.

ROLDAN: Or some other.

COLUMBUS: And we shall discover it.

ROLDAN: Who knows?

COLUMBUS: You still doubt its existence?

ROLDAN: What does it matter whether I doubt it or not, provided I follow you?

COLUMBUS: Have we not struck bottom at 42 fathoms? Yesterday it was 128.

ROLDAN: Perhaps we are approaching a sandbank.

COLUMBUS: Why do you never cease to struggle against my hopes?

ROLDAN: Because I love you.

COLUMBUS: You afflict me.

ROLDAN: I am sorry for it. Then don't ask me.

COLUMBUS: There! Look at those gulls, that albatross circling around the ship. (*Sea birds are seen flying across the rear of the stage.*)

ROLDAN: We have seen them during the whole voyage, or almost the whole voyage.

COLUMBUS: And you conclude from that?

ROLDAN: That they have followed us.

COLUMBUS: How?

ROLDAN: By landing in alternation on one of our ships.

COLUMBUS: By what mischance do all your thoughts work to destroy my theories?

ROLDAN: I would like some proof.

COLUMBUS: I can give it to you . . . at least I think so. You see that bird perched on the yardarm of the topsail. If I am not mistaken, it is a parrot.

ROLDAN: We'll soon find out. (*He fires the arquebus, killing the bird, which falls on the bridge.*)

DIÈGUE (*appearing, frightened*): What was that? (*He disappears.*)

COLUMBUS: Yes, that's what it is.

ROLDAN: I begin to hope.

COLUMBUS: And I no longer doubt. This bird, as you know, is too heavy for long flights. It could not even cross a bay of more than eight to ten leagues.[11] The plumage of this one is different from those of Africa, so it is certain that it comes from some land that is not more than ten leagues away from us.

ROLDAN: It is proof positive.

INIGO (*entering*): I will run to take this good news to signor Diègue. (*He runs off to the right, carrying the parrot.*)

ROLDAN: But which direction?

COLUMBUS: Always the same. I will consult the compass and tell the pilot to keep sailing west. (*He raises his eyes to heaven.*) Oh thou, who hast inspired this bold project and given me the strength to carry it out, bring me to set foot at last on this

---

[11] Buffon, *Histoire Naturelle des Oiseaux*, vol. II, p. 117 [*Author's note.*]

unknown land! If the day which reveals this great discovery is the last of my life, I am content. What more could I desire? I have made my country illustrious and my name immortal! (*He goes out to the right with* ROLDAN.)

MARGARITA (*on the bridge. He has overheard the last words of the Admiral*): So! You have asked heaven that this day be the last of your life. I will try to satisfy you. (*He gestures to three* SAILORS *and leads them to the port railing, as if to show them something in the sea. He checks to see if the portholes are closed and then speaks to them in a hushed voice.*) I know that you are the most determined. Are you ready to deliver us at last from Columbus? (*The* SAILORS *make an affirmative sign.*) The occasion is perfect. Perhaps we won't get another such chance. Load your arquebuses and during the drill . . . (*The* SAILORS *indicate that they understand.*) Make haste . . . (*The* SAILORS *leave.* MARGARITA *rings the bell.*)

The men of the crew assemble on the deck with their arquebuses. When they have formed two regular lines, COLUMBUS *appears from the right and passes them in review. It should be noted that* DIÈGUE *speaks in a low tone to his father, and that the latter then gives an order in a low voice to* INIGO. *The three* SAILORS *who are the accomplices of* MARGARITA *are in the first row. They should be distinguishable.*

COLUMBUS: My friends, as we approach the moment when we are to set foot on unknown lands it becomes particularly important for your own safety that you be familiar with military procedures. I am as ignorant as you of what sort of people inhabit this continent. It may be that we will be forced to fight them, and then you will thank me for having the foresight to assure your safety and prepared the way for a glorious victory. Dress right, dress! . . . Ready, front! . . . Present arms! . . .Order arms! . . . Present . . . arms! This drill was badly executed. I need to instruct you. Diègue, Roldan, imitate me. (*To the* SAILORS) Everyone, at ease . . Now watch and learn. (*Without affectation,* COLUMBUS, DIÈGUE, *and* ROLDAN *disarm the three sailors who are followers of* MARGARITA *as if carrying out a drill.* COLUMBUS *both participates and gives commands.*) Present arms . . . Prepare to fire! (COLUMBUS, DIÈGUE, *and* ROLDAN *each train their arquebuses on the terrified* SAILORS.) You tremble, and rightly so. On your knees, wretches . . . On your knees! . . . If I heeded only my just resentment, you would receive at this very moment the death that you have deserved.

MARGARITA: What has aroused you to such anger?

COLUMBUS: Perhaps you know better than anyone.

MARGARITA: I, Signor, I protest . . .

COLUMBUS: However that may be, I want the whole crew to know. My son saw three rascals loading their guns in preparation to assassinate me. (*To demonstrate the truth of his charges,* COLUMBUS *pushes a ramrod into his arquebus, so that they can see that it is loaded.*) I command that they be put in irons and shut up in the hold.

SAILORS (*movement. One can hear the murmured words*): We will not tolerate this.

COLUMBUS: You will not tolerate it, you say? . . . It is I who will not tolerate defiance of my authority. (INIGO *is seen at the left. He walks stooped over and appears to pick up something on the bridge.*) Approach. (INIGO *gives* COLUMBUS *a lighted fuse.*) You see this trail of powder. It connects to the Sainte-Barbe.

INIGO: Nothin' so sure as that. I just did it myself.

COLUMBUS: Lower your arms, or I'll blow up the ship.

MARGARITA (*placing himself between* COLUMBUS *and the* SAILORS): Admiral, your anger is justified, and I cannot plead for your mercy in regard to these three criminals. They deserve to die. (*In a low voice, to the* SAILORS.) I will save you. (*Aloud.*) But they cannot be condemned except by a Council of War, in which the commanders of the other two ships must participate.

COLUMBUS: That is just.

MARGARITA: It is doubtless your opinion that they ought to be placed in irons until we have landed on this new continent or until we have returned to Spain. (*To the* SAILORS.) Obey the Admiral, I advise you.

ROLDAN: Obey, or by heaven . . . !

The SAILORS *hand over their arms, which are immediately carried off by* DIÈGUE, ROLDAN, *and* INIGO. MARGARITA *chains the three accused.*

COLUMBUS: Be fearful lest I finally tire of granting pardons.

ROLDAN: Yes.

DIÈGUE: From now on, endeavor by irreproachable conduct to make the Admiral forget your rebellion.

MARGARITA *prepares to lead off the chained* SAILORS.

ROLDAN: (*to* MARGARITA, *taking the chains from him and pushing him away*): Did you think that I was going to entrust them to you?

MARGARITA: And why not?

ROLDAN: Don't force me to explain, you hypocrite! (THE LOOK-OUT *cries from above without being seen:* Master, beware the storm.)

COLUMBUS: Roldan, the lookout has sighted a storm. Leave Margarita in charge of looking after these men and order the necessary manoeuvres.

ROLDAN: Look to the halyards! All hands on deck! (*The* SAILORS *follow their orders.*)

COLUMBUS (*turning toward the members of the crew*): I make you responsible for guarding them. If I have been severe with you, I believe that I have proved oftener still that one can always hope for my clemency. A sincere repentance wipes away all wrongs.

ROLDAN: It is stronger than he is; he will never punish.

DIÈGUE (*low to* ROLDAN): Without calling any attention to myself, I am going to follow the prisoners to their destination.

ROLDAN: You are wise. (*All depart.*)

ROLDAN *comes and goes, giving orders, and finally stands at the foot of the main mast to oversee the activities. Each order is preceded by a whistle to which all the crew responds:* "Order."

ROLDAN: Lower the main jib!

COLUMBUS (*he has gone to consult the astrolabe, and looks at the sky, which is covered with clouds*): The lookout was right. A major storm is approaching. (*Several flashes of lightning are followed by faint rumbles of thunder. Rain falls heavily, the sea swells, and the ship begins to pitch more and more strongly. To* ROLDAN.) We must slow down. Night is approaching. We could run aground or hit a reef at water level.

ROLDAN: Yes, yes. That's very wise. (*Whistle.*) Lower and furl the topgallants! (*The ship's boys clamber up the stays; all is movement on the bridge.*) That's not it. Bear down on the small topgallant to starboard! Let out the sheet of the grand topgallant to port! (*Whistle.*) Take in the mizzen!

All these manoeuvres are carried out in silence and with complete coordination. In the middle of the turbulence of the elements, COLUMBUS *continues his observations.*

ROLDAN: It's nothing. (*Looking at the sky.*) There is no longer anything in the storm but rain. We have nothing to fear. Everyone below! (*Whistle.*) Clear the decks!

SAILORS: Right!

DIÈGUE (*running in, speaks low to* ROLDAN): They are below and I have the key.

COLUMBUS: What does the crew say?

DIÈGUE: They are divided. Some are muttering, but the great majority support you.

COLUMBUS: They will hold the others in check. (*To* ROLDAN.) Now, I advise you to go get some rest.

ROLDAN: Who will take care of the ship?

COLUMBUS: My son and I. You have not closed your eyes all night.

ROLDAN: Nor have you.

COLUMBUS: You must be exhausted.

ROLDAN: Like yourself.

COLUMBUS: You need to sleep.

ROLDAN: No more than you.

COLUMBUS: You are not needed here. This night is too important for me not to spend it on the bridge.

ROLDAN: And what gives you the right to expect me to sleep while you remain awake?

COLUMBUS: It is my desire.

ROLDAN: But not mine.

COLUMBUS: I wish it.

ROLDAN: You are wrong.

COLUMBUS: I order it.

ROLDAN: It is not just.

COLUMBUS: Go, I beg you.

ROLDAN (*aside*): The man is a devil! (*Aloud.*) You will drive me away then. I displease you?

COLUMBUS: Not at all, brave Roldan! The affection that I have for you forces me to care for your health. I repeat, your presence is useless until further orders. If I have need of you, I will call you . . . without ceremony.

ROLDAN: What obstinacy! I won't sleep a wink. (*Aside to* DIÈGUE.) If those rascals . . .

DIÈGUE (*aside to* ROLDAN): I will not leave him for an instant. We are armed. I will awaken you at the slightest noise. (*Aloud.*) What! Roldan, the chief of the crew, the one who ought to provide an example of subordination . . .

ROLDAN: It is just. (*Aloud.*) I will obey, but I will not sleep.

COLUMBUS As you wish. My authority does not go that far.

ROLDAN *exits right. The sky is dark.*

DIÈGUE: It is time to furl the sails.

COLUMBUS: Yes, the wind might drive us aground.

DIÈGUE : Truly, father, it seems as if we were in the vicinity of Spain or Portugal. You speak of this coast as if it were familiar to you, as if we were certain to land there.

COLUMBUS: I have no doubt that we will find it tonight or tomorrow morning. Yes, my son, clearly God has protected my undertaking. If the positive signs that I have gathered during the course of this long voyage, and particularly today, could be regarded by me as insufficient, if I were enough of a disbeliever not to attribute to His grace the inconceivable good fortune with which I have overcome every obstacle so far and confronted numberless dangers. Could I mistake the all-powerful hand which has brought about our miraculous reunion at the most critical moment of my life? (*He presses his son to his breast.*) Oh, no, there is no doubt! My dear Diègue, let us unite our thanks, let our grateful voices merge and rise up to the sovereign master of the world! I fear no more evil, since he has permitted me to press to my bosom a beloved son, the support of my age, and my dearest hope. (*They embrace.*)

DIÈGUE: I don't know if I am mistaken, father, but I have just experienced a new sensation. I thought that I breathed an air that was not the same as what we have experienced during our voyage. It reminds me of those fragrant breezes that arise from a vast prairie after a rain, or rather that scented atmosphere in which I found myself more than once while walking in the gardens along the banks of the Tagus.

COLUMBUS: Indeed . . . you are not mistaken, my son, and this unquestionably indicates to us that we are indeed close to land. From this side the difference can be sensed even more clearly.

DIÈGUE: It is true.

COLUMBUS (*looking left into the distance where he points*): Look, I have just seen a point of light.

DIÈGUE: In which direction?

COLUMBUS: There, opposite . . . to the south-west.

DIÈGUE: Perhaps it is the lantern of one of the other two ships.

COLUMBUS: No, they are behind us. So it must be . . .

Six members of the crew, headed by MARGARITA, *creep up silently onto the bridge. Three throw themselves upon* COLUMBUS, *three others upon* DIÈGUE. *At the same moment, and before they realize what is happening, their mouths are covered with a sash and their arms and legs are secured in such a way that they are unable to offer any resistance.* MARGARITA *disarms them. The three who attacked* COLUMBUS *raise him above the bridge railing on the port side and prepare to throw him into the sea.*

MARGARITA (*stopping them*): No. That will make a noise. We are not all agreed on this. His supporters will come running, will perhaps save him and then we are lost. We must tie his hands and feet so that he is unable to swim, then lower him quietly into the sea with the capstan. Tie the son to the mizzenmast and we will return to him after we have gotten rid of the father.

All is carried out as MARGARITA *proposes, with the least possible noise.* COLUMBUS *is suspended by a cable attached behind his back. Three men work the capstan.* MARGARITA, *sitting on the bridge, guides the cable and releases it slowly, letting it slide over a pulley attached to the rail.*

INIGO (*opening porthole no. 7 and bringing over* ROLDAN): I tell you, something extraordinary is going on on the bridge.

ROLDAN: You think so?

INIGO: I was sneakin' around up there and I ran into two big bruisers with arquebuses sittin' at the top of the stairs . . . I'm sure they mean no good to my godfather. Just listen . . .

ROLDAN: I hear nothing. (*He listens.* INIGO *looks to his right, and sees* COLUMBUS *descending, his feet now touching the water.*)

INIGO: Oh! The rascals! They're drownin' him!

ROLDAN: Damnation! Run!

INIGO: This way. (*He closes the porthole.*)

MARGARITA (*to the* SAILORS): Wait a moment . . . I though I heard something . . . don't move. (*The* SAILORS *stop to listen.*) It's nothing. Go on, a bit more quickly.

Indeed, they double the turning speed and COLUMBUS *disappears beneath the waves. Two portholes, nos. 3 and 4, open. They are those to the left and right of the area where the cable is unwinding.* INIGO *hangs onto this cable with all his strength and continues to pull on it in order to make the evil sailors believe that their victim is still attached to it.* ROLDAN, *with a strong arm pulls up* COLUMBUS, *removes the sash that covers his head, cuts the rope that binds his arms, so that the Admiral, standing on the wale, holds onto the porthole with one hand and unties his legs with the other. When he is free, he re-enters the ship through porthole no. 4.* INIGO *still continues his scheme, which completely fools* MARGARITA. *It becomes extremely dark.*

MARGARITA: He must be at least twenty fathoms down. He will have to be clever indeed to escape this time. Cut the cable. The others go take care of the son. Bring him here while we get ready. (*They cut the cable.*)

THE LOOKOUT: Land ho! Land ho!

MARGARITA (*terrified*): Land! Oh, great heaven!

THE LOOKOUT (*louder still*): Master! Land ho! Land ho!

MARGARITA: We are lost! . . .

ROLDAN (*without*): Here I am!

MARGARITA: Brazen it out.

Following his advice, the guilty SAILORS *surround the mizzenmast and thus hide* DIÈGUE *from* ROLDAN's *sight.*

ROLDAN: The lookout has sighted land . . . Where is the Admiral?

MARGARITA: I don't know.

ROLDAN (*seizing him by the collar and shaking him rudely*): The Admiral, I tell you! What have you done with him?

MARGARITA: What have I done with him? . . .

ROLDAN: Restore him to me, or . . .

MARGARITA (*totally disconcerted*): Where can I flee?

ROLDAN: To Heaven.

MARGARITA: What are you saying?

ROLDAN: Hanging or drowning. Choose.

MARGARITA: But . . .

ROLDAN: Hanging or drowning. Choose.

MARGARITA: Still . . .

ROLDAN: You do not want to choose? . . . Someone must announce to the inhabitants of the sea our arrival in the new world, and I command you to do so. (*He throws him into the sea on the starborad side.*) Ho, lookout! Where is the land?

THE LOOKOUT: To starboard by the foremast.

ROLDAN (*going upstage and thus turning his back toward* DIÈGUE): Admiral! Admiral! Land to starboard by the foremast.

The SAILORS *release* DIÈGUE *and beg his forgiveness. The entire crew runs onto the deck crying "Land! Land!" It is a veritable delirium.*

COLUMBUS (*appearing, throws himself into the arms of his son and of* ROLDAN. INIGO, *following him, shares in the common joy*): There is at last that land, the object of all our vows! . . . (*The guilty* SAILORS *fall to their knees.*) Arise.

Foam coats the guy ropes. All the portholes are open and occupied by men of the crew waving their caps. The clouds, slowly parting, reveal the land. One can see, not far off, a heavily wooded island of picturesque aspect. The scene is illuminated by moonlight. COLUMBUS *appears overcome with joy. The entire crew cries "Long Live Columbus!" The cannon fires. The curtain falls.*

End of the Second Act

Act Three

The stage represents part of the island Guanahani. At the rear, a wooded mountain with several peaks. Before this mountain, an incline toward the left, leading to the sea, which is offstage. From the top of a rock, rising twelve to fifteen feet and situated at the fourth wing on the right, a thin stream of water falls into a first basin, grows larger and forms a sheet of five to six feet which falls again in a double cascade[12] into a stream the banks of which are sown with flowers and garlands. This stream disappears off right. Downstage, on each side, conical huts, covered with the leaves of bananas, palms, and so on. The one on the left, larger than the two facing it, is the dwelling of the chief. Flowering trees and plants in abundance give great beauty to the site and render it very picturesque. As the curtain rises, the inhabitants of the island--men, women, and children--sitting on their heels, elbows on their knees and holding their heads in both hands, form a diagonal line which extends from the cascade to the hut of the chief. Each one has a large golden ornament on the chest, a large golden ring in the nostrils, and a small gold leaf at the end of the nose. Old KARAKA leaves her hut and consults the tribe to find if they approve of her intention to ask the chief for the hand of his beautiful daughter AZAKIA for her son KEREBEK, who she depicts as handsome, well-built, and endowed with all graces. All the SAVAGES nod their heads three times to signal their agreement. Then KARAKA goes to her hut and calls KEREBEK. KEREBEK appears. He is tall, thin, dry, and horribly tattooed. Everyone finds him quite acceptable and urges him to puruse his suit. KARAKA orders him to go back inside, telling him that she will take care of this and will summon him when it is time. He obeys.

KARAKA (*goes to knock three times on the chief's hut. Prostrating herself, her head against the earth, she cries out*): ORANKO!

All the SAVAGES rise, turning in the same direction as KARAKA, and

---

[12] This cascade is natural. [*Author's note.*]

take up the same attitude, awaiting the appearance of the chieftain.

ORANKO (*appears. He wears a golden crown and has a long red feather above each ear. He orders the tribe to rise and addresses* KARAKA.): Cati louma [What do you wish]?[13]

KARAKA: Amouliaca Azakia Kerebek [To ask for your daughter Azakia for Kerebek].

ORANKO *hesitates. To convince him,* KARAKA *calls her son.* ORANKO *wants to know how he can please* AZAKIA. KEREBEK, *after having displayed his person, and especially his face, takes up a club and with a single blow breaks a nearby tree, takes up his bow, points to a coconut, and then splits it with an arrow. Then he asks* ORANKO *to point out the strongest member of the assembly to engage him in combat.* KEREBEK *lifts him like a feather and throws him to the ground at their first encounter.*

ORANKO: Inalaki [Well done].

All the SAVAGES *applaud this triple triumph, lowering their heads three times. Having demonstrated his power,* KEREBEK *wishes to show his skill, and, entering his hut, he returns with baskets, rush mats, and a belt of red feathers.* KARAKA *affirms that all these are the work of her son. How can so many collected perfections be resisted?*

ORANKO: Chicalamai [I consent].

He enters his hut, and everyone shows the greatest impatience to see AZAKIA. KEREBEK *in particular expresses his joy in ridiculous gambols.* ORANKO *leads in* AZAKIA. *She is young and beautiful, delicate of build and modest in bearing. Her father tells her that he has promised her to* KEREBEK.

---

[13] The language of Guanahani is taken from the Carribean Dictionary published by P.D. Breton in Auxerre. [*Author's note.*]

Pixérécourt places the translations of the "Carribean" speeches in footnotes. I have placed them instead in brackets in the text. [*Translator's note.*]

ORANKO: Itara a moutou Koule ouekelli [Will you take him for
your husband]?

*The young savage, raising her eyes to the mate that has been chosen for her,
appears to find him quite ugly. KEREBEK squats down, skips around her
in a flattering manner, and attempts to win her over by all sorts of apish
tricks. AZAKIA remains indifferent. Finally KEREBEK goes back into
his hut, carries out the presents destined for his future bride and lays them
at her feet. AZAKIA makes up her mind; what most pleases her is the belt
of red feathers. KARAKA, aided by the other women, immediately puts it
on her. AZAKIA goes to look at herself in the waterfall, and likes what she
sees. Now she agrees to marry KEREBEK, who is overcome by joy.
ORANKO goes into his hut to get a shell. The others line up on either side
of the cascade. KARAKA fills the shell and gives it to her son, who, after
having drunk from it, gives the rest to AZAKIA. ORANKO gives the
couple a small white loaf of bread. Each takes an end and they break it.*

ORANKO: Areskoui, Azakia Karaititi-arou [In the name of the Great
Spirit, Azakia is your wife].

*Drunk with love, KEREBEK wishes to show this to the company. He
thanks ORANKO by pressing his nose against that of the chief, dismisses
all the SAVAGES assembled to participate in the ceremony, and begins to
carry off his new wife immediately into his hut. KARAKA wants to follow
him, but he requests her to do nothing of the sort and absolutely insists on
being left alone with AZAKIA, who does not appear too much alarmed by
this haste. As they are all about to separate, a noise of cannon fire is heard
from off left. This unknown noise astonishes the SAVAGES.*

ALL: Anakilika [What is that]?

ORANKO: Ouallou hougourou [It's thunder].

*A second crash, closer, reveals that this is wrong. General fright. Some run
up the mountain and behave in a completely grotesque manner. They run
off, seeing the firing of the caravels, and return to announce, with broad
gestures, that they have seen three ships at the sea shore off left and that
from them is coming this noise, so deafening that they must cover their ears.
A trumpet fanfare is heard. This sound, equally unknown to them, stuns*

them again. KEREBEK, who has run to the rear, comes back and explains as best he can that he has seen men coming off of the ships, that these men are dressed from head to foot, that they have hats with plumes on their heads, and that they are marching this way, preceded by drums and trumpets. Indeed, a military march is heard, at no great distance. KEREBEK proposes to go in arms to meet them. ORANKO opposes this. After assuring himself of the truth of this report, he thinks on the contrary that it would be prudent to withdraw and to take refuge in the neighboring woods, to spy out the movements of the newcomers and to discover their intentions. His advice is adopted and all exit to the right. COLUMBUS enters from the left, preceded by drums and trumpets and a part of his retinue, and followed by ROLDAN. He holds his son DIÈGUE around the waist and in his right hand carries unfurled the banner of Spain.

COLUMBUS (*kneeling and uncovering his head. All the others imitate him*): Before all else, let us give thanks to Him who has deigned to lead us through our trials and to protect this great enterprise. (*He rises.*) In my capacity as Admiral of this Ocean and Viceroy of the Indies, I take possession of the New World in the name of their Catholic Highnesses Ferdinand and Isabella. (*He plants his flag in the ground. Drum roll, fanfare. The cannons continue to sound from the ships.*)

ALL: Long live Columbus! Long live the King!

DIÈGUE: I will be responsible for the box.

ROLDAN (*brightening*): My thanks. This is a commission that will compensate me for the trials of the voyage.

COLUMBUS: Then you are no longer in a bad humor?

ROLDAN (*still rather brusque*): Not at all, since you are happy.

COLUMBUS (*taking his hand*): Good man! Always the same.

ROLDAN: Why would you want me to change? Would you change from being good?

COLUMBUS: It's my duty.

ROLDAN: You follow the precepts of your heart, do you not? I only
follow your example.

COLUMBUS: Go, and return soon. We will reassemble here. This
cascade will serve as a meeting-point for all those who wish to
go out exploring.

DIÈGUE *and* ROLDAN, *accompanied by several* SAILORS, *go off in
front of the cascade.*

COLUMBUS (*to* PINSON, *who comes in with several* SAILORS *from the
left*): Well, Captain, what do you think of all this? Am I still only
an adventurer?

PINSON (*bowing*): Illustrious Columbus, after God, you are our
savior. You will be the source of our fortune.

COLUMBUS: I hope so, and I will do whatever I can to realize this
hope. Has your brother rejoined us?

PINSON: The thick fog that surrounded us yesterday separated him
from us, but the cannon firing from my caravel guided him back
and he has just dropped anchor in the bay half a cable's length
from the shore.

COLUMBUS: I do not want him to disembark. Prudence warns us
not to leave the fleet without a captain. This land appears to be
inhabited. (*He points out the huts to his* SAILORS *who open and
enter them, then indicate that they have found no one.*) And we
should for the time being forbid anyone to approach our ships
whose intentions are unknown. I am therefore provisionally
placing all three ships under the command of Alfonso Pinson,
the captain of the Pinta, and I want all the crews to recognize him
in this capacity while we are on shore. (*He writes several words on
a roll of parchment or a tablet.*) Inigo, return to the ship and give
this note to captain Alfonso. It contains my authority and an
order to send here twenty-five men with barrels. It is possible

that we will not have an opportunity to take on water for some days. This cascade is at our disposal, and in less than two hours will give us an abundant supply (*The cascade stops; only a very small trickle of water continues.*)

DIÈGUE (*on the rock above the cascade. He has heard the last words of* COLUMBUS, *which were spoken loudly because* INIGO *was some distance away*): Come back, Inigo! It seems that the Admiral is going to change the order he gave you.--Father, as I was climbing up the mountain with Roldan we came upon the spring that fed this cascade and we observed that if we placed a slight barrier on one side its waters would soon flow off toward the sea, following a gentle slope that extends all the way to the shore. In this manner it will be sufficient to dig a hole thirty paces from the edge and our men can renew their supply of fresh water with little difficulty and, in effect, without disturbing themselves.

COLUMBUS: The idea is ingenious, and I am all the more willing to adopt it since the crew will then not be out of sight of our ships.

PINSON: That is essential (*Aside.*) and suits my own plans much better.

COLUMBUS (*to* INIGO, *who has come back to him and returned his order so that he can make the necessary changes in it*): Go on . . . Let everyone set his hand to the task. (INIGO *leaves. To* DIÈGUE.) It is only right that you direct the work, since it was your idea. Men will be sent to you. (DIÈGUE *leaves. To* PINSON.) As for us, Captain, we will look around the area without going too far away. According to all appearances, it was the noise of our artillery that caused the natives of this country to flee, and yet we must encourage them to approach us since it is only from them that we can obtain the information we need to make use of this important discovery. (*To the* SAILORS.) If you encounter anyone, I advise you to treat them with the utmost gentleness. Even if they approach in a hostile manner, I forbid you to engage them until I have given you an express order to do so. I see over there a small group of dwellings at the far end of this pleasant valley, and I am going to visit them. You, Captain, follow the banks of this small river for two or three leagues, and we will meet again here. (*To the* SAILORS.) While we are away, go back on board the Santa Maria and get the gifts that I have brought for the inhabitants of this new hemisphere. (COLUMBUS *disappears into the valley to the left, followed by five or six men.*)

PINSON: Carry out the orders of the Admiral at once and leave me alone. I am armed; if I need any help, I will soon have it. We will not be far apart, a shot will be enough to signal my danger. Beside, I see Roldan coming from that direction. (*The* SAILORS *depart by the mountain path that leads to the sea.*) I am not mistaken. My plan will fail unless I am able to seduce this man. His courage, his quick energy, his affection for Columbus, all this impresses the crew. I need him to lead the sailors. He is experienced and not lacking in intelligence. I must win him over to my side at whatever cost. I expect some difficulties, but doubtless, like all other men, he is susceptible to pride and self-interest, those two rulers of the world. I cannot do without him; let us make an approach.

ROLDAN (*aside, seeing* PINSON): Unpleasant meeting. (*He pretends not to have seen him and takes the mountain path.*)

PINSON: Roldan!

ROLDAN: What?

PINSON: Come this way.

ROLDAN: What do you want?

PINSON: To ask you if you have discovered anything.

ROLDAN: No.

PINSON: What? You have seen nothing?

ROLDAN (*looking at him unblinkingly*): Nothing. Only a snake.

PINSON: You should crush it.

ROLDAN: That is what I was planning to do.

PINSON: Do it then, or he will get away from you.

ROLDAN (*taking his arm*): No, I have him.

PINSON (*trying to keep control of himself and pretending to take this as a joke*): What! Are you still angry with me?

ROLDAN: Angry? . . . (*He regards him with scorn.*) No.

PINSON: Good. I would like for us to make peace.

ROLDAN: Impossible.

PINSON: Why?

ROLDAN: Ask your conscience.

PINSON: What? That old quarrel? Relax, I tell you. Everything is changed, dear friend . . .

ROLDAN: Bah! Have you become an honest man?

PINSON: You will see.

ROLDAN: That's a different matter, then.

PINSON: But before I disclose an important secret to you, you must give your oath . . .

ROLDAN: A good precaution! Traitors do as much every day. An honest man gives his word and keeps it.

PINSON: But . . .

ROLDAN: I give you mine.

PINSON: And if you were not honest with me?

ROLDAN: I have told you already that we are not friends.

PINSON: Fair enough. Listen to me, Roldan. I am going to open my heart to you. You are rough; your character is harsh, even a bit savage . . .

ROLDAN: Enough flattery.

PINSON: But your heart is open and true.

ROLDAN: You do not know me.

PINSON: You are well aware . . .

ROLDAN: Of my place.

PINSON: You are courageous.

ROLDAN: Yes.

PINSON: Capable of taking command.

ROLDAN: Perhaps. Where is this leading?

PINSON: I have figured you out.

ROLDAN: I don't believe it.

PINSON: You are ambitious.

ROLDAN: Absolutely.

PINSON: Ah!

ROLDAN (*insisting, angrily*): Absolutely.

PINSON: Couldn't you persuade me that you would like to have command of one of the three caravels?

ROLDAN: Yes.

PINSON: Would you refuse that?

ROLDAN: Indeed, yes. I would refuse it. If everyone remains in his place, things can only get better, the world will be better governed.

PINSON: But if circumstances required it . . .

ROLDAN: What? What circumstances?

PINSON: For example, if I were called to another post?

ROLDAN: Called! . . . By whom?

PINSON: If by some unexpected occurrence the Admiral . . .

ROLDAN: I begin to understand.

PINSON: Wouldn't you then accept the rank of captain with its salary of six hundred . . .

ROLDAN (*threatening him with his hatchet*): Say another word and I will lay you out at my feet. Wretch! Do you dare to make such a proposition to me, Roldan? It is fortunate for you that I have given my word. If you did not have my vow, I would go at once to denounce you to the Admiral, and within an hour you would be hanged.

PINSON: You have misunderstood . . .

ROLDAN: Quiet!

PINSON: It is not . . .

ROLDAN: Silence!

PINSON: One word.

ROLDAN: Not a one. (*Aside.*) I am returning to the ships and staying there.

PINSON: My dear Roldan . . .

ROLDAN: My dear Roldan! . . . I forbid you to sully my name. Give up your vile schemes. I will be watching you. You will find me everywhere. I will have the eyes of a lynx to see into your heart and the strength of a lion to crush you. Farewell. (*He leaves by the mountain path.*)

PINSON: That man has an iron character, and I am lost. Columbus has the power to set up a court here. (*He considers.*) But, if I wish it, this land could become the tomb of the Admiral, his son, and Roldan. Yes, before the day's end they will be massacred by the natives of this country. Doubtless these men are distrustful, suspicious. After I have insinuated myself into their confidence by gentle manners and gifts, I will describe Columbus and his friends to them as traitors who wish to enslave them, bind them in chains, and ravish their wives. Then I will furnish them with arms and teach them their use. After that I will return to the ship while some of our men set fire to their huts and carry off all they find there. It is inevitable, after the information I have given them, that these disasters will be attributed to the Admiral. The vengeance of the natives will know no bounds; Columbus will fall their victim. Certain that he can never return to Europe, I will set out at once for Spain. I will present myself to Ferdinand and Isabella as the author of this great discovery, and receive the rewards and honors which are due for it. Now, quickly to carry this out. I will rejoin Columbus, and profit by whatever he has discovered. (*He exits left.*)

ORANKO, KEREBEK *and* KARAKA, *followed by several armed* SAVAGES, *appear to the right, remaining close to the ground and sliding through the undergrowth. They advance with caution up to the edge of the clearing at the left and seem inclined to follow* PINSON, *but then* INIGO *is heard singing as he returns by the mountain path. The* SAVAGES *enter the huts,* KARAKA *hides in that of* ORANKO.

INIGO (*from offstage*): Mist. Admiral! . . . I done your orders. Where is you, Mist. Diègue? . . . Say sump'un (*He appears.*) They said they'd come back to the waterfall. Here I is . . . Shucks, I'll just rest my bones a bit afore they come . . . I'm beat . . . and anyhow, long as I'm here I can see the ships, and that makes me easy. Looks like this is where the natives live. I wonder how these huts are put together. Maybe I should take a look while nobody's around. Our folks was lookin' in them just a while ago. This is funny. Looks like these leaves . . . when it rains . . . I wouldn't care much for that . . . (*He opens the door of the first hut on the right.* KEREBEK *comes out of it.*)

KEREBEK: Mabouica [Greetings].

INIGO (*frightened, crying out*): My lord! What an ugly mug!

KEREBEK (*advancing as* INIGO *retreats and extending his hands to him*): Kerebek mabouica [Kerebek greets you].

INIGO: Rebeca bouya . . . What's that mean? (*Turning to flee, he finds himself face to face with* ORANKO.)

ORANKO (*striking him on the shoulder*): Catabou [Who are you]?

INIGO: Another one. There's no end to 'em. (*Trying to evade* ORANKO, *he encounters a third* SAVAGE *on the right.*)

SAVAGE: Kata boyen tibouyete [Why are you here]?

INIGO: Tribulette! Whatta boygon!

ORANKO: Cate biti [What is your name]?

INIGO: What the devil have I got into?

SAVAGE: Allia rabia tabou [Where do you live]?

INIGO: My blood's frozen solid.

SAVAGE: Carabou ibaounale [Are you friendly]?

INIGO: Maybe they take me for an enemy. I'll tell 'em no. (*He shakes his head.*)

ORANKO, KEREBEK, THE SAVAGES (*angrily*): Oua [No]!

INIGO: That made 'em mad. I musta been mistaken. I better always say yes.

ORANKO: Meerra ka tibanao [Are you making fun of us]?

INIGO (*nodding his head*): Yes, yes.

A SAVAGE: Niouebemali [Vengeance]!

INIGO: What? Does that make 'em mad, too?

KEREBEK: Acharamoun [Kill him]!

INIGO (*rushing toward the hut at the left*): Yi! Yi! My time has come! (*They fall upon him, raising their clubs.*)

KARAKA: Cheulleba linokatilone [Mercy for him].

INIGO: That one doesn't look as bad as the others.

KARAKA (*simperingly*): Bouetoui ouellematoum [Handsome stranger] . . .

INIGO: Looks like that one's making eyes at me. But I'm not surprised; it's a woman.

KARAKA: Anake-bouyatina akimatitibou [Although I am old, the sight of you pleases me very much].

INIGO : You can say whatever you like, then get along. I'm not so dumb.

KARAKA (*tenderly*): Nayou mouragoyem [Let us be lovers; that's what I want].

INIGO (*imitating her intonations*): It's like you was singing.

KARAKA (*to* ORANKO): Enocali bouikenli [He scorns me]!

ORANKO: Cati epecantini [What an insult]!

INIGO: There they go! They're mad again!

THE SAVAGE: Kiri kiri bana keyetou [Traitor]!

ORANKO: Katitaeraka [Crush him]!

KEREBEK (*poking* INIGO): Tikateni [He's fat]!

INIGO: They're deciding what sauce would be best for me.

ORANKO: Robouca boucae [Carry him on our shoulders].

INIGO: I have only a few minutes left!

KARAKA: Maboya [Evil spirit]!

THE SAVAGE: Oumekou [Wretch]!

ORANKO: Ietounnoucou [Enemy]!

KEREBEK: Kouloubi [Devil]!

The three pick him up as easily as a feather, place him on their shoulders, and carry him off to the right. KARAKA *follows them in triumph.*

INIGO (*struggling*): Help! Save me! Lord Columbus! . . . Lord Diègue! . . . I'm about to be murdered! Help!

During this scene and the previous one, the SAVAGES *furtively approach* INIGO. *One takes his hat and puts it on his own head, another takes off his doublet, a third slides between his legs and removes his boots, and finally, a fourth, noticing a ring with red glass on the little finger of his right hand, attempts to pull it off. Failing in this, he sets to work cutting off the finger with the sharp edge of a shell, which raises a piercing cry from the Portugese peasant. These activities continue all during the dialogue;* INIGO *is too intimidated to notice the loss of his possessions.* SAILORS, *followers of* COLUMBUS, *enter left and cross the stage, following the tracks of* INIGO, *who continues shouting from a distance to them.*

INIGO (*to* COLUMBUS, *who enters left*): Ah, lucky for me that you're my godfather, Lord Columbus. Without you and these brave fellows (*Indicating the* SAILORS.) I would'a been roasted.

During this scene, SAILORS *carrying boxes and trunks appear on the mountain path.*

COLUMBUS: So you have seen men here?

INIGO: Devils, Columbus, Sir.

COLUMBUS: What did they say?

INIGO: They said "Chaboya . . . Karamel . . . Ciboulette . . ." Who knows what! . . . They have some sort of gibberish that would stump the devil hisself.

PINSON: Did they harm you?

INIGO: Not much! Only wanted to eat me, that's all. (*Lower, to* COLUMBUS.) Listen, godfather, these discoveries are OK for some, but I've had enough of 'em and also of storms at sea. When you're ready to send me home, that'll suit me just fine.

DIÈGUE (*leading in* AZAKIA, *who is resisting him*): Look, father! What a lovely girl!

PINSON: Charming!

COLUMBUS: What becoming modesty!

INIGO: Oh, yes! She's very nice. Too bad she's a savage.

AZAKIA *breaks free, but her path is barred.*

COLUMBUS: We will tame her by flattering her vanity.

DIÈGUE: That always works in Europe.

PINSON: As it does throughout the world.

INIGO: Really, it is possible that women are vain over here, too?

COLUMBUS: It's true everywhere, and we don't mind it at all.

AZAKIA *turns her back on* COLUMBUS *and* PINSON. DIÈGUE *goes to open one of the boxes brought by the sailors and takes out a necklace made of bits of colored glass. He shows it to* AZAKIA, *who finds it pretty and tries to take it.* DIÈGUE *withdraws it from her and leaves. She pursues him. Resistance increases her desire. Finally, after teasing her a bit,* DIÈGUE *lets her have it. She quickly adorns herself with it and runs to the cascade to view herself, but its course is dry.*   DIÈGUE *shows her a mirror, which enchants her. He also allows her to obtain it only after teasing her with it a bit, all of which brings out the piquant and impish charms of* AZAKIA. COLUMBUS, PINSON, *and all the* SAILORS *are much entertained by this little struggle.* DIÈGUE *asks* AZAKIA *if she is alone; she responds that her companions have fled.*   DIÈGUE *assures her that they have nothing to fear from the Europeans. He shows her the boxes filled with presents and tells her to go look for the other women. She hurries off.*

COLUMBUS (*to* INIGO): Draw a line in the sand from this hut to the
    waterfall. That will serve as a barrier between us and the
    Indians. (*To the* SAILORS.) I forbid you to cross it, and especially
    to take for yourselves any of their possessions, however unusual
    they appear to you.

INIGO *caries out* COLUMBUS'*s order and stands behind the line with*

the others.   Two trunks are placed on the other side, one of them closed.
AZAKIA *returns with one of her companions.   They approach shyly.*
AZAKIA *gives her friend a necklace and a mirror. The friend goes to bring
a third, who calls a fourth, and so on.*   COLUMBUS *enjoys their
astonishment and joy, but their pleasure would be incomplete if their
husbands and lovers were not witnesses to it. They go to look for them and
to lead them back also, one after another, and not without difficulty.   They
are armed and suspicious of the strangers.*   AZAKIA, *to prove to*
KEREBEK *that they are not evil, calls* DIÈGUE, *takes him familiarly by
the hand and urges him, with much charm and insistence, to open the other
trunk.*   DIÈGUE *gives her the key and everyone is amused by the
confusion of the young savage, who does not know how to use it.* DIÈGUE
*shows her. She finally opens the trunk and finds in it pretty little hats with
red feathers. She gives them to all of the men, who, as child-like as herself,
are delighted with these playthings and put them on.*   Old KARAKA
comes forward in her turn and requests a gift. INIGO *gives her a little hat.*
KEREBEK *blows in a shell, the sound of which is rather similar to an
English horn. This signal summons* ORANKO. *Seeing him from afar,*
AZAKIA *runs toward him. All the* SAVAGES *follow her.* ORANKO
*comes forward solemnly, led by his daughter and escorted by all the natives,
who show him the presents they have received. They express their joy by
gamboling about with amusing contortions.*   AZAKIA *goes up to*
COLUMBUS, *takes his hand and places it in that of her father.   She
presents the peace pipe alternately to the two men; then the chief rubs his
nose against that of* COLUMBUS *as a sign of peace and alliance.*
COLUMBUS *has another trunk brought, from which he draws a scarlet
cloak and a glass necklace with large beads and several strands.* AZAKIA
*dresses her father in them, who cannot suppress his joy and who offers gifts
in turn to* COLUMBUS.   *The* NATIVES *depart for a moment, soon
returning to lay at the Admiral's feet coconuts, tortoises, sugar cane, and
nuggets. These are in the form of large crude plates just as they have been
found in the earth. This particularly draws the attention of the Spanish. A
seat is hastily put together from the branches of trees and covered with a
canopy of rushes.* ORANKO *urges* COLUMBUS *to sit there and would
sit on the ground near him.* COLUMBUS *opposes this, insisting that he
remain at his side.* ORANKO *gives a sign and the* SAVAGES *display all
their talents in pantomime and dance to please the Europeans.* AZAKIA
absolutely insists that DIÈGUE *join in their sports.   She seems to look
upon him with great pleasure and lets pass no occasion to demonstrate this*

to him. This much irritates KEREBEK, *whose jealousy, long held back, finally breaks forth. He roughly separates* AZAKIA *and* DIÈGUE. ORANKO *seeks to reprimand him, but* KEREBEK *makes it understood that his wife is his property. He therefore shuts her in his hut, which is the first on the right, and places himself as sentry at the entrance. When the dance ends, the* SAVAGES *rub noses with the Europeans.*

COLUMBUS (*to* PINSON): I will take advantage of the good terms we are now on to inform myself and find out if this land is an island or a continent. (*To* ORANKO.) Take me up there . . . onto the mountain.

ORANKO: Inalekia. Acaboyete none [All right. Come with me].

COLUMBUS: Let us follow him. Come, Diègue.

PINSON: I will await you here. Prudence requires that we do not remain all in the same location.

COLUMBUS: I have no misgivings.

COLUMBUS, DIÈGUE, *and* INIGO, *led by* ORANKO *and some of the* NATIVES, *leave to the right.* KARAKA *and the women leave to the left.*

PINSON (*aside*): Let us profit from these moments. (*To the* SAILORS.) Pick up those presents and carry them on board. You can put down your hatchets; they will be a hindrance. You will find them here . . . I will be responsible for guarding them. (*The* SAILORS *carry off the gold plates and other presents offered by the* SAVAGES.) Now that the treasures are safe, let us look to Columbus. (*He adjusts his bearing, assumes a sad air and gathers the* SAVAGES *around him, appearing to pity them. He looks for every means and utilizes the most meaningful gestures to make them understand that the man who was just before them and who is now accompanying their chief is a villain who desires to make them into slaves, burn their homes, and carry off their gold and their women. He addresses* KEREBEK.) No more Azakia for you. (*He makes him understand that she will be carried off by* COLUMBUS, *taken onto the ships, and transported far away. This lively pantomime produces a*

*great effect on the islanders, who easily grasp the message and appear
extremely agitated.   They appear to seek* PINSON's *advice.)*

KEREBEK: Cate achicabouria? [What is to be done?]

PINSON *advises them to kill the Admiral and his son, and hands out to
them the* SAILORS' *hatchets.   He gives one of them a Moorish scimitar
that is hanging at his side and his arquebus to* KEREBEK, *after showing
him how to use it.   The* SAVAGES *fondle and examine with curiosity the
arms he has given them.*

PINSON (*aside*): To give them further encouragement, I will drink
    with them in token of friendship.   This novelty liquor,
    overheating their brains, will further assure the Admiral's
    demise. (*He takes a bottle from one of the trunks, pours the liquor into
    a shell, drinks first from it himself and then passes it to* KEREBEK,
    who finds it excellent and shares it with all of his fellows.) Now they
    are well prepared. Within the hour, Columbus will pass from
    life into nothingness. Following my plan, I will set fire to the
    nearest huts, then, if possible, I will carry off that pretty young
    savage. (*During this aside, the* SAVAGES *have continued to drink.*
    PINSON *takes their hands, rubs noses with* KEREBEK, *points out to
    them that* COLUMBUS *is returning, then departs, advising them to
    kill him.*)

Enter COLUMBUS *and* DIÈGUE.

INIGO: Where's the crew? I better ask Captain Pinson; I see him
    over there. (*He goes out to the right.*)

COLUMBUS (*enthusiastically*): What a beautiful country! Oh, my
    dear Diègue, what delicious fruit I have gathered from my
    labors! My name will be famous forever . . .

DIÈGUE: You are giving to the sovereigns of Europe what may be
    an immense kingdom, with new subjects, an inexhaustible
    source of wealth . . .

COLUMBUS: My family's fortune is assured.   Ah, how many

blessings at once! This island appears to be twelve to fifteen leagues in circumference; but its good king has made known to us that there exist many others at no great distance. I am on fire to discover them. Let us hasten to take our leave of these hospitable islanders. (*During this dialogue,* KEREBEK *has detained* ORANKO *at the rear. He and another* SAVAGE *gesture excitedly and seem to threaten the two Europeans. As soon as* COLUMBUS *and* DIÈGUE *turn around, they are surrounded and immediately disarmed.*)

ORANKO, KEREBEK, SAVAGES: Licotamali! [Death!]

COLUMBUS: What horrible treachery!

DIÈGUE: This is Pinson's doing.

COLUMBUS: No doubt. He has given them arms.

KEREBEK, *who has constantly displayed hatred toward* DIÈGUE, *is the most fervent. He would like to kill him with his arquebus, but he is unable to do so.* COLUMBUS *is confined in* ORANKO's *hut and* DIÈGUE *is put in bonds.* ORANKO *orders the savages to guard the prisoners until he has gathered the entire tribe to kill and then to eat them. He blows on the shell, but seeing that no one is coming, he charges* KEREBEK *to watch over them until his return, and he goes away anticipating the pleasure he will have in destroying those he believes to be his enemies.* KEREBEK *throws the arquebus that he has been unable to use into the corner of his hut, and goes to dig through the trunks, which remain upstage. He finds another bottle in them, tastes it and returns to offer some to his companions, who have stretched out* DIÈGUE *on the ground. According to their custom, they squat around him after having attached to their right hands one end of the bonds that restrain each limb of their victim, so as to prevent his escape in case they fall asleep.*[14] KEREBEK, *squatting like them and placed above, that is at* DIÈGUE's *head, gives signs that the liquor has reached his head and that he feels his eyelids becoming heavy. Still the bottle is passed around again. Each of them feels the same effects; they fall down one after the other. But they make it clear before doing so that they are not*

---

[14] An historical fact. [*Author's note.*]

concerned, since the prisoner cannot make a movement without awakening them and their weapons are close at hand. Indeed, they have their clubs to one side and on the other the hatchets given them by PINSON. AZAKIA *quietly leaves her hut to see what is happening. Touched by the situation of the young Spaniard, she wishes to shield him from the death which threatens him. She moves around the group and, satisfied that all her countrymen are sleeping, she picks up a hatchet and uses it to cut carefully the vines that are restraining* DIÈGUE. *She shows him the way which he must flee, assures him that she will never forget him, and urges him to be gone. But* DIÈGUE *makes her understand that his father is shut in the chief's hut and that he will never agree to leave without him. Two* SAVAGES *squatting before the door make entry impossible. Their situation is extremely difficult.*

DIÈGUE: How can I deliver him? . . . Pinson himself has given me a way.

DIÈGUE *takes the scimitar that one of the* SAVAGES *has near him and cuts the vines that serve as hinges for the hut's door. When the door is detached,* COLUMBUS *pulls it into the interior, but this is not enough. He still must get past the guards, who are seated next to each other.* DIÈGUE, *aided by* AZAKIA, *goes to find two empty boxes. He passes one of them to his father and places the other at the* SAVAGES' *feet. Climbing up on the upright boxes, the* ADMIRAL *can step from one to the other across the heads of his guards.* DIÈGUE *offers his knee to his father to use as a step.* AZAKIA *supports him gently with her right hand. In this way he is able to escape. He embraces* DIÈGUE *and both thank* AZAKIA, *who accompanies them as far as the mountain path. They disappear.*

AZAKIA, *pleased with the good deed that she has done, slips quietly back through the* SAVAGES *and shuts herself in* KEREBEK's *hut. She anticipates gleefully the astonishment of her father and his countrymen when they discover the disappearance of their prisoners. She has already opened the door when* PINSON *slips through the trees, surprises her from the rear, and attempts to drag her away, threatening her with his dagger.* AZAKIA *resists and defends herself, but cannot cry out.*

PINSON: The huts are on fire. There's not a moment to lose. Here she is. (*He seizes* AZAKIA *around the waist. She fights back.*) Oh! She resists! Quickly, back to our ships!

Enter ROLDAN.

ROLDAN (*throwing himself between them*): I will protect you.

PINSON (*allows* AZAKIA *to escape and runs here and there awakening the* SAVAGES): That madman again. Sent by the devil.

ROLDAN: No, I'm the devil in person. Your brother, thinking me in league with you, told me everything, and I have come just in time to upset your plans.

PINSON: Is this how you keep your word?

ROLDAN: I promised to say nothing, and I have remained silent. But I never promised to do nothing, and I will pursue you without rest until you are expunged from the list of the living. God be thanked, it won't be long, I hope.

AZAKIA *tells the islanders about* PINSON's *attack. She points him out to them.*

KARAKA (*frantic, runs in followed by all the women*): Lira chayoucaeti icabouiali! [He set fire to the huts!]

She points out PINSON, *and all the women also point to him. The rage of the islanders is turned against the rascal. He is thrown to the ground, but* KEREBEK *wishes to have the pleasure of killing him. He goes to find his arquebus and tries to recall the lesson he was given. At last he levels the weapon at* PINSON; *then, by chance, he discharges it. The bullet fires and kills the villain.* KEREBEK *and all the savages fall to the ground, sitting down.*

ROLDAN: A fitting punishment! . . . He himself furnished the fatal weapon.

The sound of ORANKO's *horn is heard from the right. At the left, on the mountain, drums and trumpets announce the arrival of* COLUMBUS *and his company. The* SAVAGES *in* ORANKO's *train, joining those already on stage, prepare to attack the Spaniards who are occupying the mountain. The parties face each other menacingly.* AZAKIA *throws herself before her father and seeks to disarm him, while pointing out to him the lifeless* PINSON.

ROLDAN (*throwing himself before the Spaniards and forcing them to put down their arquebuses*): Stop, Columbus. Thanks to me, your enemies no longer exist.

COLUMBUS: In that case, nothing should further disturb our relations with these good Indians.

DIÈGUE: Let a kiss of peace be the token of our eternal friendship.

DIÈGUE *leads* COLUMBUS *toward* ORANKO, *who, for his part, is pulled toward the Admiral by his daughter.* DIÈGUE *embraces* AZAKIA, *to the great displeasure of* KEREBEK.

INIGO (*to* KARAKA, *who approaches him with the same intention*): Thanks, old lady, but I don't need that from you.

COLUMBUS (*giving his sword to* ORANKO, *who offers him his bow*): Oranko, I give you this weapon as a sign of alliance, and I accept the one you offer me in exchange. (*To his men.*) My friends, we are going to set sail and pursue our discoveries. Let the memory of what has happened since our departure from Spain not be lost among your experiences. Those wretches, your cruelest enemies, whose sole aim was to sow conflict among you to elevate themselves, brought you to the brink of major crimes and of depriving your king of possession of this beautiful country. In the future, turn a deaf ear to the whispers of treachery, remain calm in tempests, steadfast in your duty, faithful to your sovereign. Always rally to the voice of the leader who speaks to you in his name and I promise you long-lasting prosperity.

ALL THE SPANIARDS: Long live Columbus! Long live the King!

They throw their hats in the air. The cannon is fired, banners wave, a drumroll and fanfare are heard. The WOMEN *take up the left side, the* SAVAGES *to the right, the* SPANIARDS *cover the mountain. They say farewell and the curtain falls.*

End of *Christopher Columbus*

Alice

or

The Scottish Gravediggers

Translated by Daniel Gerould

Translator's Foreword

Alice is noteworthy for three reasons: it is a true crime story, it is a collaborative work, and it ends unhappily.

Pixérécourt wrote three plays dealing with true crime stories—which would prove to be a rich and inexhaustible mine of material for subsequent melodrama. These are *The Suicide, or the Old Sergeant* (1816), *The Chapel of Wood* (1818), and *Alice, or the Scottish Gravediggers* (1829). *The Old Sergeant* was based on an incident that took place many years ago in Caen where a servant, in order to remove the stigma of a suicide, was falsely accused of murdering his master. *The Chapel of Wood* dramatized the recent murder of Fualdes, former magistrate of Rodez in the south of France; the horrors of this case had been exploited by newspapers, pamphlets, and lithographic prints as well as by Géricault in a series of drawings.

Alice dealt with a much more famous case, the serial killings by Burke and Hare in Edinburgh that led to the most celebrated murder trial in the history of Scotland, immediately publicized by local pamphlets, ballads, and broadsides. Pixérécourt, who read about the *fait divers* in an Edinburgh journal, appears to be the first literary figure to seize upon this lurid and grisly subject that later would attract such authors as Robert Louis Stevenson ("The Body-Snatcher"), James Bridie (*The Anatomist*), and Dylan Thomas (*The Doctor and the Devils*) as well as the makers of horror films. Here Pixérécourt shows himself to be the great progenitor of melodrama in its most basic and enduring form.

A word about the case. The first serial murderers to achieve international celebrity were two Irish resurrectionists or body snatchers, William Burke and William Hare, who provided cadavers for Dr. Robert Knox, a brilliant professor of anatomy at the University of Edinburgh Medical School. Rather than rob graves, the two decided to make corpses out of the destitute and downtrodden staying in the flophouse run by Hare and his wife. From November 1827 to October 1828, they killed sixteen penniless and homeless derelicts whom they first got drunk. They delivered the "anatomical subjects" to Dr. Knox's experimental laboratory in a tea chest or herring barrel and were paid ten pounds a piece for fresh merchandise, no questions asked. Burke and Hare were arrested at the end of November 1828; the trial began on Christmas Eve and ended twenty-four hours later on December 25, 1828, when the verdict and sentence were pronounced. Hare, who gave evidence against his partner, went free; Burke was hanged in January 1829. Ten months later Pixérécourt's *Alice* was playing in Paris.

After Burke was hanged, his carcass was flayed, his hide tanned, and his skin sold in different size pieces, cost depending on size. Sir Walter Scott bought a piece. Burke's skeleton went on display at the Anatomical Museum of Edinburgh University (where it still can be seen), Burke and Hare went into the murderers' gallery at Madame Tussaud's, and the Anatomy Act of 1832 was passed, making it possible for medical schools to obtain corpses legally. To "burke" became an English verb, meaning "to murder, as by suffocation, so as to leave no or few marks of violence." Films on the subject include *The Body Snatcher* (1945) based on Stevenson, *The Greed of William Hare* (1948) starring Tod Slaughter, *Burke and Hare* (1971), and *The Doctor and the Devils* (1985), Ronald Harwood's revision of Dylan Thomas's scenario.

Despite his proclaimed distaste for collaboration, Pixérécourt worked with other playwrights throughout his career, which helps to explain his prodigious output. However, he insisted on total control himself and allowed his collaborators little freedom.

Written in his "romantic period," *Alice* is one of Pixérécourt's melodramas that ends badly for the protagonist. The others are *Valentine* (1821), *The Escape of Marie Stuart* (1822), and *Death's Head* (1829). In Alice's harrowing tale Pixérécourt has moved close to the somber tonalities and grim aesthetics of black romanticism, behind which lurks the Marquis de Sade's *Justine, or the Misfortunes of Virtue*. Sir Jack himself has been a Byronic wanderer full of nihilistic thoughts on human existence. And no amount of moralizing can disguise the sheer horror of the final discovery of Alice's corpse on the dissecting table. The critic Julien-Louis Geoffroy had declared that the public demanded "strong emotions, violent shocks, no matter how and at whatever price." Pixérécourt was ready to provide these thrills, while avoiding questions of medical ethics and the misery of the poor.

ALICE

or

THE SCOTTISH GRAVEDIGGERS

A Melodrama in Three Acts

by

René-Charles Guilbert de Pixérécourt

In Collaboration with Charles Desnoyers and B. Edan

Music by Alexandre Piccini

Presented for the first time in Paris at
the Théâtre de la Gaîté on 24 October 1829

CAST OF CHARACTERS

SIR JACK

EDWARD, a medical student

GEORGE, another student

TOBY, Mistress Butler's son

MACDOUGALL

ROSBEEF   } GRAVEDIGGERS

BURKE

A STUDENT

WAITER IN THE TAVERN

MISTRESS BUTLER, innkeeper

ALICE, her niece

FRIENDS and RELATIVES of Mistress Butler

STUDENTS, SERVANTS

The action takes place in London at MISTRESS BUTLER's *inn during the first two acts, and in Inverness, Scotland, during the last act.*

ℱct Onℰ

The stage represents a common room in the inn of MISTRESS BUTLER; *to the right,* SIR JACK's *room, no. 3; and to the left, no. 4,* GEORGE *and* EDWARD's *room.*

TOBY *and the porters arrive from the market; they are carrying fowl, vegetables, and fruit in dossers and baskets.*

TOBY (*sitting down*): Oh! . . . I can't take any more! . . . Alice! . . . Alice! . . . Mistress Butler! . . . Mama! . . . Where are they? It's a crying shame to overburden a poor young man, weak and delicate like me; while that little Alice plays the princess all day long and gives herself the airs of a lady. Help me take this off. Put those provisions in the kitchen, and tell them to bring me a bottle of porter . . . That's it . . . fine. You can go now, I'll wait.

The porters leave, taking off the provisions.

TOBY (*still seated*): Did you ever hear of anything like that. I'm of a peaceable disposition and good natured, but there's no way I'm going to put up with that, I simply won't stand for it. Mama! . . . Mistress Butler! . . . (*He bangs on the table.*)

MISTRESS BUTLER (*entering*): Who have you got it in for, Toby, to make such a racket? You must be out of your mind to disturb the travelers' sleep like that.

TOBY: So much the worse for the travelers; but I can't stomach the fine airs that little girl gives herself. I know she can't go to the market for me, but at least she ought to be here when I come back.

MISTRESS BUTLER: You're really a fine one to be complaining! I'm the one who does everything in this house, aren't I? . . . I'm always here when the travelers arrive and when they leave, aren't I? If a gentleman goes to bed, if a groom gets up, it's Mistress Butler come here, and Mistress Butler go there! . . . Upstairs, downstairs, in the kitchen, everywhere, it's always Mistress Butler! . . . It's simply intolerable. Oh! if my hotel is one of the best frequented and most comfortable in London, it certainly isn't in any way due to you or to Alice; the two of you are equally useless to me.

TOBY: All right! Let her do her work, and I'll do mine, that's fine; but I have no intention of breaking my back from dawn till dusk, while my lady spends her time sweeping the garden paths with the hem of her gown, her nose stuck in a book, or stays shut up in her room scribbling all sorts of things I don't understand a word of.

MISTRESS BUTLER: That's not surprising: you don't know how to read.

TOBY: Look here, mother, you're at it again! . . . I don't know how to read! . . . Why don't you scream it from the roof tops? . . . Well, all right, no, I don't know how to read, and it's your fault.

MISTRESS BUTLER: My fault? . . . Ungrateful boy! . . . How many times did I beat you without its doing you any good? That's how children are . . . And then it's my fault! . . .

TOBY: Yes, it's your fault. You should have hit me harder and oftener. If I'd had that kind of upbringing, chances are I wouldn't have turned out such a blockhead. Now it's too late. I'd be easily consoled for not knowing how to read, if Alice hadn't got the idea of being a scholar; because after all, if some day I decided to make her my wife . . .

MISTRESS BUTLER: Well, would it be such a misfortune for your wife to know more than you did? . . .

TOBY: I'm not so dumb as to have a clever wife! I want my better half to be stupider than me.

MISTRESS BUTLER: You're asking a lot, my poor boy, and I'm afraid you'll die a bachelor.

TOBY: You see, I'm jealous . . . Jealous . . . (*In a tragicomic tone.*) Like Othello.

MISTRESS BUTLER (*laughing*): And just who are you jealous of? . . .

TOBY: That will do; I'll explain it all to you. (*He goes upstage, and opens the door to the rear.*) Well now, what was I telling you? . . . There she is, a book in her hand as usual, and always dolled up like an elegant miss. Look at her.

MISTRESS BUTLER: I see her.

TOBY: And you're not saying anything to her? Scold her, mother.

ALICE *comes out reading.*

ALICE (*noticing her aunt. She puts her book in the pocket of her apron*): Oh!

MISTRESS BUTLER: Still engrossed in reading, despite my forbidding you to? Alice, you would do much better to make yourself useful around the house.

TOBY: My mother's right.   What kind of a book is that anyhow? . . . Let's see. (*He takes the book, opens it, and spells out the title.*) P, a, pa, m, e, me; l, a, la, Pamela. . . . What does that mean: Pamela? . . .

MISTRESS BUTLER: Pamela? . . . She was a virtuous young lady.

TOBY: It doesn't take much virtue to be a serving girl in an inn.

ALICE: Oh! My cousin! . . .

MISTRESS BUTLER: You just said something foolish; there's no law against virtue in any of the stations of life.

TOBY: That may be, but I hold it against her. She only shows consideration and concern for that odd character in no. 3, her tutor. I'll bet he's the one who lent her . . .

ALICE: Quite right.

TOBY: Well, then! So much the worse, that hurts me . . .   that affects me; that affects me a great deal; not to mention those two madcaps in no. 4 . . . I dislike one of them especially, Mr. Edward! . . . I'll be really glad when he leaves.

ALICE *reacts involuntarily at* EDWARD's *name.*

MISTRESS BUTLER: If you carry on like this, Niece, what will come of it? . . . You'll become brainy, you'll want to appear above your station, and those of your own class won't want to marry a woman who knows more than they do; and yet you don't intend to stay an old maid.

TOBY: Sir Jack with his books and his maps is not the one who'll want you for his wife. Besides (*bluntly*), if you're pretty enough, you don't have to have a brain in order to please men.

MISTRESS BUTLER: So no more reading; pay less attention to your clothes and bit more to the concerns of the house.

ALICE: Yes, Aunt.

TOBY: That's right, pay a bit more attention to your clothes, and a bit less to the concerns of the house . . . (*They exit to the right.*)

ALICE (*alone*): They've gone, and I can weep to my heart's content. How I'm treated here!   Fortunately from time to time I find people who take pity on poor Alice. For instance, there's Mr. Jack, so eccentric, but so good! . . . and then this young traveler, who seems so kind and who talks to me in such a gentle tone!

Because of the predicament I'm in, I blush in their presence and especially in his; but he doesn't disdain me on that account, and every day, when he can find a moment . . .

EDWARD (*running over to her*): Alice! . . .

ALICE: Mr. Edward! . . .

EDWARD: Oh! What? Did I frighten you? . . .

ALICE: Oh! No, not at all; it's only . . .

EDWARD: You didn't expect me so early? I heard you were here, and I came running . . .

ALICE: I'm very grateful.

EDWARD: You do not owe me any gratitude. We students have few pleasures. Smoke, drink porter, read the newspapers, and discuss politics, that's the extent of our amusements. Well, then! Although I'm no Cato, far from it, I don't like these noisy get-togethers, and I have no greater pleasure than coming here and chatting with you, and having you confide in me. What's the matter? You're not saying anything . . . do you have some new cause for distress? . . .

ALICE: Good gracious! Yes.

EDWARD: Tell me the whole story, I beg you.

ALICE: I've been scolded again . . . But it's not my fault; I do the best I can.

EDWARD: And you stay in a house where you are treated so unjustly? What keeps you from leaving?

ALICE: Leaving is impossible; Mistress Butler is my aunt.

EDWARD: All the more reason. To treat one's niece with such

inhumanity!

ALICE: She says it's for my own good.

EDWARD: For your own good? Do you believe that?

ALICE: What else can I do? She's my sole support in the world. My mother was the wife of a lawyer at Oxford. My father had a small inheritance; but speculations made with public funds soon ruined him. He died of the shame of having lost his fortune, and my mother followed him soon after. Before she died, she sent for me. "My girl," she said to me, "I raised you for a class which you must relinquish; because you have nothing, and I regret that your tender age did not allow me to provide you with an education which could have given you a few resources; but now there is only one possibility left. Go find my sister in London; she will receive you cordially, although during my life . . . " She died while uttering these last words, and I was taken to my aunt's.

EDWARD: Who took you in out of charity.

ALICE: What would have become of me without her?

EDWARD: She makes you pay dearly for her hospitality; I have been a witness scores of times. . . .

ALICE: Yes, but I have a protector here.

EDWARD: Oh! You have a protector?

ALICE: Sir Jack. . . . You don't know him?

EDWARD (disdainfully): Just who is Sir Jack? A young man, I dare say!

ALICE: Good heavens, how you look at me! . . . No, sir, no, he is not a young man.

EDWARD: And what is he? Tell me. . . .

ALICE: What is he? I know nothing about him; but he is the best and most generous of men. It is he who has taught me the little that I know.

EDWARD: Oh! He's the one. . . . Alice, watch out for him.

ALICE: For Sir Jack? . . . Why should I? He has never done me anything but good.

EDWARD: All the more reason to be suspicious. He is a dangerous man.

JACK (*off-stage, to the right*): Alice! . . .

ALICE: Oh! Dear God! I recognize his voice.

EDWARD: Whose voice? . . .

ALICE: Sir Jack's voice.

EDWARD: Oh! It's different if it's Mr. Jack who's calling.

JACK (*coming out of his room*): It seems no one wants to answer me. Oh! There you are, Alice? Here, take this letter to your aunt. (*He notices* EDWARD.) No, give it back to me. . . . give it back to me, I tell you. (*He grabs the letter out of* ALICE's *hands, makes a movement as if to go back into his room, and on reflection turns around.*) Wait. On second thought, take the letter to her. (*He gives her the letter and goes back into his room.*)

EDWARD: He's delightful, that kind gentleman of yours; I congratulate you on him.

ALICE: He is a bit eccentric.

EDWARD: A bit? . . . He's the most peculiar, the most bizarre person I've ever seen.

ALICE: If you knew him, you would respect him, I'm sure.

EDWARD: Well! I don't believe it . . . One can say what one likes about the face not proving anything, but I do not believe that a decent person could look like that.

ALICE: You cause me much pain by talking that way.

EDWARD: Forgive me. . . . God knows that was not my intention. . . . Let's make up. I was wrong, I admit it; I made a superficial judgment. Will you forgive me? . . . And, look here, as a sign of reconciliation . . . (*He kisses her hand;* GEORGE *appears at the door of no. 4.* ALICE *runs off to the rear.*)

GEORGE: Bravo! Bravo! Well done! . . . You said you were going to see our anatomy professor, didn't you? . . . A charming professor! I should like to take lessons with her.

EDWARD: Always the same old George! . . .

GEORGE: I ask you, to get up at the break of day to go chat with the chamber maid.

EDWARD: You're not going to suppose . . .

GEORGE: I'm not supposing anything, I saw.

EDWARD: Alice is a decent girl . . . incapable . . .

GEORGE: Don't get so worked up, for heaven's sake! All right, I believe you; but that makes you all the crazier. To wake up a friend who's fast asleep, in order to come kiss the hand of . . . (*ironically*) a decent girl!

EDWARD: My friend, all these jokes . . .

GEORGE: All right! Are you going to get angry? . . . Look here, let's calm down and talk sense. Here you are, an exemplary student, famed for your good sense and principles, ready to forget everything for the pretty little face of a serving girl in an inn. Farewell the noble profession! Farewell the studies that occupied you exclusively!   Farewell the hope of one day being one of the foremost doctors of England . . . in a word, one of the . . .

Voices off-stage.

EDWARD: Be quiet. I hear sounds; come back to our room.

GEORGE: All right, let's go back. But I won't stop telling you . . .

EDWARD: I won't listen.

GEORGE: I want to convince you . . .

EDWARD: Be quiet.

GEORGE: Let me speak, without interrupting me, for just half an hour.

EDWARD: Oh! Be quiet, chatterbox! . . .

They go back to their room.

MISTRESS BUTLER *and* TOBY *enter from the right.* ALICE, *who comes in from the rear, approaches them.*

ALICE: Aunt, here's a letter that Sir Jack gave me for you.

MISTRESS BUTLER: A letter? . . .

TOBY: I wonder what could be in it?

MISTRESS BUTLER: You're quite curious.

TOBY: Always have been. It's my weakness.

MISTRESS BUTLER: Leave us, Niece.

TOBY: Yes, our business concerns only us.

ALICE: I'll leave you. (*She goes out to the rear.*)

TOBY: Now we're alone; read it, mama.

MISTRESS BUTLER: Let's see. (*She peruses the letter.*) Oh, good heavens!

TOBY: What's the matter?

MISTRESS BUTLER: I can't believe my eyes.

TOBY: What is it? . . .

MISTRESS BUTLER: That good Sir Jack! . . .

TOBY: Well, what's he done? . . .

MISTRESS BUTLER: What generosity! Who would have suspected it?

TOBY: I beg you, mama, read it a little louder and more distinctly; I don't understand a word.

MISTRESS BUTLER: Listen, and you'll be as surprised as I am. (*She reads.*) "Mistress Butler, I have stayed in your hotel five or six times, so you know who I am well enough. But what you do not know is that I am very unhappy. . . . "

TOBY: Oh! I can guess: he wants us to give him credit.

MISTRESS BUTLER (*continuing*): "I have lots of gold . . ."

TOBY: Well, then, what's he after?

MISTRESS BUTLER (*continuing*): "But not a single relative, not a single friend with whom I can share it."

TOBY: Look here, he had only to tell me that, and I would have shared it with him right then and there.

MISTRESS BUTLER: Listen then if you're so anxious to know. (*Reading.*) "In my loneliness I resolved to unite my life to the first woman whom I found worthy of such an attachment. I have searched for a long time ... for a very long time; I even began to despair, but I believe that I have found her."

TOBY: Wow! I'll bet he's going to ask for your hand in marriage.

MISTRESS BUTLER: My hand! What an idea! ...

TOBY: Golly, listen, mama, you're not yet too ...

MISTRESS BUTLER (*reading*): "And that woman is Alice, your niece."

TOBY: Alice? ... Hey, come on? ... What are you saying? ... I didn't expect that.

MISTRESS BUTLER (*continuing*): "At my age it is probably sheer folly to marry someone so young."

TOBY: Sure, it's sheer folly.

MISTRESS BUTLER (*continuing*): "But I am unable to resist it, it is stronger than I am."

TOBY: That is his misfortune.

MISTRESS BUTLER (*continuing*): "As it is customary to ask the nearest relatives ..."

TOBY: He's asking my permission, that's what.

MISTRESS BUTLER: Will you be quiet, chatterbox? ... (*Proceeding.*) "I am ready to conform to this usage; but I warn you in advance that nothing you can say will make me abandon my resolution . . ."

TOBY: Then it's not worthwhile even asking.

MISTRESS BUTLER: "Only Alice's refusal could deter me. Yours very truly. Signed Jack Spleen." Well, what do you think of this letter.

TOBY: I think it's splendid, it's magnificent; but I refuse to give my consent.

MISTRESS BUTLER: Oh! Who is asking for your consent? . . . No one needs it. Don't you see the advantage we gain from making such a marriage?

TOBY: All I can see is that I'll lose my intended.

MISTRESS BUTLER: Good heavens! What a terrible disaster! As if there weren't plenty of young girls in London.

TOBY: In the meantime, the one I love is taken away from me.

MISTRESS BUTLER: How like a man! Now that you are about to be parted from her, you are madly in love, and just a moment ago you were showering her with reproaches.

TOBY: You were the one, mama.

MISTRESS BUTLER: It was you.

TOBY: It was you, you scolded her and abused her; whereas I was the one . . .

MISTRESS BUTLER: You set me against her.

TOBY: What an idea! . . . I loved her blindly, I completely lost my head over her! . . . I was the one who . . .

MISTRESS BUTLER: All right, have it your way, I was the one who abused her. It doesn't matter which one of us did. The important thing now is to make her forget it ... (*Calling.*) Alice! Alice! ...

TOBY: That's it, ask her pardon! Look here, mama, you don't have any strength of character.

MISTRESS BUTLER: Self-interest comes first.

TOBY: All right, I'm going, because I won't be able to keep myself from telling her just what I think. You see, I was right to be jealous; your Alice is a flirt, and your Sir Jack is an old hypocrite. (*He leaves, pouting at* ALICE *as she comes in.*)

ALICE: You called me, Aunt?

MISTRESS BUTLER Yes, I have something to tell you. How deeply moved you seem! ... Poor child! Why are you trembling so?

ALICE It's because ...

MISTRESS BUTLER: I don't think I have ever treated you harshly.

ALICE: I know what I owe to your benevolence, Aunt.

MISTRESS BUTLER: I rescued you from destitution, that's true; without me, I don't know what would have become of you; these are the things that close relations do for one another. Besides, your mother was my best friend. But that's not the issue now. I had you come here ...

ALICE: This morning you scolded me, and I swear to you I didn't deserve ...

MISTRESS BUTLER: I was too sharp, I admit it, and I ask your pardon.

ALICE: My pardon, Aunt?

MISTRESS BUTLER: It's quite simple when one was in the wrong.

ALICE (*aside*): Good heavens! My aunt must have something unpleasant to tell me, since she's proceeding so cautiously.

MISTRESS BUTLER: Well, then! You're not saying anything, you're not curious to know . . .

ALICE: On the contrary. I beg you, Aunt, what is this secret?

MISTRESS BUTLER: Well, now, no, I won't tell you; I prefer to give you the pleasure of being surprised.

ALICE Then it's something agreeable?

MISTRESS BUTLER: Truly agreeable, no doubt about it. Good heavens! Look at how you're dressed! . . . What clothes! . . . One would take you for a servant, whereas you are my niece, my own niece.   Come now, go get dressed properly; from my wardrobe take what is the most beautiful: my grandmother's dresses, her finery.

ALICE: Yes, Aunt.

JACK (*coming out of his room*): That's not necessary; I find her quite fine just as she is. Stay, Alice. Well, then, Mistress, what's the answer? What have you to tell me?

MISTRESS BUTLER: How enchanted I am and overcome by the honor . . .

JACK: The devil take the honor as well as your enchantment. In this whole matter I have not once given a thought to you.

MISTRESS BUTLER: All the same . . .

JACK: Get to the point. Does your niece consent?

MISTRESS BUTLER: I should like to see her not consent; I would order her to on the spot . . .

JACK: You will do nothing of the sort, I don't want anyone to order her; I want her to consent of her own accord . . .

MISTRESS BUTLER: She'll consent; I'm going to tell her . . .

JACK: I prefer to tell her myself.

MISTRESS BUTLER: Very well. Come here, Alice; Sir Jack wishes to speak to you. (*In an undertone.*) Just be sure you are courteous and answer properly.

JACK: Why are you interfering in this? What you think is courteous may perhaps seem quite ridiculous to me; that will do, leave us.

MISTRESS BUTLER: As you wish. (*She goes out.*)

SIR JACK *remains a moment without speaking; he sits down, then on reflection stands up and goes to fetch a chair which he offers to* ALICE. *She looks at him uneasily.*

ALICE (*aside*): Good heavens! What a severe look! What does he have to tell me?

JACK: Undoubtedly you've guessed what it's all about.

ALICE: Oh! Good heavens, no; but I presume it's something I've done wrong without meaning to . . .

JACK: Poor child! . . . She doesn't understand. Alice, you are not happy here in this house.

ALICE: Sir . . .

JACK: These people treat you harshly. You wish to excuse them . . . I know how things stand.

ALICE: They are my benefactors.

JACK: They are benefactors of the sort one sees everywhere nowadays, who get rich from their benevolence.

ALICE: Gratitude obliges me to ... (*She gets up.*)

JACK: What you've just said is fine, very fine. Sit down ... (*She obeys.*) But I know what I'm talking about. You cannot stay any longer in this inn.

ALICE: Good gracious! ... And for what reason? ... Could my aunt have chosen you to ...

JACK: Not in the least; your aunt asks nothing more than to keep you, and you must have seen that just now ... I'm the one who doesn't want it.

ALICE: You believe that there are dangers ...

JACK: Who has said anything about dangers?

ALICE: Then I'll stay here?

JACK: No, I'm telling you. I don't want you to.

ALICE: What have I ever done to make you want to take away my sole place of refuge?

JACK: Who has ever said you'll be without a place of refuge?

ALICE: I am alone on this earth.

JACK: I'll be your support.

ALICE: You?

JACK: Why not?

ALICE: I shall never accept the charity of a stranger.

JACK: And why should I be a stranger to you? . . . I have known you for a long time. Each time I came to this house, I noticed that you were not cut out for the situation in which you found yourself. I said to myself: "She's not like other women; she lacks their deceitfulness!"   Alice, I love you. . . . (*Regaining his self-control.*) I'm very interested in you.

ALICE: I have not forgotten the many kindnesses . . .

JACK: Don't interrupt me. Scores of time a thought has come into my head; but I always hesitated . . . One is so often mistaken! . . . And only today did I make up my mind, this very day, when I witnessed the ill treatment you were subjected to and the sweetness with which you endured it. I told your aunt that I wished to marry you.

ALICE: Marry me! . . . you marry me, Sir Jack?

JACK: Would that displease you?

ALICE: No, sir. But the surprise . . . You are not deceiving me?

JACK: No, certainly not; but I want a frank answer: yes or no.

ALICE: Remember I am a poor orphan.

JACK: I know that as well as you do. Yes or no, I tell you. You hesitate? . . . Could I be mistaken! . . . Might you feel repugnance? . . .

ALICE: Might I feel repugnance? . . . for such a kind, generous man! . . . My sole fear is accepting a fortune . . .

JACK: And what do you want me to do with it if I don't have you? . . . My existence is a burden to me, and I feel that a refusal . . .

ALICE: I do not know if I should . . .

JACK: You are free to choose. Yes, you are free; but your choice will decide whether I live or die.

ALICE: Oh, heavens! . . . I accept.

JACK: You accept? . . . how obliged I am to you! . . . and you're doing it, without its causing you any grief? . . .

ALICE: Can you doubt it? . . .

JACK: I have never been so happy! . . . We must call them: Mistress Butler! . . . Toby! Come here. (*They come running.*) It is all arranged.

MISTRESS BUTLER: Oh! So much the better.

JACK: She has consented. The wedding is for tomorrow.

TOBY: He's in a hurry.

MISTRESS BUTLER: Why not today? . . .

JACK: Today, so be it.

TOBY: Has any one ever seen . . .

JACK: And the notary? . . .

MISTRESS BUTLER: Toby has sturdy legs, he'll be able to get there in a trice.

TOBY: Oh! That's going too far! I won't go.

JACK: Hey? . . . What's that, what's that, young man! . . . Go immediately and fetch me a notary. Just a minute . . . and where will you find the witnesses?

MISTRESS BUTLER: Those two young men in no. 4 . . .

ALICE *gives a start.*

TOBY: That won't be possible; they are going to leave straight away.

ALICE: Straight away! . . . (*Aside.*) Mr. Edward didn't say anything to me . . .

TOBY: When I say straight away, I don't know exactly; but I think so: they were talking about it between themselves.

MISTRESS BUTLER: All right, Toby, go to the notary's; it's close by.

TOBY: To tell the truth, mama, it's going a bit too far to insist that *I* go . . .

MISTRESS BUTLER: Do what you're told, Toby! . . .

TOBY (*without stirring*): I'm going . . .

JACK: All right, get moving! . . .

TOBY: I'm going, I'm already on my way. (*He leaves slowly.*)

JACK: Seriously, Alice, does this marriage please you?

ALICE: Yes . . . Yes, Sir Jack.

JACK: You're crying. . . .

ALICE: Am I? It's from happiness.

JACK: Oh! That's different. As for me, I've never shed a single tear, either from happiness or from grief. I'm going back to my apartment for a few minutes to draw up the articles of the contract. Until we meet again, my charming future wife.

SIR JACK *goes back to his room, after kissing* ALICE'*s hand.* EDWARD *and* GEORGE, *who have come out of no. 4, have overheard* SIR JACK'*s last words.*

EDWARD: His future wife?

MISTRESS BUTLER: Dear gracious, yes. She's going to marry him; we're going to sign the contract in a moment.

GEORGE: In a moment? . . .

MISTRESS BUTLER: Certainly. In matters of business this good Sir Jack goes at it briskly. "Are you willing?" . . . "Yes." . . . "Well, then, let's get going!" . . . And it's all taken care of.

EDWARD: But at least shouldn't you know . . .

MISTRESS BUTLER: Oh! We know him well enough; it's not the first time that he's been a lodger here. He's a bit brusque perhaps; but he has the best heart! . . .

EDWARD: And does Alice consent?

MISTRESS BUTLER: Does she consent? . . . It would be ridiculous for her not to consent! A marriage that will make her the richest woman in the neighborhood; a marriage that will assure the happiness of her entire family; a marriage that will bring her aunt very special consideration . . . Oh! That would be ridiculous! . . . I would like to see that! . . . Your servant, gentlemen. (*She goes out.*)

EDWARD: Well, now, my friend, what do you say to this development?

GEORGE: A fool commits an act of folly, there's nothing astonishing in that.

EDWARD: What was I telling you this morning? There's something in that young woman that shows she's . . .

GEORGE: A princess in disguise, is that it? . . .

EDWARD: All right, stop it! . . . are you going to start all over again? . . . are you going to keep on making those bad jokes of yours?

GEORGE: I forgive you your excesses; you're in love.

EDWARD: In love? . . . You think that after such a betrayal . . .

GEORGE: A betrayal? . . .

EDWARD: No doubt about it. When I pressed her hand tenderly this morning, didn't I feel it tremble in mine? Didn't I see her blush? . . .

GEORGE: From habit. You can well imagine that a serving girl in an inn must often find herself in similar circumstances.

EDWARD: No, I cannot be mistaken, I read in her eyes . . .

GEORGE: The secret of her love? . . . and she is marrying another!

EDWARD: That's what bothers me! . . . But, when I think about it, who knows if she's acting of her own accord? Or if force . . . Yes, the more I reflect on, the more I believe it . . . That Sir Jack may have taken advantage of his power over a timid young girl, and Alice's aunt, dazzled by the hope of a fortune . . . Yes, yes, there's no doubt about it, that's what it is. The aunt looked so delighted! . . . and that poor Alice, how sad she seemed! Did you see her when she left? . . . It's settled, I've made up my mind, I'm going to find Sir Jack.

GEORGE: No, my friend, you won't go.

EDWARD: Your attempts to hold me back are all in vain. I'm going to find him, I tell you, to ask him what right he has to force a young woman . . .

GEORGE: To accept a large fortune.

EDWARD: If Alice's aunt alone is guilty, I won't let her sacrifice her niece to considerations of material well-being.

GEORGE: Oh! This time, my friend, you're going too far! I am a madcap, a fantastical fellow; scores of times you have reproached me for my follies. . . . Now you will allow me to have my turn preaching at you. Come now, what the devil do you mean to do?

EDWARD: I want . . . I want to see her, to talk to her; because there's no question about it, I'm in love with her . . . wildly in love with her! . . . And that miserable Jack! . . .

GEORGE: He's done you great wrong!

EDWARD: He's carrying off a woman I adore.

GEORGE: And if she doesn't love you?

EDWARD: If she doesn't love me? . . . all the more reason; I'll fight him.

GEORGE: A duel!

EDWARD: Yes, a duel. Why not? . . . Men have fought scores of times for far less serious reasons.

GEORGE: Think it over carefully: a serving girl in an inn.

EDWARD (*angrily*): And suppose she is a serving girl in an inn! Is that any reason why she cannot love with ardor?

GEORGE: On the contrary. Those girls love everybody with ardor.

EDWARD: Insulting Alice is the same as insulting me personally!

GEORGE: Oh! Indeed! Get angry if you like; but my respect for you cannot go so far as to respect . . .

EDWARD: And I'm telling you that you're overstepping the rights of friendship.

GEORGE: Solely in your interest.

EDWARD: And who's asking you, sir, to think of my interest? Allow me to act as I wish, and do not interfere in my affairs. You are not my guardian to the best of my knowledge.

GEORGE: No, certainly not; but since you want to do something foolish, I'll stick by you, and I'll do all in my power to keep you from dishonoring yourself.

EDWARD (*furious*):   Dishonor myself? This time you've gone too far; you'll answer me for it.

GEORGE: I will? . . .

EDWARD: You have insulted me in what I hold most dear; you'll answer me for it, I'm telling you.

GEORGE: And our friendship . . .

EDWARD: It no longer exists; you have destroyed it. Let us go.

GEORGE: Edward!

EDWARD: Let us go, I say, or I shall think that there is another reason . . .

GEORGE: Edward, you know the opposite is true.

EDWARD: Well, let's get a move on. We'll obtain arms there . . . two steps from here.

GEORGE: Friends, to fight over the virtue of a servant in an inn! . . .

EDWARD: At it again! . . . You wretch!

He strikes him in the face with his glove.

GEORGE: Oh! That's too much! Let's get moving!

EDWARD: Let's get moving! ... (*They leave to the rear.*)

SIR JACK *comes out of his room.*

JACK (*alone*): Hey? ... What's this? ... A quarrel! ... Perhaps they're going to fight ... That's too bad! ... They're young, they're relatives, friends ... I am going to separate them. ... No, in faith. (*He goes and sits down by the table.*)

TOBY (*entering*): How amusing to go fetch a notary for the marriage contract of a rival; because after all, there's no denying it, he's my rival. My rival! ... Must I be such a good sort?

JACK: Well! Where's the notary?

TOBY: He's coming; don't worry.

JACK: Is Alice ready?

TOBY: She'll be ready soon enough, Cousin. Cousin! ... What an agreeable name that is! ... Oh! I'm in a rage!

JACK: What's the matter with that odd chap?

TOBY: What's the matter with me? Nothing. I'm fine. ... Just fine. That's all.

JACK: Why aren't they coming? Go find them.

TOBY (*aside*): If he's in such a hurry, he can go himself. (*Aloud.*) Look, here they are.

Enter MISTRESS BUTLER, *a* NOTARY, FRIENDS *and* RELATIVES.

MISTRESS BUTLER: Come in, come in, my dear relatives, my good friends. You don't yet know why I've had you come here. You are going to find out. There's going to be a celebration, an important ceremony, a feast, and a ball ... And first, I present to you my nephew, Sir Jack, a worthy merchant, or some other trade, because I don't know exactly. But in any case the best of men; my benefactor and Alice's benefactor. She will owe him everything, he is going to marry her. (*A stirring among the* FRIENDS *and* RELATIVES.) You're astonished? . . . Such a rich man! . . . I know that Alice has admirable qualities and that she will make him very happy; but nowadays there are so few men who want happiness without a dowry; and then what modesty! See how thoughtful and absent-minded he looks! One would think that he doesn't hear the praises offered up in his name. Oh! My friends, join me in thanking this generous man. (*They surround* SIR JACK, *who is plunged in reverie.*)

JACK: Well, what is it? . . . What do all those people want of me? Oh! That's true. I had forgotten . . .

MISTRESS BUTLER: These are our friends and relatives.

JACK: Friends, relatives? I have no need of all that. Notary, follow me into my office, there you will find all that is necessary for drawing up your document.

He goes into his room; the NOTARY *follows him.*

MISTRESS BUTLER: He's a bit brusque, but we shall be able to cure him of his bad humor; we'll prove to him how deeply we are impressed by the honor he does our family.

TOBY: Thanks.

MISTRESS BUTLER: Let the celebration begin.

TOBY: A celebration! . . .

MISTRESS BUTLER: So that when he comes back he will find here the very picture of pleasure and happiness.

TOBY (*looking furious*): Yes, jump, dance, it's the most wonderful day of my life . . . I've never laughed so much in my life!

BALLET
[*Danced by the* FRIENDS *and* RELATIVES.]

At the end of the ballet, SIR JACK *comes out of his room with the* NOTARY.

JACK: What do I see? What does this mean?

MISTRESS BUTLER: We're celebrating your betrothal, my dear nephew.

JACK: You're making my head split! . . . Alice is what I want; where is she?

MISTRESS BUTLER: Here she is.

JACK (*to* ALICE): Have you thought it over? You won't have any regrets?

ALICE: Regrets? Never.

JACK: I believe you, I want to believe you. The contract is ready, we have only to sign it.

NOTARY: The only thing missing is the profession of the bridegroom.

TOBY (*aside*): Oh! That's a lucky chance! . . . I was curious to learn that . . .

JACK: Put: without profession.

TOBY (*aside*): That's how it is, he's an adventurer, a sort of vagabond! . . . and that's the man who is preferred to me! . . .

MISTRESS BUTLER (*to the* NOTARY): Put: "rich capitalist."

TOBY (*aside*): What does she know about it?

JACK: Come, my dear Alice. (*He conducts her to the table where she signs the contract.*) She has signed! (*He signs too.*)

MISTRESS BUTLER: I'm putting my initials. It's your turn, Toby.

TOBY: Not likely I'm going to sign! Mama, I told you that he wouldn't ever have my consent, and he won't.

JACK: It's all over. Thanks be to heaven for the first happiness that has been granted me in my whole life.

Two pistol shots.

MISTRESS BUTLER: What's that?

TOBY: Oh! My God! . . .

GEORGE (*running in pale and haggard*): Help! Help! Edward! My friend! And I'm the one . . . I'm the one! . . .

ALL: How did it happen? . . .

Servants carry in EDWARD *who is wounded and unconscious. They place him in an armchair by the door to the rear.*

ALICE (*running to him*): Heavens! . . . Dear Edward! . . .

She falls on her knees in front of EDWARD, *one of whose hands she grasps and bathes in tears. General reaction of surprise.*

JACK: Oh! . . . Give me that contract.

TOBY (*eagerly*): Here it is, my dear cousin.

JACK: Thanks.

He tears it up. Stupefaction on the part of MISTRESS BUTLER; TOBY *overjoyed; surprise on the part of the* FRIENDS *and* RELATIVES.

End of the First Act

Act Two

The theatre represents the garden of the hotel run by MISTRESS BUTLER. *To the right, a stone table and two chairs; to the left, a kind of grove formed by rose bushes, in which there are also two garden chairs. Here and there, orange trees and bushes in wooden boxes.*

TOBY (*alone downstage*): What's that? . . . I hear someone. It's her! . . . No, it isn't any one. Here's the door (*He points to the left.*) where she went out this morning; and through which she comes back every day. Oh! Miss Alice, you're up to some pranks! You gad about town from early in the morning; you haunt the young students' academy . . . That's a pretty business! . . . But not every one is asleep here, and I've seen her . . . yes, I've seen her! Oh! I've good eyes, and ears too! Gracious! What ears I've got! Sssh! Here she's coming back.

ALICE *comes back furtively by the left, and steals warily between the trees and the plant boxes, for fear of being seen.*

Yes, that's it; take care, no one sees you, go, don't worry.

ALICE (*approaching the grove*): I can barely keep on my feet! . . . (*She sits down. Her face is pale, she often raises her hand to her left arm. She holds a little vial wrapped in a piece of paper.*)

TOBY (*aside*): That's the effect of long walks.

ALICE: This blood-letting has weakened me more than the previous times. Dear Edward! . . . May my devotion have the reward I hope for! May I restore life to you, even at the expense of my own! Fortunately, so far I have been able to hide from everyone the means I employ to earn money and give him help. Alas! He would have died without me . . . Perhaps I shall perish myself in the process; but it was a duty; I am only discharging a legitimate and sacred debt.   Wasn't it in defending my reputation that he received that fatal wound? Oh! To pay back such a great act of generosity all my blood would not be too much! . . . Let's go in. Thank God, no one has seen me.

TOBY (*barring her way*): No, no one, except me.

ALICE (*staggering back*): Good heavens! Toby! . . .

TOBY: Yes, Toby, who has followed you.

ALICE: Dear God! . . .

TOBY: I know where you have been going so often for a month now.

ALICE: You know . . .

TOBY: Yes.

ALICE: For mercy's sake, my dear Toby, don't tell any one.

TOBY: That's how it is; my dear Toby, all sweetness now because you're afraid of me. Well, not on your life, I'll tell the whole world.

ALICE: Don't do it, I'd be lost.

TOBY: I believe it. A young girl who should keep her self-respect, to do such things! . . . To go to such a place . . . surrounded by thirty young men! What horror!

ALICE: For heaven's sake, silence!

TOBY: No, no, I won't keep quiet. Who do you take me for? . . . I'll make every effort not to keep quiet . . . Oh! What an idea! . . . (*Noticing the vial that* ALICE *is holding.*) What's that?

ALICE: It's . . .

TOBY: It's? . . .

EDWARD (*off-stage*): Alice! . . . Alice! . . .

ALICE: That's his voice! He's calling me! . . . He needs my help . . . Here I am. (*She runs to the right.*)

TOBY (*alone*): "He's calling me! . . . He needs my help! Here I am! . . ." How edifying that is! In the morning, she gads about the town, God knows for what reason; and the rest of the time, she sits by Mr. Edward's bedside, her dear patient. Stay there, stay near him; don't leave him, I beg you . . . Try to save him . . . I certainly hope you won't succeed. As for me, I've always counted on Providence. (*He sits down in the grove.*) Then, I'll only have Sir Jack as a rival . . . He's the one I fear more. He's rich . . . Oh! There's no denying he's the best match she could have made . . . after me. But he doesn't want her any more; he's pouting, and he's right. I'll pout too; I won't give her either my heart or my hand. I'll be cruel and inflexible . . . Look out! Here's Sir Jack! Let's watch and listen. I don't want to praise myself, but with a talent for observation like mine, I could be a success; I have all the makings of a good spy. (*He stands to one side.*)

SIR JACK *enters slowly to the right, lost in thought.*

TOBY: What's that? . . . What's he saying? . . . Nothing! . . . Oh! Oh! If that's the way it goes, he won't reveal a thing.

JACK: Poor child! . . . she makes me suffer.

TOBY (*aside*): Poor dear man! . . . He makes me sad.

JACK: Her eye dull, her features drawn, her pallor ever increasing . . . Truly, if that young man doesn't recover soon, the poor little creature will precede him to the grave.

TOBY: Well and good, he's started talking . . . He should have a lot to say since he hasn't opened his mouth for a month. If that had happened to me, my words would have choked me a thousand times over.

JACK (*turning around*): What's that? . . . Oh! Oh! It's you, blabbermouth!

TOBY: What does the gentleman desire . . .

JACK (*indicating the stone table to the right*): Tea. Over there.

TOBY: I'm on my way. (*Aside.*) That's too bad, I might perhaps have ended up hearing something.

JACK: Tea!

TOBY: Yes, Sir Jack. It's on the way. (*He goes out to the right.*)

JACK (*alone. He sits down at the table*): I'm angry at myself for staying so long in this inn. I should have beat a retreat the very day that young man was wounded . . . but no; against my own will I took pleasure in staying here: it made me suffer, that was something. Everywhere else I was bored. No emotion, no feeling, not even of pain. In my travels, I went from France to Italy, from Spain to England without experiencing either sorrow or pleasure; each of those countries that I traveled through was for me only an inn where one is more or less well nourished, lodged . . . and where, one is at least always robbed. One fine day, weary of roaming, I returned to my native land. No desire, no hope brought me back home: I wished to die . . . it might as well be in my birthplace as elsewhere. At this table, alone, a pistol in my hand, I was prepared to end it all, when Alice came into my view, and for the first time I was moved. What features! . . . What a face! . . . It seemed to me that my task here on earth was not yet accomplished; I wanted to save Alice from the snares of seduction, to shape her soul, her mind, to make her rich . . . what else did I want? . . . to find a sweetheart. A sweetheart? . . . An ingrate! I didn't think so then. Ridiculous plaything of destiny! Do you know neither fate, nor men, nor yourself? . . . Yes, I lost my head. She loves another! . . . For almost twenty days, her

Edward has lain unconscious, unable to speak . . . She has not left him. Neither Mistress Butler's hardheartedness nor her son's inane jesting have damped her courage for an instant. . . . Dear child! . . . Oh! She is an angel . . . an angel!

TOBY (*setting the tea on the table*): Yes, yes, she's an angel . . . a fallen angel.

JACK: Meaning what?

TOBY: Fallen from Heaven to deceive us all.

JACK: Deceive us?

TOBY: You must have seen how she's changed in the past month.

JACK: That's true . . . she's suffering.

TOBY: She gets up too early in the morning.

JACK: What of it?

TOBY: And then, she takes too long walks.

JACK: What's that you're saying about walks?

TOBY: Oh! why, you see . . . we know what we know.

JACK: All right, what do you know?

TOBY: I know that the innocent Alice likes to enjoy the morning air.

JACK: Where's the harm in that?

TOBY: I didn't say that she enjoyed it all by herself.

JACK: How's that? What do you mean?

TOBY: Just a minute, you're getting carried away! . . .

JACK: You're going to explain yourself without further delay.

TOBY: All right, since you're so curious, I'm going to tell you the whole story.   I had already noticed that Alice went out in the morning . . . so today I kept an eye on her; I followed her, and I saw her . . .

JACK: What then?

TOBY: I saw her enter a house . . .

JACK: Finish your story.

TOBY: No, it's not worthwhile telling you that; I'll keep it to myself.

JACK: Speak!   Speak up!   . . .   Damn!   Will you speak up?   . . . Wretch!!

TOBY: All right, I saw her enter a house where several young men were gathered.

JACK: Young men?

TOBY: Oh!   Very respectable; very well-behaved fellows: medical students.

JACK (*seizing him by the throat*):   You're lying, rogue!

TOBY: I saw her with my own eyes.

JACK: You're lying, I tell you.

TOBY: Let me go!   You're hurting me!

JACK: And if at this very instant you don't give me proof . . .

TOBY: Proof?   . . .

JACK: I'll throttle you!

TOBY (*struggling*): Oh! Oh! You're strangling me!

JACK: Oh! You won't get away from me! Brute, take me to that house you've just been telling me about.

TOBY: Yes, Sir Jack.

JACK: Infamous slanderer! . . . To accuse Alice! . . . in my presence! . . . Woe, woe be on your head! . . . (*He pushes* TOBY *out. They both leave to the left.*)

MISTRESS BUTLER *runs in from the right.*

MISTRESS BUTLER: Oh! my God, what a racket! . . . It must be Toby . . . To tell the truth, for a month now, I don't have any idea of what's going on here. Sir Jack is sulking and doesn't say boo; my son runs all over the place to gather some new libel against Alice; my niece is sad, rapidly declines, and soon will be more gravely ill than the wounded patient. As for me, I don't know where I am any more. If things go on at this pace, I'll be driven out of my mind.

ALICE (*coming in from the right*): Heaven be praised, now he's almost entirely well. I'm so happy! . . . Oh! Aunt!

MISTRESS BUTLER: Well, how's he feeling?

ALICE: Much better.

MISTRESS BUTLER: That's most fortunate!

ALICE: The cordial he's just taken should complete his cure.

MISTRESS BUTLER: And who's paying for all that?

ALICE: Aunt . . .

MISTRESS BUTLER: The pharmacist apparently trusts him. . . . That's his misfortune; he'll be taken advantage of. As for me, I was asked to stand security for Mr. Edward . . . I said no, and I'll always say it.   Who will pay the doctor's bills?

ALICE: Aunt, everything is paid for.

MISTRESS BUTLER: That's odd! . . . Where did that money come from? . . . I didn't see anyone bring it to him . . . It doesn't matter, I'm glad to know about it, because now it's my turn; I'm going to ask him for what he owes me.

ALICE: No, don't speak to him about it yet, Aunt; wait . . . you won't lose anything.

MISTRESS BUTLER: In faith, it's not a sure thing: no one knows where his family resides, or even if he has one. Mr. George, his comrade, ran off without saying a word: thinking that he had killed his friend, he wanted to flee from the pursuit of justice. Thus it wasn't possible to notify the relatives of the wounded student or to ask them for money for more than twenty days because he has been unable to utter a single word. Still, I need my money.

ALICE: Aunt, I'm telling you once again, you won't lose anything. You will be paid, I promise you.

MISTRESS BUTLER: When?

ALICE: In two days.

MISTRESS BUTLER: How do you know?

ALICE: Aunt . . .

MISTRESS BUTLER: Maybe you're the one who'll lend him money?

ALICE: Oh! Aunt . . .

MISTRESS BUTLER: Listen, Alice, all this is beginning to irritate me. I curse the moment that Mr. Edward set foot in my inn.

ALICE: You are so severe.

MISTRESS BUTLER: He's the one who caused your marriage with Sir Jack to fall through, and a suitor like that will never be found twice. You could have become a great lady, and thanks to Mr. Edward you will remain a serving girl in an inn for the rest of your life. You certainly weren't paid for looking after him, and yet God knows how much trouble you have taken for him during his illness! I put up with him, because after all we couldn't push him out the door in the state he was in. . . . But finally all this cannot continue. He's feeling better, isn't he?

ALICE: Yes, my aunt, the doctor has given him permission to take a walk today.

MISTRESS BUTLER: Then your caring for him becomes unnecessary, and I forbid you to speak to him in the future.

ALICE: What, you want . . .

MISTRESS BUTLER: I insist on it, and I expect you to obey me.

ALICE: Oh, heavens! Poor young man!

MISTRESS BUTLER: What? . . . Are you saying . . .

ALICE: Nothing, my aunt, I'll obey.

MISTRESS BUTLER: That vexes you? . . . Too bad!

EDWARD (*off-stage*): Alice!

ALICE (*running toward the house*): It's him!

MISTRESS BUTLER: There! My orders are already forgotten! . . .

ALICE (*entering from the right with* EDWARD *whom she supports*): Be careful, don't walk so fast . . . To come out like that, alone; it was unwise. Isn't that so, Aunt?

MISTRESS BUTLER: It's all right, it's all right.

EDWARD: Alice, you weren't there any more . . .

ALICE (*taking a chair in the grove*): Sit down.

MISTRESS BUTLER (*pushing her away*): Mind your own business; I'm going to call Toby.

ALICE: How can you think of it? . . . He's so careless and brusque!

EDWARD: Whereas Alice is so good, so attentive! I beseech you, my dear hostess, let her stay a few more days by my side.

MISTRESS BUTLER: Not a chance, not a chance.

ALICE: Remember, his life perhaps depends on it.

MISTRESS BUTLER: I know you always have some excuse for disobeying me. Get out . . . Did you hear me? Leave, I'm telling you.

ALICE: But after all . . .

MISTRESS BUTLER: Will you leave! (*She grabs her niece vigorously by the arm.*)

ALICE: Oh! . . .

EDWARD: What's the matter with you?

ALICE: Nothing.

EDWARD: But that cry . . .

MISTRESS BUTLER: That's true, she frightened me . . . What's the matter with you? You're going pale.

EDWARD: Are you in pain? . . .

ALICE: It's nothing, I assure you.

MISTRESS BUTLER: Did I hurt you when I squeezed your arm?

ALICE: I don't think so.

MISTRESS BUTLER: I barely touched you, and I can't understand . . .

Someone rings.

ALICE: Someone rang, I'll go see. (*She leaves.*)

EDWARD (*coming forward*): But tell me . . .

MISTRESS BUTLER: Where are you rushing off to, Mr. Edward? In your condition, you could do yourself harm.

EDWARD: To tell the truth, I am still deeply moved . . . Alice . . . That cry of pain.

MISTRESS BUTLER: All right. Don't worry, she's not really ill. And even if she were, you are not the one I'd give the task of curing her.

ALICE (*returning*): Aunt, it's someone asking for you.

MISTRESS BUTLER: What for?

ALICE: It's about money, I think.

MISTRESS BUTLER: That they're coming to ask for?

ALICE: No, that they're bringing you.

MISTRESS BUTLER: Oh! That's different, I'm going. Money that they're bringing me. . . . Finally a bit of luck! There are so many bad debtors . . . Good day, Mr. Edward. Follow me, Niece.

She goes out. ALICE *prepares to follow her.*

EDWARD: Alice, are you abandoning me? And I don't know if you're still in pain.

ALICE: No, sir, no, I tell you again, I haven't suffered any pain . . . and now I'm not thinking about it any more at all. Good-bye.

EDWARD: I beg you . . . Stay.

ALICE: What are you doing? . . . Weak and ailing as you are! . . . Mr. Edward, you're not being reasonable.

EDWARD: You are fleeing from me . . . I am obliged to follow you. What do you expect, Alice, I can no longer exist without seeing you and hearing you.

ALICE: Rest a little and stay quiet.

EDWARD: But if you go away again . . .

ALICE: All right, I'll stay near you.

EDWARD: What kindness, what patience! . . . Oh! I do not deserve all your generous attentions; I am ashamed to ask for them still. What does health, life itself matter; if it means that you will be taken away from me, if my lips henceforth cannot address to you a word of thanks? Oh! I must regret having received your kindnesses, since I have been forbidden to express my gratitude.

ALICE: Yes, it is too soon to deprive you of my cares, and for some time yet my presence would not have been unavailing to you; but my aunt insists and I must obey. At least, promise me that you will not commit any more rash acts.

EDWARD: None.

ALICE: You will behave as if I were always here, won't you? . . .

EDWARD: Yes.

ALICE: I count on your promise.

EDWARD: Alice, how pretty you are!

ALICE: Sir, you are not listening to me.

EDWARD: Yes, yes, keep on talking. Wait, sit next to me, I shall hear you better.

ALICE: Oh! No, I cannot.

EDWARD: Alice, it seems to me that I'm sicker than I was just a moment ago.

ALICE: Really?

EDWARD: And it's your fault; you like to oppose me.

ALICE (*sitting down*): Well, here I am.

EDWARD: Dear Alice! . . . at this price I would be glad to be sick all of my life.

ALICE: Mr. Edward!

EDWARD: Mr.! . . . always Mr.! . . . That word is cruel, and I would give a lot not to have heard it.

ALICE: Why?

EDWARD: Am I a stranger to you then? And did those cares that you lavished on me spring only from compassion and pity? . . . Would any one's misfortune other than mine inspire in you the same devotion?

ALICE: Oh! No, I do not think so.

EDWARD: Well, prove it then . . . prove the contrary to me.

ALICE: Edward!

EDWARD: Oh! Good! Good! . . . It's already better than just a moment ago. Dear Alice, I owe you my life. I entreat you to let me owe you even more! . . . If you knew . . . There is a word which, uttered by you, would make me the happiest of men. Alice, I love you.

ALICE: Be quiet. If someone heard you!

EDWARD (*lower*): I love you! That is the word so easy to say and that you won't refuse to repeat after me.

ALICE: I beg you, let me go.

EDWARD: Alice! . . . My sweetheart! . . . (*He presses her against his heart. ALICE, during this scene, has appeared to suffer more and more; she cannot keep on her feet any longer; she falls on her chair almost unconscious.*)

ALICE: Oh! . . . The pain! . . .

EDWARD: What's the matter?

ALICE: I cannot endure any more . . . (*She tears her dress convulsively, and pulls a bloody bandage from her arm.*)

EDWARD: Heavens! What is this I see? . . . Help! Help! . . .

Enter MISTRESS BUTLER.

EDWARD: Oh! Come here, Mistress Butler, come here!

MISTRESS BUTLER: What is it?

EDWARD: Look at your niece, help her . . . I cannot understand . . .

MISTRESS BUTLER: Oh! Dear God! . . . Blood! . . . What does this mean? . . . Where does this wound come from?

JACK (*off-stage*): Come here, come here, wretch! . . . (*He comes in from the left to the rear with* TOBY, *whom he holds by the collar.*) Come pay homage to the truth. On your knees! On your knees! . . . Entreat her to grant you a pardon that you do not deserve.

TOBY (*on his knees*): Pardon! Pardon! . . .

JACK: Admit that you're a wretch!

TOBY: It's true.

JACK: A liar!

TOBY: It's true.

JACK: A slanderer!

TOBY: It's true.

EDWARD: Silence! For Heaven's sake! Silence!

JACK (*noticing that* ALICE *has fainted*): Good heavens!

TOBY (*on his knees*): What's going on?

ALICE (*coming to*): Oh! It's you, Mr. Edward? . . . (*Frightened.*) My aunt!

MISTRESS BUTLER: Come, come, Niece; you're not comfortable here.

EDWARD: But Alice, explain to me . . .

JACK: You are going to hear the whole story, Sir. Take your niece inside, Madam; lavish on her all the cares that her condition demands and that so many virtues deserve; do not leave her, do not leave her for a moment ... I shall soon call you back. Alice, until the present I did not think you worthy of my friendship, of my esteem ... now I admire you ...

ALICE: Oh! Sir, if you have been informed, do not betray me.

JACK: I know what I must do.

ALICE *goes out by the right with her aunt.*

EDWARD (*seeing them out*): Poor Alice, what am I about to learn?

JACK (*to* TOBY): Get up.

TOBY: Yes, Sir Jack.

JACK: Get out.

TOBY: Yes, Sir Jack.

JACK: Summon all the neighbors.

TOBY: Yes, Sir Jack.

JACK: All those in whose hearing your hellish tongue has slandered the purest virtue; bring them here, this very instant.

TOBY: Yes, Sir Jack.

JACK: And you will declare to them in front of me and in front of Alice that you lied about her.

TOBY: Yes, Sir Jack.

JACK: Come, get a move on! Hurry up, and tremble if you disobey me.

TOBY: Yes, Sir Jack. (*He goes out running.*)

EDWARD *comes back on stage at the moment* SIR JACK *turns round.*

JACK: Now, listen to me. I do not like you. (EDWARD *reacts.*) No, Heaven is my witness, I do not like you, and if I said the contrary, you would not believe me. Weary of life, unhappy almost from my earliest childhood, one sole instant I believed in the hope of happiness, and you came to steal it from me. I offered young Alice the heart and hand of a decent man; but she had seen you. Led astray by your fine words, she preferred you to me, and you wanted to seduce her.

EDWARD: What are you saying? An accusation like that . . .

JACK: Is just. Your vanity would have prevented you from marrying a simple serving girl in an inn.

EDWARD: My love ennobles her; and from the moment I loved her, she was worth as much as I am.

JACK: I'll say more; she is worth a hundred times more.

EDWARD: Sir!

JACK: Let us proceed. You wanted to seduce her, and she preferred you to me. Your duel, your wound, happened to reveal in time the secret of her soul. I tore up the marriage contract that I had just signed; and soon, seeing all the love that you inspired in Alice, her continual anxieties and the tender cares that she lavished on you, I envied your fate, and I detested you still more than all other men.

EDWARD: Yes, I know it. Alice is my guardian angel, I owe my life to her and to her alone.

JACK: Yes; but do you know at what cost she has preserved your life?

EDWARD: No.

JACK: If Alice had had more confidence in me, if she had come and told me: "Sir Jack, my life is linked to that of Edward; unknown in the great city of London, without family, without help, he is going to perish as a result of his wound. To take an interest in him, he has on earth only me, only poor Alice, who is concerned with him; but I want to save him . . . I want him, were it at the cost of all my blood! . . ." If she had made such a declaration, I would immediately have put into her hands all the gold that I possess.

EDWARD: What generosity . . .

JACK: Not at all; you're wrong to feel gratitude to me; I wouldn't have acted that way for you . . . Only for her, for her alone. What do I care about your existence? Hers I would have tried to preserve. Well, then! Alice did not dare turn to me; she feared a refusal, and the poor child has herself been able to meet all the expenses, by an act of devotion, both admirable and sublime, of which she alone was capable. Her cares and her vigils were not enough, she has given her life. Yes, Sir, her entire life! . . . It's a miracle that she still exists.

EDWARD: For pity's sake, finish your story.

JACK: You know, sir, since you have studied the art of healing, that it is indispensable for your young colleagues sometimes to practice on living specimens. Well, then! Every other day, for the past month, Alice has been seen going out early in the morning, and staying away for almost an hour. In return for a guinea, the hapless child went to proffer her arm to the unskilled blade of a young surgeon.

EDWARD: Oh, Heavens! Is it possible?

JACK: Yes, sir, yes; it is at that cost that she has preserved your days.

EDWARD: Alice! . . . Oh! How can I ever make amends . . .

JACK: You have seen to what degree she has become weakened . . . transformed!

EDWARD: Indeed, just a moment ago, that blood which flowed before my eyes . . . Oh! Why can I not in my turn offer her my life as a sacrifice? . . . Why can I not endure for her all the torments, all the misfortunes?

JACK: No, Sir, no; that is not what I am asking of you. Are you a man of honor?

EDWARD: That question . . .

JACK: It is a question like any other question. But it is not by fine phrases, but by actions that you will give your answer. After all that Alice has done for you, you should love her.

EDWARD: I adore her.

JACK: Oh! You adore her, do you? That is a word I put little faith in . . . but, after all, I'm ready to believe you. You love her, or you would be the worst ingrate, the vilest of men.

EDWARD: Sir! . . .

JACK: I do not retract what I have said. Let me finish. Your family?

EDWARD: Comes from Scotland.

JACK: Your father?

EDWARD: I have lost him. His widow lives in the little town of Inverness.

JACK: Your financial expectations?

EDWARD: Are mediocre; but I am counting on soon exercising an honorable and lucrative profession.

JACK: I know. Well, Sir, were you the richest man in the three realms, you must marry Alice; it is the sole means of proving that you are not unworthy of her generous devotion.

EDWARD: Oh, Sir, I shall marry her.

JACK: You promise me?

EDWARD: On my word of honor.

JACK: I count on it. Remember that I too loved her, that I gave her my hand; that marrying her was for me the sole boon on earth; that I gave it up of my own free will when I saw that she loved another; remember finally that if you ever went back on your word, I would be your cruelest enemy.

EDWARD: No, Sir, you will always be my friend.

JACK (*squeezing his hand*): Always? . . . May it be God's will! (*Calling to the right.*) Come, Mistress Butler! Come, Alice!

EDWARD: Dear Alice, yes, I swear to you in the face of Heaven, I will be your husband.

ALICE: My husband!

MISTRESS BUTLER: What this I hear?

EDWARD: I have learned everything; I know your soul through and through. Oh! Would I had to offer you a fortune equal to my gratitude, equal to my love! . . . But, if I am poor at present, in the future I shall enjoy a decent income, and I shall be proud to share it with you.

ALICE: With me!

MISTRESS BUTLER: How's that? How's that?

JACK: Be quiet! . . . (*In an undertone.*) I undertake to look after the dowry.

MISTRESS BUTLER (*making a deep curtsy*):   That's different; I'm keeping quiet.

TOBY (*entering with the neighbors*):   Come in, come in, ladies and gentlemen, and pay careful attention to what I am going to tell you. I am a wretch, a liar, a backbiter. (*At each epithet, he turns toward* SIR JACK *to see if he approves.*)

MISTRESS BUTLER: Are you mad, Toby?

TOBY: No, mama, I am not mad, or at least, Sir Jack has forgotten to tell me that I am. But except for that, I have all the bad traits in the world. Everything that I said about my cousin Alice was a pack of lies. My cousin Alice is the most chaste, virtuous and admirable of women. There now, are you satisfied with me, Sir Jack?

JACK: Yes, be quiet.

TOBY: If you want me to say more . . .

JACK: No, be quiet

TOBY: Yes, Sir Jack.

EDWARD: Alice, Sir Jack, and you, Mistress Butler, let all those who stand round us be witnesses of my vows. Alice Butler, take this ring; from this day forth, you are the fiancée of Edward Belton.

TOBY: His fiancée! What an idea!

JACK: Silence!

TOBY: Yes, Sir Jack.

EDWARD: Soon I shall leave for Inverness . . .

TOBY (*aside*): Inverness!

EDWARD: And I shall not delay in returning provided with the consent of my family.

ALICE: Dear Edward!

EDWARD: My sweetheart! My wife!   (*He kisses her hand.*)

ALICE: No, I dare not believe in so much happiness.

TOBY (*aside*): Yes, yes, kiss her hand; perhaps I am going to make some mischief. (*Aloud.*) Speaking of Inverness, that reminds me that just a moment ago someone gave me a letter from that country for mama.

ALL: From Inverness?

MISTRESS BUTLER: Give it to me . . . (*Unsealing the letter.*) That's odd! . . . I don't know anyone . . . "Inverness, October 24. Dear Mistress Butler: If, as I hope, my friend Edward has recovered from his wound . . ." (*She opens the letter to see the signature.*) The letter is from Mr. George Fleming.

EDWARD: George?

ALICE: Go on, Aunt.

MISTRESS BUTLER (*reading*):   "It is absolutely necessary upon receipt of this letter that he leave for Scotland and come rejoin me."

EDWARD: What this I hear?

ALICE: Leave! So soon?

TOBY: It's a very well written letter

JACK: Finish reading, Mistress Butler.

MISTRESS BUTLER (*continuing*): "His mother is dangerously ill."

EDWARD: My mother!

TOBY: Poor woman!

MISTRESS BUTLER (*continuing*): "She calls his name, she asks for him; she needs his presence and his help."

TOBY: It's quite obvious.

MISTRESS BUTLER (*reading*): "She is afraid of dying without having seen her son again."

TOBY: That would be most unfortunate!

MISTRESS BUTLER (*reading*): "Before dying she would like to carry out a plan for uniting our two families conceived long ago."

ALICE: Oh, Heavens! . . .

EDWARD: Have no fear, Alice; when my mother learns of all that you have done for me, when she knows that you single-handedly preserved my life, she will give up her plans; she will hasten to call you her daughter. No one other than Alice will ever, ever be my wife.

MISTRESS BUTLER (*continuing*): "There is not a moment to lose; have him come immediately; his mother's life may well depend upon it."

EDWARD: I am off.

MISTRESS BUTLER (*concluding*): "This bill of exchange should cover the cost of his trip.   Mistress Butler, I am yours respectfully." (*Giving* EDWARD *the bill of exchange.*) There, Sir, here it is.

JACK: You must leave, Sir.

EDWARD: Yes. I have to go.

TOBY: Do you want me to do your packing?

ALICE: Oh! Good heavens! Weak as he is, will he be able to endure the fatigue of the journey?

JACK: Under any other circumstances, such concern is just fine; but here, duty makes stern demands. Sir, my carriage is at your orders.

TOBY: Harness the horses to Sir Jack's carriage! . . . (*He leaves running.*)

EDWARD: Dear Alice! How cruel it is to part from you, at the very moment . . . But dry your tears; the day of our marriage will only come more swiftly. I shall soon be at my mother's side and have her consent.

ALICE: Do you think so?

EDWARD: I'm sure of it. Good-bye, Mistress Butler. Good-bye, Sir Jack . . . My friend, you will see me again in two weeks.

JACK: Alice, you will be happy with Edward; because you love him! . . . I see it in your tears. Well, then . . . and I am weeping too! . . . for the first time in my life, I am weeping!   I am happy! . . . Alice, Edward, may Heaven bless your engagement!

TOBY (*returning*): Mr. Edward, your carriage is waiting for you.

EDWARD: Good-bye, good-bye.

TOBY (*aside*): Pleasant journey to you and don't bother to come back.

Every one gathers round EDWARD; *he says good-bye to* MISTRESS BUTLER, *to* SIR JACK, *to* ALICE, *and departs. All follow him with their looks.* TOBY *does a dance in the grove.*

End of the Second Act

Act Three

Scene One

The stage represents a neighborhood in the town of Inverness, Scotland. To the left, the entrance of a tavern with this sign-board: Good Fellows Tavern. *A bench in front of the door; to the right, several houses near a tree-lined path; another bench at the front of the stage; to the rear, a dilapidated wall about seven feet high, forming the enclosure of a cemetery. Above the wall are visible the top of a funeral monument and the crowns of cypresses. It is night.*

MACDOUGALL *is seated astride the wall;* BURKE *is in the cemetery.*

MACDOUGALL (*speaking to* BURKE, *who cannot be seen*): Burke, are you there?

BURKE (*in the cemetery*): Yes.

MACDOUGALL: Have you discovered some new grave?

BURKE: No; nothing for today.

MACDOUGALL: Damn! That's bad. We made a promise . . . Our night is a total loss!

ROSBEEF (*coming along the length of the wall from the left*): Not at all. This evening, in that tavern, there's to be a celebration.

MACDOUGALL: Is that you, Rosbeef?

ROSBEEF: Yes, it's me.

MACDOUGALL: You say there's to be a celebration in that tavern.

ROSBEEF: Yes.

MACDOUGALL: Well, what's that celebration to us?

ROSBEEF: You know that the young men of Inverness make it a practice to celebrate, glass in hand, the last day of life as a bachelor. Today it's Mr. Edward Belton's turn.

MACDOUGALL: Edward Belton, the one who passed his exams and became a doctor some time ago, and from whom we earn the most money in the exercise of our calling?

ROSBEEF: The very same. But be careful; speak lower.

MACDOUGAL: Why?

ROSBEEF: Our calling! . . . If someone heard you.

MACDOUGALL: Well, who the devil could figure out . . .

ROSBEEF: That wouldn't be difficult, seeing you perched on the wall of a cemetery at this late hour.

MACDOUGALL: That's true; the law is absurd! . . . (*He comes down from the wall and goes to sit down on the bench at the front of the stage, to the right.*) Trying to keep poor people from engaging in commerce, and a form of commerce so useful to science and the humanities.

ROSBEEF: Certainly: it's a profession like any other.

MACDOUGALL: After all, without us, what would become of doctors? To learn to cure the living, they first have to have their dead.

ROSBEEF: We keep them supplied. That's all well and good; but the trade is too dangerous.

MACDOUGALL: Coward! . . .

ROSBEEF: No matter how brave you are, no one likes to be hanged.

MACDOUGALL: Nonsense! It's just a moment to be got through.
   Besides, when you're working in the interests of society, that
   gives you courage.

ROSBEEF: Thanks. To be hanged, in the interests of society or
   otherwise, is always . . .

GEORGE (*in the tavern*): Waiter! . . . Champagne! . . .

MACDOUGALL: Quiet! I recognize the voice of one of our
   customers.

ROSBEEF: Mr. George Fleming.

MACDOUGALL: The future brother-in-law of Mr. Edward.

ROSBEEF: Take it from me, that Mr. George is no enemy to joy.

MACDOUGALL: No.

ROSBEEF: I see that tonight it will be difficult for us to do anything.

MACDOUGALL: Who knows? Let's go rejoin Burke, and lie in wait
   behind the wall.

ROSBEEF: That's it.

MACDOUGALL: Come on, since you're afraid, climb over first.

ROSBEEF: With pleasure.

ROSBEEF *climbs up and disappears;* MACDOUGALL *follows his lead;
but as soon as nothing can be seen except his head, lively music is heard,
announcing the arrival of the students who are assembling at the tavern.*

MACDOUGALL (*speaking to* ROSBEEF, *who is no longer visible*):
   Look, we just made it in time; there are the new guests heading

toward the tavern.

ROSBEEF: Hurry up then!

MACDOUGALL (*disappearing*): Here I am.

GEORGE (*coming out of the tavern, and going to meet the students who are arriving from the right*): This way, comrades; we've been waiting for you, laughing and drinking all the while. Well, now, Edward is not with you?

STUDENT: He'll come later; he didn't want to stop working.

GEORGE: As though one should work on the eve of one's wedding.

STUDENT: He has such zeal for his studies!

GEORGE: For the past six months, he hasn't been recognizable; he works night and day, and says it's to drive away his sorrows.

STUDENT: His sorrows? Is he still thinking about that girl?

GEORGE: I'm afraid so.

STUDENT: What folly! . . . Just when he's about to marry a charming woman.

GEORGE: The sister of a friend.

STUDENT: And a magnificent dowry!

GEORGE: What can you expect? . . . He has become sad, serious . . . One might take him for a pupil of Doctor Faustus.

STUDENT: It's frightful!

GEORGE: Here's an idea! . . . Let's conspire to convert him.

ALL: Motion adopted.

GEORGE: During the celebration tonight, let's see that his glass is never empty.

STUDENT: But if he doesn't come?

GEORGE: If he doesn't come? . . . That's impossible. Besides, there's a way . . . Waiter!

WAITER (*hurrying over*): What will the gentlemen have?

GEORGE: You know where Dr. Belton lives?

WAITER: Yes, sir.

GEORGE: Run over to his house immediately; tell him that we're waiting for him at the Good Fellows Tavern . . . Add, if you like, that one of us has fallen ill.

WAITER: Yes, sir.

GEORGE: Run, and come back as soon as possible.

WAITER: Yes, sir.

GEORGE: Now, gentlemen, we can go in. (*They go into the tavern. The* WAITER *is ready to leave when* GEORGE *calls him back.*) Oh! Waiter! Waiter! . . . I also wanted to tell you that . . . No, no, that's not necessary; go.

WAITER (*bumping into* ALICE *as she comes in*): Oh! Excuse me, miss . . . or mistress; I don't know which . . . No doubt you've come for the party? You'll find those gentlemen in the large salon..

ALICE: You are mistaken. I have just arrived in Inverness; I do not know the town, nor do I know where I am. Voices that I heard a moment ago drew me in this direction . . . I am looking for Dr. Belton's house.

WAITER: It's nearby, just a stone's throw.

ALICE: I thank you. (*False exit.*)

WAITER: Well, now? Where are you going?

ALICE: To his house.

WAITER: To his house? . . . You don't know Dr. Belton, do you?
He admits no one . . . He works night and day . . . Thus it's
impossible, as you see. Anyhow it comes out all right; at this
very moment I am going to look for him . . . He's going to come
here in a minute, wait for me over there. (*He points to the bench
to the left, and goes out to the right in the rear.*)

ALICE (*alone*): He works night and day . . . (*She sits down.*) That's
undoubtedly why he has gone so long without writing me . . .
Six long months! . . . His silence has done me much wrong . . .
And Sir Jack, who always said to me, "Poor Alice! That young
man will deceive you; perhaps he already is unfaithful to you."
Edward unfaithful! . . . Oh! No; after all the oaths he swore me,
it's impossible. And yet that idea alone has spurred me into
undertaking such a long trip. Some one is coming . . . it must
be him . . . Oh! How my heart is beating!

EDWARD (*to the* WAITER): A young woman, you say?

WAITER: Yes, Doctor, a young woman who seems very anxious to
see you . . . And look, there she is.

ALICE: Edward, it's me.

EDWARD: Alice! . . . (*To the* WAITER.) Go; leave us.

WAITER: Yes, Doctor. (*He goes back to the tavern.*)

EDWARD: You here? . . . How does it happen . . .

ALICE: You went so long without writing me, I wasn't able to fight
off my anxiety. And then I lost my aunt . . . I had no more hope
left except in you, my dearest . . . I set out for Scotland.

EDWARD: You had promised me to wait for me.

ALICE: I waited for you; but you didn't come . . . I came myself.

EDWARD: Alone?

ALICE: No. Sir Jack, always good, always generous, offered to accompany me.

EDWARD: Is he here?

ALICE: Oh! I did not want him to come with me to find you; because you know his character. He has reproaches to address to you, he says . . . I prefer to address them to you myself, and he stayed in one of the inns of the town. What's the matter? . . . Did I do wrong to come find you? You're pleased, aren't you, dearest? . . . You don't say anything to me . . .

EDWARD: Excuse me, excuse me, Miss Alice . . . Yes, very pleased . . . (*Aside.*) Good God, if she knew . . . (*Aloud.*) Miss Alice, believe me . . .

ALICE: Well . . . What does that mean: Miss Alice . . . Previously you chastised me when I called you Mr. Edward, and now it's you who speak to me that way . . . What have I done to offend you, dearest?

EDWARD: Nothing . . . Nothing.

ALICE: I am the one rather, sir, who should complain of you. For six months, not a letter, not a word of consolation for poor Alice! . . . Oh! it's very wrong! . . . But I am forgiving, I pardon you, Edward dearest . . . I know the reason that prevented you . . .

EDWARD: How's that, you know? . . .

ALICE: When one is working, one doesn't have the time to think of the person one loves; and if you seek to acquire a reputation, it is in our common interest . . . When I am your wife . . .

EDWARD: For heaven's sake, speak more quietly! . . .

ALICE: Why? . . .

EDWARD (*aside*): Poor child! With a word I am going to destroy all her hopes.

ALICE: Speak.

EDWARD: I have a troublesome piece of news to tell you, Miss Alice.

ALICE: Miss Alice! . . . Again and again Miss Alice! . . . Say what you have to say, Mr. Edward.

EDWARD: I often told you that my father, a merchant in Inverness, left me only a middling fortune. . . . Well, then! The little that my mother possessed she now has lost . . . Ill-advised investments cost her everything.

ALICE: And you hesitated to tell me about it? That was the cause of this misunderstanding, this difficulty and this eternal silence? . . . Poor dear Edward! . . . You were afraid that my affection would not withstand any blow? On the contrary; I shall only love you the more, because at least we shall be equal.

EDWARD: But my mother . . . at her age . . . ailing as she is . . . It's for her that sake that I've been uneasy . . . It's for her sake that I had to . . .

ALICE: Oh, you are right; I shall do everything to lessen her suffering, to make her happy. I do not wish to leave her for a sole instant. You have talent, you will work. For my part, by my thrift and management . . . And first of all you are going to present me to her.

EDWARD: To my mother? Impossible.

ALICE: I do not understand you.

EDWARD: At her age, a person thinks differently than at ours. She has expectations for me, hopes, ideas of wealth.

ALICE: Of wealth?

EDWARD: Yes. I can offer nothing to my fiancée.

ALICE: What does it matter? Edward dearest, you do not share those ideas, say you do not?

EDWARD: Oh! No, certainly not. . . . But . . .

ALICE: But?

EDWARD: She is my mother . . . and I must stop to consider before disobeying her . . . It is necessary . . .

ALICE: For us to wait still, isn't that it? . . . For you to succeed in eliminating her prejudices? . . . Well, then, I agree, since it is necessary, I shall wait. To tell her everything, to convince her to unite us in marriage, we only need a favorable moment . . . we shall be on the lookout for it, and I shall always be there at your side to help you find it.

EDWARD: At my side? . . . That's impossible.

ALICE: Impossible? . . . That word again!

EDWARD: Miss Alice?

ALICE: What now?

EDWARD: It is imperative . . . that you return to London.

ALICE: What are you saying, sir?

EDWARD: It is imperative.

ALICE: Oh! No, I would be too miserable.

EDWARD: Here, in a small town, our secrets would soon be known; people would not take long to discover . . .

ALICE: Well, then, I am proud to belong to you, to be your sweetheart, your fiancée, sir.

EDWARD: Miss Alice . . . (*Aside.*) Oh! My heart is torn! . . . (*Aloud.*) I implore you, for pity's sake, tomorrow morning, return to London, which you never should have left without consulting me.

ALICE: Oh! I am beginning to believe that I would have done well to pay heed to Sir Jack's words.

EDWARD: That man again! . . . What did he say to you? . . .

ALICE (*weeping*): He told me that you would forget me . . . or that you would betray me!

EDWARD: Miss Alice! . . . (*Aside.*) She's crying! . . . Oh, Heavens! And I am the one who is causing those tears to flow! (*Aloud.*) For heaven's sake, calm down.

ALICE: Leave me alone, sir.

EDWARD: No, whatever happens, I shall never, never forget you. But if you knew . . . destiny . . . circumstances . . . Oh! I am quite miserable!

GEORGE (*in the tavern*): Edward! Edward! . . .

EDWARD: It's George! . . .   Flee, flee, Miss Alice! If he should surprise us together! . . . Recognize us! . . . Good-bye, I'll see you again before you leave for London.

GEORGE (*at the door of the tavern*): Look here, Edward, are you finally coming or aren't you?

EDWARD: Here I am, here I am. (*Softly to* ALICE.) Dear Alice, wait for me. I'll be back in a moment. (*Aloud.*) Here I am, my friend.

GEORGE: It's about time.

They go into the tavern.

ALICE: Dear Alice, wait for me, he said . . . Is he going to come back? Oh! no, I mustn't believe him any more . . . All my illusions have been crushed . . . I am no longer loved!

GEORGE (*in the tavern*): To the health of Edward and Caroline, his fiancée!

ALICE: His fiancée! . . . Heavens! . . . What do I hear? Oh! This final blow was all I lacked! Now everything is finished for me! . . . Oh! Good heavens! Give me enough strength to rejoin Sir Jack . . . Alone, in the dead of night, how can I make my way back? . . . Just a moment ago, this darkness did not frighten me . . . I was coming to be close to him. Now I am afraid! . . .

At this moment, the THREE GRAVEDIGGERS, MACDOUGALL, BURKE, *and* ROSBEEF, *climb over the wall of the cemetery, and come downstage where they watch closely all of* ALICE's *movements.*

ALICE: Edward! Cruel Edward! . . . Oh! Despite everything, I still love you! . . . Good-bye, good-bye forever! . . . I can scarcely stand . . . No, I shall never, never be able to retrace my steps . . .

Staggering, ALICE *heads toward a street to the right. No sooner has she disappeared than her body can be heard falling; the* THREE GRAVEDIGGERS, *who have followed her stealthily, pounce on their prey and disappear as furtively.*

EDWARD (*coming out of the tavern, followed by* GEORGE *and the* STUDENTS): Let me go, my friends, let me go!

GEORGE: Oh, nonsense, you are going to have to explain your lack of good manners.

EDWARD: George, my friend, my conduct and my language must surprise you, incense you against me; but you are going to know everything. I am no longer addressing the young student, my comrade in follies; I am appealing to the man of honor . . . Listen, listen to me. I have seen Alice again, this very evening, right here; she wept, and her tears rent my soul. You know all that she has done for me. . . . You know that I owe her my life. Answer me, now: am I permitted to marry Caroline? What guarantee of happiness could I offer her? What oaths would I dare swear in receiving her hand? I, a perjurer towards another! . . . I, a murderer perhaps of the unfortunate Alice! . . . No, no, that marriage would be a crime . . . And you, George, you the dearest of my friends, would not force me to commit such a crime . . . Good-bye. I must see her again. . . . I must find her, speak to her, tell her: "Alice! Dear Alice! You will be my wife!" Good-bye, good-bye, my friends. (*He dashes off.*)

GEORGE: Yes, Edward is right; my sister would have been unhappy. Whatever distress I feel because of his new resolve, I cannot blame him. In any case, my friends, let us not abandon him; he is suffering; he deserves our consolation. . . . Let us follow him.

ALL: Yes, let us follow him.

Exit all.

End of the First Scene

Scene Two

The stage represents EDWARD's *study. A door to the right and to the left, opening into the library. To the rear, a glass partition discloses an anatomy cabinet; a black marble table stands in the middle of the room, and suspended above it hangs a lighted lamp. At the front of the stage to the right, an armchair; to the left, a table loaded with surgical instruments, books, papers, vials, etc. It is ten o'clock at night.*

A servant ushers in SIR JACK *by the side door on the left and shows him the armchair to the right, indicating that he should wait for Mr.* EDWARD BELTON. *The servant leaves instantly.*

JACK (*alone*): Everything here bears witness to the presence of a scholar, the retreat of a studious man. There is the anatomy cabinet . . . here the library . . . There it is that after having meditated upon the learned writings of the famous men who have preceded him, he comes to put their lessons into practice, and to steal from death useful secrets for the living. All that is very fine . . . (*He sits down.*) But it does not prevent one from writing, from fulfilling one's engagements, from being a man of honor . . I am curious to hear what he will tell me to justify himself. The poor little creature! . . . With me she would not have had all those risks to run. But Edward is twenty-five years younger than Sir Jack . . . There lies the whole secret to unlocking women's hearts. (*Getting up.*) Here he is.

EDWARD (*coming in*): You here, sir? . . .

JACK: The very same.

EDWARD: It seems to me that you could have put off your visit till tomorrow.

JACK: By no means. I need an answer today, this very instant.

EDWARD: In the middle of the night?

JACK: I do not know how to wait.

EDWARD: What is the cause of your visit?

JACK: The cause? . . . You cannot guess it? . . . It appears, young
man, that memory is not your strongest quality.

EDWARD: Sir!

JACK: What did you tell me, seven months ago tomorrow, in
London, at Mistress Butler's?

EDWARD: Sir, you speak to me in such a tone! . . .

JACK: It suits me. Answer, what did you tell me? . . . You
promised to write to your fiancée often and you did nothing of
the sort. A few infrequent letters during the first month alone
attested to your existence . . . Since then, not a single letter . . .
total abandonment.

EDWARD: Constant studies . . . duties to fulfill . . .

JACK: The first of all duties is to be an honest man, and you failed
in that.

EDWARD: Sir!

JACK: Don't yell so loud! You should know that you do not
frighten me.   I repeat it, and you must hear it first; afterwards
we can fight: you went back on your word of honor.

EDWARD: Word of honor!

JACK: Yes; because you played fast and loose with oaths made to a
young girl knowing full well that she could not exact vengeance
for it. I too had sworn to make her happy; I had sacrificed my
happiness for yours, because I believed that you were sincere,

and you have deceived me shamefully. I took your word, and your word was only a lie. I have come to demand satisfaction from you. In this heart of mine which has never been able to find another heart capable of understanding it, there is nothing left at present but one sole idea: vengeance. I must have your blood, I offer you provocation, you will accept my challenge; because a man may be vile enough, cowardly enough to take advantage of a weak woman, and proud enough not to refuse a challenge. Have I made myself clear? . . . It is eleven o'clock . . . I shall come back at midnight; I shall bring weapons and be accompanied by a minister, to divest you of even the slightest excuse. You will choose: Alice's hand, or we shall fight until one of the two of us is dead.

EDWARD: Sir, I deeply regret that you have felt you must accost me with insults and threats on your lips; you have placed me in the cruel necessity of spilling your blood, perhaps of taking your life! . . . When I was more than ever disposed to righting my wrongs.

JACK: How's that?

EDWARD: Yes, sir. I have seen Alice again, and I have understood better than ever before all my obligations to her. I have felt that I always loved her. Family interests, considerations of friendship, the importunities of my mother, had made me, despite myself, consent to another match . . .

JACK: Another match?

EDWARD: Do not interrupt me, sir. Yes, I was about to comply, all the while bewailing my fate, when, made stronger by the presence of Alice, my decision was reached; I was going to find my mother and implore my friend to release me from my promise.

JACK: Well, sir, that is all that I ask of you; we are in accord.

EDWARD: No, Sir. You might believe that now in taking the road that honor has prescribed for me, I was yielding to your threats and to fear. Rather death than allow such a shadow on my good name! I shall marry Alice, it is my wish and my duty; but first we shall fight.

JACK: No, we shan't fight.

EDWARD: We shall fight, Sir.

JACK: Oh! No, it is impossible! . . . If I had the misfortune to kill you, the same blow would strike the poor child . . . You can certainly sense . . .

EDWARD: You have insulted me.

JACK: It is true, it is true, yes, I have insulted you . . . I ask your pardon . . . Damn it, you will have to be content with my excuses.

EDWARD: But, Sir . . .

JACK: But, Sir, but Sir . . . that is the way it is, and it cannot be otherwise. Come, give me your hand . . . You are a worthy young man; yes, you are worth more than I thought, and I am glad of it for my little friend. Once again, I ask your pardon . . . Let us clasp hands.

EDWARD: I agree.

They clasp hands.

JACK: Fine; tomorrow we shall go together to your mother's.

EDWARD: Yes, Sir.

JACK: She desires a brilliant marriage for her son, well, I'll tell her: Alice is my sole heir.

EDWARD: Sir, I won't accept that.

JACK: Sir, you will accept it.

EDWARD: Never.

JACK: Yes indeed.

EDWARD: Not ever.

JACK: Oh! Hang it all! ... Do you want us to fight again? ... My wealth is mine, and I am free to do with it what I wish. As to your friends, you'll tell them ...

EDWARD: I am sure that I can persuade them. Despite his apparent frivolity, George is a man of honor and sensibility, he won't refuse to release me from my promise ... he will consent.

JACK: I should like to see him not consent ... So everything is settled ... You do not bear me any more ill will?

EDWARD: Bear you ill will, when I owe you everything! ... Oh! Take me to Alice; I must have cruelly wounded her heart, and I cannot wait to repair the harm that I have done her. Let us not lose an instant.

JACK: No, it is too late ... She is doubtless sleeping ... the proprieties do not allow it ... Tomorrow I shall get her to receive you.

EDWARD: You are right. Tomorrow, my noble friend, tomorrow, at the break of day, I shall come see you.

JACK: At the Yorick Hotel.

EDWARD: I shall lay at the feet of my fiancée my repentance and my love.

JACK: Yes, we are all happy. Good-bye, my friend, until tomorrow.

EDWARD: Until tomorrow! ...

They shake hands. SIR JACK *goes out, escorted by* EDWARD.

EDWARD (*alone*): I am satisfied with myself. I must admit to my shame that absence had made my heart grow cold . . . I had become an ingrate; I yielded without love to family arrangements: who knows if I would have made Caroline happy? I doubt it. Within all men there is a secret voice that speaks louder than calculations and proprieties . . . the voice of honor, and to ignore it is never permitted.

At this point there is the sound of a loud bell rung by a cord leading outside and which is located in the library where EDWARD *is seated.*

That ringing of the bell is the signal agreed upon with MacDougall . . . (*He gets up.*) Yes, it's those wretches . . .

He enters the study and goes to open the hidden door to the right, which cannot be seen; then he comes back. Soon after we see passing behind the glass partition the THREE GRAVEDIGGERS *carrying a lifeless corpse wrapped in a shroud; they deposit it on the black table in the anatomy cabinet. During this time,* EDWARD *has come back into the library.*

The THREE GRAVEDIGGERS *appear on the threshold of the door to the library.*

MACDOUGALL: Doctor, sir, there's what we promised you; you can't have anything better.

ROSBEEF: It's not more than an hour . . . you can take that on trust.

EDWARD: How much do I owe you?

MACDOUGALL: Twelve guinea . . . that's not steep. You know that getting caught means nothing less than the gallows. Doctor Oswald wouldn't have haggled at fifteen pound sterling; but I've given you preference because one's got to favor youth. Your colleague hasn't got anything more to learn, while you've . . .

EDWARD (*paying*): There you are.

MACDOUGALL: Thanks.   There, you fellows each get three
   guineas. (*To* EDWARD.) You see what's left for me . . . It's a
   pittance for being responsible; because if we got nabbed, I,
   MacDougall, would be the first to hang.

ROSBEEF: That would be only just; you're our chief.

EDWARD: Leave now.

THREE GRAVEDIGGERS: Good night, Doctor, sir.

EDWARD (*escorting them out*): Be careful not to say a word to any
   one . . .

MACDOUGALL: Don't worry.

ROSBEEF: Our own interest assures you of our silence.

They disappear in the same direction by which they came. EDWARD
*closes the door and approaches the table, where he sets out his instruments
as he speaks.*

EDWARD (*alone*): Just an hour ago, that man said! . . . How short
   the interval that separates life from death! . . . How rapidly it
   arrives . . . unforeseen! . . . And yet we torture our existence as
   if it were in our power to fix the limit or to prolong it as we wish.
   We do not fear being unjust or ungrateful, although we never
   know if we will live long enough to repair our injustices or cause
   our ingratitude to be forgotten. The unfortunate creature who
   lies there perhaps made these same reflections a few minutes
   ago, and death surprised him before he had time . . . Oh! I'll
   hesitate no longer: tomorrow Alice will be my wife.

He makes his way towards the door of the cabinet and stops.

What is this I am feeling! . . . I feel cold . . . an involuntary
   tremor . . . From long experience have I not become familiar
   with the sight of death? For the first time I am shuddering as I
   approach a shroud . . . Death is frightful! . . . Overcome your

weakness . . .

He opens the door, draws near the table, and lifts up the shroud.

Good God! . . . what do I see! . . . Alice! . . . Alice!!! . . . Oh! Unhappy man!

Hearing his cries, servants bearing torches run in and gather round the corpse in the anatomy cabinet. SIR JACK and some STUDENTS enter the library by the side door to the left.

JACK (*coming in without seeing* EDWARD): She has not been seen again . . . I've come to find out . . .

EDWARD (*coming out of the anatomy cabinet in the wildest disorder*): There . . . There she is! She is dead! . . . And I killed her! . . . I killed her!! . . .

He falls lifeless at SIR JACK's feet, with his face to the ground. General stupefaction.

End of Alice

Theoretical Writings by Pixérécourt:

"Melodrama"

&

"Final Reflections on Melodrama"

Translated by Daniel Gerould

"Melodrama" (1832)[1]

To avoid all confusion in our little literary debate, I shall divide melodrama into two clearly distinct parts, classic and romantic. [. . .] I shall speak to you only about the former. I abandon romanticism to its frenetic admirers. It will share the fate of all that lies outside the bounds of reason.

Undoubtedly, melodrama could never have been, nor should it be classical in the manner of Corneille or Racine. Nonetheless, for thirty years it has had its own poetics; it has been subject to the unity of action and of time. It was, properly speaking, a form of lyrical drama patterned on the model of Sedaine's plays. And what proves it is that the best melodramas have been translated into Italian, into German, and set to music by the most famous foreign composers. Without venturing any further, *Victor, or the Child of the Forest,* the first born of the modern melodramas, was an opera accepted by the Théâtre-Favart and for which Solié composed the music; Madame Saint-Aubin, Michu, Chénard and Solié were to play the roles of Clémence, Victor, Roger and Valentin. They tried to do me an injustice [by persuading the management to put on another opera, also based on Ducray-Duminil's novel, with the same title and subject], at which my young pride revolted. I took my opera to the Ambigu-Comique, suppressing only the sung portions. Such is the origin of melodrama. [. . .]

For twenty years it has been the height of good taste to run down this genre of dramatic work. This word was the trite weapon with which one attacked the interest felt by the spectator, the unique and inexhaustible source of our pleasures at the theatre. A thousand times I have heard old carping critics exclaim: "A melodrama! Disgraceful! I've never seen one, God forbid! But it must be awful, it couldn't possibly be good," and I answered them: "Within twenty years melodrama will invade all the theatres." That was also the

---

[1] In *Le Livre des cent-et-un, Vol. 6.* Bruxelles: Louis Hauman, 1832.

opinion of Chénier and Monvel. My predictions have been realized. Melodrama is spoken, it is sung, it is danced, it is mimed; it has replaced everything else, turned everything upside down. There is only one genre, only one theatre in Paris; the sole difference lies in the actors. But the same thing will happen with melodrama as has happened with everything else in this world; out of chaos order is born. Soon this confusion will come to an end and each theatre will go back to its initial reason for being. [. . .]

Why should I care what a dramatic work is called if I find nothing in it contrary to morality and reason? Who has the right to force me to be entertained only by such and such a thing that often is extremely boring? If I like to be moved, if I am gratified by seeing well painted stage sets, costumes that are accurate and new, well designed ballets connected to a reasonable action written in a natural style, executed by actors who make every effort to please me, and all of that at a modest price which allows me from time to time to provide this pleasure for my family; what right has anyone to compel me to pay a high price for the tedious performance of masterpieces that I prefer to read and admire by my fireplace or on my solitary walks rather than to see them too often butchered by the second and third tier actors at the royal theatres. [. . .]

From 1636 to 1790, the French stage has been a repository of masterpieces . . . veritable treasures for the enlightened segment of the nation. But those who by their taste, their education, or their station have not been able to acquire the requisite learning (and one cannot deny that this class constitutes the largest part of society) are no less eager for entertainment and have no less than any others the right to be provided with such diversions; it is thus necessary to suit this entertainment to their taste, to their education, to their station, and above all to their financial means. [. . .]

The *drame,* exiled from the imperial theatres, took refuge on the boulevards. That is where for twenty-five years there were staged plays called melodramas that the newspapers and public opinion frequently placed higher than the new works that were played at the Comédie Française.

Melodrama signed letters of nobility for the old stages too long subordinate to the major theatres which enforced on them their insolent system of vassalage and kept them in the most humiliating servitude. Melodrama has refined the language of the people who, after seeing it performed, rent it for two sous at the lending library and read it until they know it by heart. Since poetry, this language of the gods, is comprehensible only to enlightened and well-educated spectators, tragedy is totally out of keeping with the education of the people. The great political interests which are almost always at the heart of tragedy demand for proper appreciation years of study and extensive and profound knowledge of many subjects. These are the reasons why it was necessary to create a popular theatre, a popular genre, and a popular interest for the spectator. That is how melodrama arose.

In support of my opinion, I shall cite once again the views of the savage Robespierre who was a lamb before turning tiger; as witness the following paragraph taken word for word from *The Eulogy of Gresset*, a speech entered in the competition for the prize offered by the Academy of Amiens, written by M. R. . . . , lawyer in the Parliament, published in 1786, which I own along with several other literary essays by the same author; all of them extremely rare and virtually inaccessible.

"In recent times we have seen the province of the theatre grow due to the birth of those productions known as *drames*. But an inexplicable mania impels a throng of critics to denounce this new genre with a kind of fanaticism. These rabid censors, convinced that nature has sanctioned only tragedies and comedies, took any dramatic work that did not bear one of these two names for a literary monster that had to be strangled at birth; as though this inexhaustible variety of interesting pictures that show us man and society must inevitably be confined in those two slots; as though nature had only two tones and there were no middle point for us between the sallies of gaiety and the transports of the wildest passions.

"But the *drames* and good sense have triumphed over all their outcries. In vain were their efforts to make us feel that the pleasure that these works gave us was shameful and to persuade us that it was permitted to be moved only by the calamities of kings and heroes. While they wrote books against the *drames*, we hastened to the theatre to see them staged, and we found out that our tears can flow sweetly for other misfortunes than those of Orestes and Andromache; we felt that the more the action resembles ordinary scenes of life, the more the characters are close to our station in life, the more complete is the illusion, the more powerful the interest for the spectator, and the more striking the instruction."

It is thus true that through performances and through reading of melodrama, the people learn to become better. You will not deny that, in plays of this genre, there are frequent portrayals on stage of fine examples of morality and virtue, acts of heroism, traits of bravery and fidelity drawn from our history. Melodrama should thus have a useful influence on our manners and morals, because the eternal morality that one finds there consists of rewarding good actions and punishing bad. [...]

For the most part, the outstanding plays in this genre conform to the three unities, at least approximately. Those of time and place above all are observed more strictly than in [Sedaine's] *The Deserter* [1769] and *Richard Coeur-de-Lion* [1784], and in [Monvel's] *Sargines* [1788], etc. [...]

I adore fine poetry, and I never tire of reading Racine's works and the sublime reveries of Lamartine or Victor Hugo. But fine poetry is not enough to make a good play; you will never prove to me that an exposition in two or three quite long scenes, made up of endless monologues which are almost always boring, can equal, from the dramatic aspect, the first act of any melodrama, where I see taking shape, from the very first words, a rapid and engrossing action; where each member of the cast appears with his own character and the language that is appropriate to him; where the interest for the spectator grows from scene to scene, from act to act, and keeps me thrilled for two or three hours until the catastrophe comes to wring my tears. I confess, to my shame, that I have never wept at a tragedy; and even if you treat me as a barbarian, I shall tell you that I go to the theatre either to laugh or to weep. Woe to the author who leaves the spectator unmoved!

"Final Reflections on Melodrama" (1843)

During the past century and a half, Molière, Regnard and Destouches produced masterpieces in comedy and Corneille, Racine, Crébillon and Voltaire produced masterpieces in tragedy. Since then, with very few exceptions, the only thing any one did was to glean. Everything had been said, everything had been done.

What was needed was to invent a new theatre.

Making use of religious and providential ideas and of moral sentiments, I embarked upon the ticklish career of theatre.

I studied the works of Mercier and Sedaine; I understood that, in order to succeed in the theatre, it was necessary first and foremost to choose a subject that was both dramatic and moral; that next what was needed was natural dialogue, a simple and truthful style, delicate sentiments, honesty, feeling, the happy mixture of gaiety combined with concern, sensibility, the just reward of virtue and the punishment of crime, in a word all that is lacking in our moderns who are so proud and so poor of heart, soul, and sentiment. I mean poor only in the sense that I attribute to theatre: because for them, fine-sounding phrases are everything. All modern characters are cast in the same mold; there is never naturalness or gaiety: the minister and the peasant, the soldier and the orator are all the same. It seems to me I'm constantly and uninterruptedly listening to a professor of rhetoric; his style is correct, often too diffuse and florid; but his language is everywhere the same. Now that's a far cry from theatre, which is nothing other than, in my opinion, a precise and true representation of nature. To all these essential qualities I add the sense of order so necessary in all matters, next the taste and severity that must govern the rehearsals which become an element of success that is almost certain when one knows how to make good use of it.

I maintain that an understanding of what is called staging (*mise en scène*) is enough to enable one to avoid the pitfalls that are so dangerous in this difficult and perilous profession.

I insist and I maintain that the dramatic author cannot be too attentive to rehearsals in order to polish his style (theatrically speaking) and to wage war on words; because for forty years I have constantly remarked that the public clings to words, not things. I have often seen on the very first day the incontestable success of works trivial in the extreme, which subsequently died from their own emptiness at the fourth performance; while others that were at high risk and hissed at the premiere became all the rage for months on end, once the appropriate corrections had been made.

Here is what I call the school of Sedaine brought to perfection, and beyond which successes are ephemeral and without fruit.

The dramatist must know how to stage his own play. This is of the greatest importance. First it is the sole means of aptly making useful corrections, next of rendering the actors as good as is possible dependent on their ability and especially their obedience; this is a difficult point. The first thing to demand of these performers is to require them to learn their roles perfectly; and, nowadays, this is almost impossible, because there are very few managers or directors who know their metier. Because of equality and progress, no one obeys; every one believes it possible to know without having learned. Superiority is ubiquitous; but where is experience? where is art? where is taste? where are they to be found? In all quarters, people chase after money, they want it at all costs and in large quantities. But it's not enough to obtain a license. To know the theatre, one must be able to control the performers, the artists, to study the moral and the matter of an enterprise of this kind. It is an extremely long study of which very few people are capable. Thus every day we see would-be managers go bankrupt and compromise the fortune that is not theirs and that they have borrowed from over-trusting friends.

Undoubtedly for half of my successes I am indebted to the minute and severe care with which I have constantly presided at the rehearsals; but I have also had the advantage of composing all my plays alone: the result being a unity (*ensemble*) that could not be achieved with several distinct collaborators often separated from one another by great distances. The only thing needed is one single and uniform thought guiding the composition, the working out, and the complete execution of a work for the theatre.

Formerly one labored conscientiously, one staked one's self-esteem and honor to become the creator and proprietor of whatever work resulted; but, at present, greed for gold has led to those regrettable collaborations that produce so many bizarre, incoherent, and defective works.

If I leave out of consideration *Charles the Bold* and *The Daughter of the Exile*, I have respected the three unities in my dramas as far as was possible. I have always thought that total unity was necessary in the total labor of a dramatic work.

But it is only in tragedy and in comedy of character that all three are scrupulously observed. In comedy of intrigue, in *drame* and in comic opera, the two unities of action and time are usually found to be sufficient. The unity of place is boring and monotonous, and almost always improbable; it has been avoided for a long time.

Sedaine stuck to the first two, and I have never hoped to do better than he did; I have never wished to do more than imitate him.

A play for the theatre can only be well conceived, well made, well dialogued, well rehearsed, well acted if it is under the control of and in the hands of a single person having the same taste, the same judgment, the same mind, the same heart and the same opinion.

For thirty years I worked alone; and consequently my works were generally successful. Since 1830 only, I have been forced by the new practices to enter into partnership, against my will, with various colleagues. What have been the results? pallid successes. It is no longer the thought of a single person, it is no longer a single impulse, everything is discordant.

What I maintain about the unities, I also demand in the name of good taste: every play should be divided into acts and not into tableaux. The reverse is a sign of mediocrity, laziness, incapacity, lack of reason, inability to produce: I don't consider any one guilty of a crime on this account, because not everybody is destined to become a dramatic author, although daily one hears the contrary.

I maintain the same thing about all the subjects that are written about today for the theatre. In the past one chose only what was good; but in these modern dramas, we find only monstrous crimes which offend our sense of morality and decency. Always and everywhere adultery, rape, incest, parricide, prostitution, vices ever more shameless, filthy, disgusting, each worse than the other. What is the result? Mothers with families have stopped attending shows where young women could no longer be seen without the risk of scandal and danger. Unfortunately there can be found in Paris a vast number of gallant and libertine women who have sufficed to legitimize this filthy and obscene genre, and to assure a large number of performances for plays that are rejected by good taste and morality. But decent society has gradually abandoned public places; it has devised for itself other private forms of entertainment. A few more years, and all the theatres in the departments will have deteriorated irreparably. It is impossible for them to keep going. Bad plays, bad actors, absence of good traditions, excessive cost of salaries, and lack of good directors have made these enterprises impossible.

For over thirty years I have watched all of France flock to the frequent performances of my works. Men, women, children, the rich and the poor, all came to laugh and to cry at well-made melodramas. Alas! Those times are over. The theatre has been forsaken forever. Due to progress, society has been deprived of an important source of innocent pleasure that will never be recaptured. Not all stomachs can tolerate sulfuric acid.

For the past ten years, a very large number of romantic plays have been produced, that is to say, evil, dangerous, immoral works, devoid of interest or truth. Well, then, at the very height of this evil genre, I wrote *Latude* [1834] in accord with the same taste, the same ideas and the same principles that have guided me for more than thirty years. This play enjoyed the same success as the earlier ones. All of France flocked to it as they previously had to *The Dog of Montargis*, *The Ruins of Babylon*, *The Daughter of the Exile*, etc. Why then don't present-day authors follow my example? Why don't their plays resemble mine? The reason is that they have nothing in common with me, neither their ideas, or dialogue, or way of working out a design; the reason is that the new plays have neither my heart, nor my sensibility, nor my conscience. So I am not the one responsible for establishing the romantic genre.

I now pose the following question with some assurance: is what writers have done since and even after 1830 similar to what I produced during the previous thirty years?

It is very painful for me, sick and nearly blind, to be compelled to touch on this burning issue. But I have been forced to do so. That is the question. These are the facts. I leave the task of judging me to the impartial public.

Selected Bibliography

Pixérécourt, René-Charles Guilbert de. *Théâtre choisi*. Vols. I-IV. Geneva: Slatkine Reprints, 1971 (Original edition, Nancy: 1841-1843).

_____ *Alice, ou Les Fossoyeurs Ecossais*. Paris: Chez Barba, 1829.

_____ *Christophe Colomb; ou, La découverte du Nouveau monde*. Paris: Barba, 1815.

_____ "Le Mélodrame," in *Le Livre des cent-et-un, Vol. 6*. Bruxelles: Louis Hauman, 1832.

_____ *Les Ruines de Babylone, ou Giafar et Zaida*. 2nd ed. Paris: Chez Barba, 1815.

Akins, William H. Jr. *Three Melodramas by Guilbert de Pixérécourt*. Translated and with an introduction. Ann Arbor: UMI, 1971.

Hartog, Willie Gustave. *Guilbert de Pixérécourt: sa vie, son mélodrame, sa technique et son influence*. Paris: Librarie ancienne, 1913.

Lacey, Alexander. *Pixérécourt and the French Romantic Drama*. Toronto: University of Toronto Press, 1928.

Marcoux, J. Paul. *Guilbert de Pixérécourt: French Melodrama in the Early Nineteenth Century*. N.Y.: Peter Lang, 1992.

ACKNOWLEDGEMENTS

All the French texts translated in this volume come from Pixérécourt, *Théâtre choisi*, except for "The Author to the Public" (the preface to *Christopher Columbus*), *Alice, or The Scottish Gravediggers*, and "Melodrama," which are taken from original editions indicated in the selected bibliography. The anonymous translation of *The Dog of Montargis* of 1816, along with Pixérécourt's "Historical Note," is reprinted from *Melodrama, New York Literary Forum*, Vol. 7, 1980. Grateful acknowledgment is made to Elizabeth Swain and Lenny Borger for help with the translations and to Frank Hentschker for advice on the cover design. The print of *The Dog of Montargis* is reproduced courtesy of the Harvard Theatre Collection, The Houghton Library. The cover design is based on a portrait of Pixérécourt by Cheralame, engraved by Bosselmann.

OTHER MARTIN E. SEGAL THEATRE CENTER PUBLICATIONS

Contemporary Theatre in Egypt, edited by Marvin Carlson, contains the proceedings of a Symposium on this subject held at the CUNY Graduate Center in February of 1999 along with the first English translations of three short plays by leading Egyptian playwrights who spoke at the Symposium, Alfred Farag, Gamal Maqsoud, and Lenin El-Ramley. It concludes with a bibliography of English translations and secondary articles on the theatre in Egypt since 1955.

Zeami and the No Theatre in the World, edited by Benito Ortolani and Samuel Leiter, contains the proceedings of the "Zeami and the No Theatre in the World Symposium" held in New York City in October 1997 in conjunction with the "Japanese Theatre in the World" exhibit at the Japan Society. The book contains an introduction and fifteen essays, organized into sections on "Zeami's Theories and Aesthetics," "Zeami and Drama," "Zeami and Acting," and "Zeami and the World."

Four Works for the Theatre by **Hugo Claus** contains translations of four plays by the foremost contemporary writer of Dutch language theatre, poetry, and prose. Flemish by birth and upbringing, Claus is the author of some ninety plays, novels, and collections of poetry. The plays collected here, edited and with an introduction by David Willinger, include *The Temptation, Friday, Serenade,* and *The Hair of the Dog.*

For further information on the
Martin E. Segal Theatre Center visit:
http://web.gc.cuny.edu/mestc